John Quincy Adams

AMERICAN PROFILES

Norman K. Risjord,
Series Editor

American Profiles

JOHN QUINCY ADAMS

Lynn Hudson Parsons

A Madison House Book

ROWMAN & LITTLEFIELD PUBLISHERS, INC.
Lanham • Boulder • New York • Oxford

A Madison House Book

Rowman & Littlefield Publishers, Inc.
4720 Boston Way
Lanham, MD 20706
www.rowmanlittlefield.com

12 Hid's Copse Road
Cumnor Hill, Oxford OX2 9JJ, England

First Rowman & Littlefield edition 2001

British Library Cataloguing in Publication Information Available

A previous edition of this book was cataloged as follows by the Library of Congress:

Library of Congress Cataloging-in-Publication Data

John Quincy Adams / Lynn Hudson Parsons.
    p. cm.
ISBN 0-945612-59-1 (pbk., alk paper)
1. Adams, John Quincy, 1767–1848. 2. Presidents—United States—Biography. 3.
United States—Politics and government—1825–1829. 4. United States—Foreign
relations—1783–1865. I. Title. II. Series: American profiles (Madison, Wis.).
E377.P37 1997
973.5'5'092—dc21
[B]   97-34987

Printed in the United States of America

♾™ The paper used in this publication meets the minimum requirements of American
National Standard for Information Sciences—Permanence of Paper for Printed Library
Materials, ANSI/NISO Z39.48–1992.

To the memory of Joseph Frazier Wall—

"And gladly wold he lerne, and gladly teche."

Contents

Illustrations

Editor's Foreword

THE COMPLAINT OF MANY PEOPLE who dislike history is that it is full of obscure names, arcane dates, and big words that always seem to end in "ism." The problem is that history, in some ways, is like a foreign language. The grammar has to be mastered before thought, discussion, and interpretation is possible. The task confronting the teacher of history is how to sugarcoat the pill.

For some years I have given a talk to educators at meetings and seminars around the country entitled "Making History Human." It is essentially a pitch for a biographical approach as a pedagogical device. I am not advocating the reduction of history to a series of human-interest stories. My thesis, instead, is that complex and often dry subjects (when presented in general terms) can be enlivened and given meaning through a focus on one of the individual stories. For example, P. T. Barnum's impact on popular amusements can add a new dimension to the concept of democracy in nineteenth-century America. The story of Jackie Robinson can add poignancy to the often legalistic (because of its emphasis on statutes and court decisions) story of civil rights in the middle decades of the twentieth century.

That is the basic purpose of Madison House's *American Profiles* series—to add a human dimension to the study of history. *American Profiles* offers relatively concise and swiftly-paced sketches that contribute significantly to the discourse on the American past. Each narrative takes advantage of the explosion of recent historiography while the author's interpretive insights serve as a basis for organizing that mass of complex and often disparate information.

What we hope to do with the books in the *American Profiles* series is to tell the American story—to tell the multitude of our national stories. Our goal is to arouse interest and provoke thought. Once that is accomplished, we can truly begin to teach our history.

NORMAN K. RISJORD
Series Editor

Acknowledgments

FOR A BOOK OF MODEST LENGTH, this one was a long time coming. It was the late Lyman Butterfield who first urged me on in the late 1970's: "The book *must* be written!" he said. While in the intervening years I was lured off the path with other projects and other responsibilities, my wife, Anne Hruska Parsons, never let me forget Butterfield's admonition. In a very real sense, this book is as much hers as mine.

I am grateful to the American Council of Learned Societies for a research grant that allowed me to get the project underway, and to the Massachusetts Historical Society for permission to quote from the microfilm edition of the Adams Papers. A number of colleagues and scholars have read and critiqued parts or all of the book, or have been of assistance in providing insights into the Adams family and its role in the American past, or both. Special thanks, then, to Bill Andrews, Owen Dudley Edwards, Steve Ireland, Ralph Ketchum, Mary-Jo Kline, Kathy Kutolowski, Walter La Feber, Walter Morris, and Mel Small. And an extra special thanks to Wanda Wakefield, student and friend, for a quick and thorough indexing of this work. As the book neared completion, Norman Risjord and Richard Ryerson were of particular help in rooting out errors of style and substance. Those that are left are my own.

Brockport, New York
September, 1997

xi

Prologue:
"A Splendid Pageant"

THE OLD MAN WAS DYING. Everyone in the room sensed it. He had arrived that morning, February 21, 1848, just as he had nearly every morning when the House was in session, for the previous sixteen years. In spite of his eighty years and the lingering effects of a stroke, he appeared alert and had followed the debates intently. On this particular occasion—to no one's surprise—he had shouted "No!" to a vote of thanks to several American generals in the recently concluded war with Mexico. The war, he had said on many occasions, was "most unrighteous," unconstitutional, and unworthy of Americans. Few saw anything unusual when he and a handful of antiwar Congressmen (including the gaunt, odd-looking member from Illinois, Abraham Lincoln) opposed the vote of thanks.

As the House clerk was calling the roll for final approval of the resolution, one of the newspaper reporters was watching the Old Man. A flush of crimson passed over the nearly-bald head. The Old Man attempted to rise, could not, and fell into the arms of a nearby colleague. "Look to Mr. Adams," called several congressmen, "Mr. Adams is dying." All was confusion. The Speaker of the House called for a motion to adjourn, several members who were also physicians rushed to assist, young pages darted out of the chamber to inform the Senate, and John Quincy Adams, former president, former secretary of state, former senator, former U.S. minister to the Netherlands, to Prussia, to Russia, and to Great Britain, was carried from the room.

Two days later, on February 23rd, without regaining full consciousness, John Quincy Adams died in the Speaker's chamber. "This is the last of earth," he was reported to have said. "I am content."

On the day of his funeral, "the whole population of the city and surrounding country seemed to be in motion toward the Capitol," wrote the friendly correspondent of the *Boston Courier*. In the House chamber, while president James K. Polk, the Supreme Court, the diplomatic corps, and members of the House and Senate watched, John C. Calhoun and seven other former friends and enemies bore the coffin. Following the service, a mile-long procession followed the casket to its temporary resting place in the Congressional cemetery. The events of the day, wrote President Polk in his diary, were "a splendid pageant."

Not all joined in the pageant. Adams' strident antislavery speeches, coupled with his opposition to Texas annexation and the Mexican War, had left him with few friends in the South. The Virginia state senate tabled the usually routine resolutions for adjournment. Daniel Webster confided to a southern colleague that Adams was little more than a narrow-minded sectionalist at heart. A young New York editor, who still called himself Walter Whitman, was not impressed. "He was a 'gentleman of the old school,' no doubt," wrote the future author of *Leaves of Grass*, "but the old school, with all its polish and grace, had its sources too near monarchy and nobility to be entirely free from their influence."

Yet some of the strongest tributes came from old foes and rivals in Congress. "Punctual to every duty, death found him at the post of duty," intoned Missouri's Democratic Senator Thomas Hart Benton, "and where else could it have found him, at any stage of his career, for the fifty years of his illustrious public life?" Declared South Carolina's Congressman Isaac Holmes, contrasting Adams with Andrew Jackson, "he crushed no heart beneath the rude grasp of proscription; he left no heritage of widow's cries or orphan's tears."

When John Quincy Adams' father, John Adams, first visited the city of Washington as president in 1800, he had arrived in a stagecoach. Few knew or cared. When the body of his son left the city for the last time in 1848, it was borne by a steam-powered locomotive, and news of his death had flashed up and down the East Coast by means of Samuel Morse's new "magnetic telegraph." Never had the body of an American statesman made a public railroad journey before. As the train made its way north through Baltimore, Philadelphia, New York, Springfield, and finally to Boston and Quincy, citizens of large and small towns turned out to watch, forming, as Massachusetts Senator Edward Everett later remarked, "one mighty funeral procession." Not until the death and funeral of Abraham Lincoln would it be matched, recalled an observer who witnessed both.

IN 1848 THERE WERE FEW PEOPLE living who could remember when there had not been a John Quincy Adams. He had been born in 1767, a subject of the British Empire under King George III, and had died in 1848, a citizen of the United States and a member of Congress in company with Abraham Lincoln. In the intervening years he had known George Washington and Benjamin Franklin, La Fayette of France, Alexander I of Russia and Castlereagh of Great Britain. He had both collaborated and quarrelled with Thomas Jefferson, Andrew Jackson, Henry Clay, John C. Calhoun, and Daniel Webster. In his lifetime Americans had fought for and established their independence, adopted a Constitution, fought two wars with Great Britain, and one with Mexico. They had expanded south to the Rio Grande and west to the Pacific. At the same time they argued among themselves over what the American Revolution meant, what the Constitution permitted, the wisdom of the wars, and the need for the expansion. At the time of Adams' death, they were beginning to debate whether American expansion meant that human slavery necessarily went with it.

John Quincy Adams had witnessed most of this. From the day in 1778 when at the age of ten he accompanied his father on a diplomatic mission to France, to his last years as an eloquent, bitter, and cantankerous opponent of his country's foreign and domestic policies, Adams was rarely uninvolved with public affairs. A product of New England culture, influenced though not controlled by the Puritan religious tradition, affected by the Enlightenment of the eighteenth century, inspired by the patriotic republican rhetoric of the American Revolution, tempered by years of residence in Europe, he was never truly "at home" anywhere. He was often alienated from his native Massachusetts, where his views on foreign policy set him at odds with the mercantile power structure. In Washington, his reticent nature placed him outside the *bonhomie* of the saloons and dinner parties that often accompany politics. In the diplomatic circles of Europe he came to be regarded as a stubborn, phlegmatic, Yankee ideologue, a "bulldog among spaniels." He certainly was not at home in the White House, where by his own admission his single term was a failure. His diary, which he began as a teenager and kept with few interruptions until his very last weeks, shows him seldom content, although by most standards he had accomplished much.

The public of his day, and historians ever since, have not known what to do with John Quincy Adams. One biographer saw him, as did Adams himself at one point, as "the man of the whole nation," rising above parties and sections to heights of dispassionate patriotism. Another scholar agreed with a critic that toward the end of his life, he was little more than a "mischievous bad old man." Ideologically Adams was neither democrat nor aristocrat. He never identified fully with any political party, and never became "a symbol for an age."

And yet, in spite of its length, there was a pattern to Adams' life. He craved order, stability, and moral purpose encouraged by enlightened government. The idea of "laissez faire," whether in economics or in morality, never appealed to him. He believed fully in the principles of the Declaration of Independence, if not in its author. Government rested on the consent of the people, who ought to choose their own governors, who in turn should be qualified by proper education and temperament. Having chosen such leaders, Adams believed, the people had best leave them alone. He believed in ordered liberty.

In foreign affairs, John Quincy Adams believed in the strictest American neutrality in the affairs of other nations, especially in Europe. For most of his life, he believed in "Manifest Destiny," although the term was not coined until shortly before his death. He looked forward, as did most people in his day, to the time when the continent of North America and the boundaries of the United States would be one and the same, when the principles of ordered liberty would be spread from coast to coast with a common language, a common religion, a common political system. Only when he became convinced that expansion would lead, not to ordered liberty, but to the extension of chattel slavery, did he change his mind. He closed his career as an opponent of expansion in the case of Texas and the Southwest, but its advocate in the case of Oregon and the Northwest. To some this was Yankee hypocrisy; to others it was evidence of rocklike integrity.

The death of John Quincy Adams, as more than one observer noted, severed one of the last ties with the founders of the Republic. "He was a living bond of connexion between the present and the past," declared a Congressional colleague. A normally hostile newspaper agreed. "His eulogy is written in the history of the last half century." For the biographer in the late twentieth century, he presents an opportunity to trace through the life of one man the evolution of America from the eighteenth-century republican world of which he was a product, to the nineteenth-century democratic world in which he found himself increasingly uncomfortable.

His life can be divided into three "careers." The first, the longest, and the most successful, was in diplomacy, culminating with his tenure as Secretary of State from 1817 to 1825. The second, the shortest, and the least successful, was his presidency from 1825 to 1829. The third, and easily the most spectacular, was as a congressman from Massachusetts from 1831 to his death in 1848. Throughout all three he confronted a series of private crises as well: a less-than-happy marriage, irresponsible siblings, frustrating children, and financial stress. His diary chronicles all of these achievements and crises, reflecting both his great strengths as a dogged and often courageous defender of principle, and his weaknesses as a censorious and uncharitable critic of those who crossed him.

John Quincy Adams was hardly a typical American. His parentage alone set him apart, not only from his contemporaries, but from later generations as well. Yet his is an American story nonetheless, for his three careers and their uneven results were shaped by the

American world in which he moved and which he himself often shaped. His greatest successes occurred when his principles of ordered liberty and expansion harmonized with those of the broader national culture. When he failed, he failed because he lost contact with the culture, or at least the ascendent part of it. By studying his life, we learn about both the culture and the man.

JOHN QUINCY
ADAMS

John Quincy Adams, portrait in oil on canvas by George P. A. Healy, 1858. *In the Collection of The Corcoran Gallery of Art, Museum Purchase, Gallery Fund.*

Chapter One

―――――――――○―――――――――

"Times in Which a Genious Would Wish to Live"

THE LAND SOUTH OF BOSTON IS rough, stony, and unyielding. The product of a retreating glacier that left nearly all of New England liberally strewn with rocks, boulders, drumlins, and other vestiges of the Ice Age, it never held much agricultural value. To the first wave of English Puritans who came to settle it in the seventeenth century, the Massachusetts South Shore must have seemed disappointing. Happily for many, their religion, which taught them that life was a series of tests and challenges, provided a buffer against the disillusion that sent less hardy souls fleeing back to England, or heading for more southerly latitudes. One of those who stayed was a maltster from Bristol named Henry Adams, about whom next to nothing is known except that he died in 1646, leaving an estate worth seventy-five pounds and thirteen shillings; and that he had a large number of descendants, two of whom became presidents of the United States.

Henry's farm was near Boston, in the town known as Braintree in the seventeenth and eighteenth centuries, and as Quincy in the nineteenth and twentieth. Here one of Henry's eight children, Joseph Adams, remained in hopes of improving upon his father's modest farm and increasing his social standing. He served in the local militia and was chosen a selectman of the town and a surveyor of the highways. His son, Joseph Adams, Jr., married a granddaughter of nearby Plymouth's most famous romantic couple, John and Priscilla Alden. He was able to send his eldest son, Joseph Adams, III, to "our university," as the people of Massachusetts liked to call Harvard College. Although Joseph III's younger brother John was unable to go to college, he did marry Susanna Boylston, daughter of one of the wealthier families in the colony. Not much is known about Susanna, other than that she was much younger than her husband, was outspoken and strong-willed, and brought financial security into the marriage. "Deacon John Adams" as he later was known in order to distinguish him from his more famous son, settled down with Susanna in a modest house on the road to Plymouth, where their son John Adams was born in 1735.

Unlike his father, the second John Adams was able to go to Harvard, after which his parents hoped that he would enter the ministry. Years later, he recalled that "it was whispered to me and circulated among others that I had some faculty for public Speaking and that I should make a better Lawyer than Divine." After a brief stint as a schoolteacher, he entered the legal profession in 1758. Lacking contacts and the financial wherewithal, young John Adams spent the earliest years of his legal career living with his parents in the house on the Plymouth Road. When "Deacon John" died in 1761, young John divided the estate with his mother and two brothers, moving into a smaller farmhouse adjacent to the family homestead. Both houses, birthplaces of two presidents, may still be seen today.

Now twenty-six years old, John Adams had yet to marry. His new independence, combined with a growing legal reputation, pushed him in that direction. Although awkward in social gatherings, he nonetheless enjoyed female company. Through his friendship with Richard Cranch, an English immigrant, Adams became acquainted with the three daughters of the Reverend William Smith of nearby Weymouth. His wife was the daughter of Colonel John Quincy, who for a dozen years had served as Speaker of the Great and General Court, the province's elected legislature. Cranch was courting their eldest daughter, Mary, and John became attracted to the second daughter, Abigail.

Like his father, John Adams had managed to fall in love with a woman from a more socially prestigious background than he himself could claim. But Abigail Smith had more to offer than that. The woman destined to be the wife of John Adams and the mother of John Quincy Adams lacked, as did most women of that day, any formal education. But her father's extensive library, with its Bible, its religious tracts, its classical tales, its English poets, and its Shakespeare, provided more than an equivalent. The letters of Abigail Adams reveal an inquiring mind, a voracious appetite for reading, a keen discernment of other people's character, and an intense love and loyalty to her husband and her family. Although her parents harbored misgivings about the match, Abigail Smith married John Adams on October 25, 1764. In the following July a daughter, also named Abigail, was born to them. Two years after that, on July 11, 1767, Abigail bore a son, whom they named John Quincy Adams, after her grandfather.

Seventeenth-century puritanism was based on two assumptions that affected those who came into contact with it. One was the notion of the "elect," which held that God chose a small handful of mortals to do His work in an otherwise hopelessly sinful world, and that the rest were doomed to eternal damnation. The other was the idea of the "calling," which asserted that God had selected a role for every one in life, rich and poor, high and low alike, and that a person's first real task was to determine his "calling," and then proceed to fill it as best he could. If one did this, the probability that he (or she) was one of the elect was vastly increased. The two ideas thus reinforced one another.

In John Adams' day, both ideas had been modified. Among educated people in New England the fear of eternal damnation for the unelected retreated before the more comforting notion that God's grace was available for all who truly sought it. The "calling" was modified to a belief in the dignity of all honest and diligent work. Adams, who first considered both the ministry and school-teaching, eventually realized, in his own mind at least, that his "calling" was the law. In time he became the most prominent lawyer in the province. His mastery of the law, and the history behind the law, made him not only a formidable opponent in the courtroom, but an effective propagandist on behalf of the colonial cause when controversy broke out between Great Britain and her North American possessions in the 1760's. His speeches, letters, and newspaper essays became a critical part of the arsenal used by the American patriot cause.

We know more about John Adams than we do about any of the founders of the Republic. The twin doctrines of the elect and the calling insisted upon a remorseless self-scrutiny. In John Adams' case—and even more so with his son John Quincy—we have a mountain of material with which to deal. "Whatever you write, preserve," John Adams remarked, and both John and John Quincy almost always did. In the case of both, the private side of their lives can be scrutinized in ways unmatched by few, if any, of their contemporaries. "Oh! that I could wear out of my mind every mean and base affectation, conquer my natural Pride and Self Conceit . . . and subdue every unworthy Passion and treat all men as I wish to be treated by all," John Adams wrote—and preserved—when he was twenty-one years old.

For many, especially his critics, John Adams was temperamental, vain, and egotistical, but to those who knew him better, he was a warm and emotional human being with a compelling sense of duty. Two years before John Quincy Adams was born, his father was appointed to draft the town of Braintree's instructions to its representative in the General Court, denouncing the Stamp Act of 1765. The following year, at cousin Samuel Adams' urging, John Adams was a successful candidate for selectman. With this new responsibility came a loss of income from his legal practice, but the loss provided Adams with justification for his political ambitions. "The only principles of public conduct that are worthy of a gentleman, or a man," Adams quoted his early hero James Otis, "are, to sacrifice estate, ease, health and applause, and even life itself to the sacred calls of his country." The problem was, Adams later wrote, that even with true patriotism, there was "an alloy of Ambition, of Pride, and avarice that debases the Composition, and produces mischievous effects." Avoidance of the sin of pride, through self-sacrifice, became an Adams trait, one that in time would be passed on to his eldest son.

Shortly after John Quincy Adams' birth came news of the passage of new tax laws, this time the so-called Townshend duties on lead, paper, glass, paint, and tea. A raucous Boston town meeting voted to boycott British imports until the taxes were repealed. In Braintree, John Adams thought he needed to be closer to the action. He moved his family to Boston, first renting a house on Brattle Square in 1768 and then moving to another house on Cold Lane the following year. In the meantime, in order to demonstrate its determination, the royal government dispatched two regiments of soldiers, who proceeded to encamp on Boston Common. Later they chose to drill on Brattle Square, in front of Adams' house.

For the next two years the Adamses lived in what many Bostonians regarded as an occupied town. Tensions rose steadily between townspeople and the British soldiers until the night of March 5, 1770, when five people were killed in what became known as the Boston Massacre. The next day Adams was approached by a friend of Captain Preston, the commanding officer of the accused men. They could find no one to defend them in court, he was told, and they feared for their lives. But if John Adams, whose reputation for integrity was unassailable, would step forward to defend the accused, others might do so as well. "I had no hesitation in answering that Council ought to be the very last thing that an accused person should want in a free Country," he recalled, and agreed to take the case, which he proceeded to win.

In defending the British, Adams risked his career and leadership position, but "Judgement of Death against these Soldiers," he wrote three years later, "would have been as foul a Stain upon this Country as the Executions of the Quakers or Witches, anciently." The town of Boston evidently agreed, for that spring the citizens elected him as a delegate to the Massachusetts General Court. He was reelected in 1773, and nominated to a seat on the Governor's Council, only to be vetoed by Governor Thomas Hutchinson as being too conspicuous an opponent of the Crown.

The tension between the colonies and Great Britain relaxed after the Massacre, but it intensified again after the granting of special privileges to the British East India Company, which helped precipitate the Boston Tea Party in late 1773. For five months, the town of Boston, the colony of Massachusetts, and Anglo-Americans in general waited for the reaction from London to the destruction of the East India Company's property. It came on May 13, 1774, in the person of General Thomas Gage, newly appointed Governor of the colony, and in the Coercive Acts, the most significant of which called for the shutting down of the entire port of Boston until the tea should be paid for. By that time, John Adams had moved his family back to Braintree, although he held on to his house. His son would later use it as a law office.

Not long thereafter John Adams was chosen as one of five delegates from Massachusetts to a Continental Congress, expected to meet in Philadelphia late in the summer of 1774. By this time John Quincy Adams was seven years old, his older sister Abigail (usually called Nabby) nine, and his two younger brothers Charles and Thomas, four and two. It was an exciting time in which to be born and to grow up, especially if one's father was a key player in public affairs.

FOR THE NEXT TEN YEARS, John Adams was to spend most of his time away from Abigail, including six years in Europe, but she rarely complained to her husband or to anyone else. As for Adams, he rationalized the separations as sacrifices that true patriots were expected to make, thus shielding himself from any self-doubts over the vanity, improper ambition or the overbearing pursuit of fame that he often detected in others.

The separation of John from Abigail Adams produced a remarkable correspondence between the two. Next to his family's safety in a troubled time, John Adams' major concern was for the proper education of his children, on which the puritan culture placed much emphasis, and the responsibility for which would now fall upon his wife. He had no doubt of her abilities, but nonetheless felt obliged to deliver little lectures on the subject from various places, both in America and later in Europe. "The education of our Children is never out of my Mind," he wrote, on his way to Philadelphia.

"Train them to Virtue, habituate them to industry, activity, and Spirit. Make them consider every Vice, as shamefull and unmanly; fire them with Ambition to be usefull—make them disdain to be destitute of any usefull, or ornamental Knowledge or Accomplishment. Fix their Ambition upon great and solid Objects, and their Contempt upon little, frivolous, and useless ones." This was the sturdy language of many of the founders, particularly the emphasis upon "virtue," which in the eighteenth century meant subordination of the private interest to the public good, or the "commonwealth." Religion, too, was tied to virtue. "My Opinion of the duties of Religion and Morality, comprehends a very extensive Connection with society at large, and the great Interest of the public," he wrote while observing the debates in the Continental Congress. "Public virtues, and political qualities therefore should be incessantly cherished in our children."

Inner moral strength and outward public virtue: these two themes Adams repeated endlessly during his absences from Braintree. They were meant for the entire family, daughter as well as sons, although the nature of their education would not be the same. Abigail was in full agreement, having the same aspirations for her family. Already "Nabby" was writing letters to her father, and John Quincy was learning Latin and reading a page or two of Charles Rollin's *Ancient History* every day. Instruction in French, which Abigail read and understood better than her husband, soon followed.

In late 1774 John Adams returned to Braintree, Congress having agreed to re-assemble in the following spring. Now, the British soldiers who drilled at one end of Boston Common were met by colonial militia marching and countermarching at the other end. The seven-year-old John Quincy Adams was taken by his father's cousin Samuel to witness the spectacle. With neither side willing to back down, the stage was set for the inevitable clash at Concord and Lexington the following April. After it came, thousands of men from all over New England streamed toward Boston in hopes of bottling up His Majesty's troops. Some of them came through Braintree, where the Adams family provided food and rest. Abigail Adams melted down the family pewter for bullets, and one militiaman—who reminded John Quincy Adams of it fifty years later when he was President of the United States—instructed the young boy in the manual of arms.

All was not grim seriousness, however, in the spring of 1775. The rocks and hills of Braintree offered a thousand mysteries to a young boy free to ramble in search of robbers' dens, pirate treasures, or simply spectacular views of Boston Harbor. But the life of such a youngster was not without hazards. While his father was on his way back to Philadelphia, John Quincy managed to break a finger, necessitating a visit from none other than Dr. Joseph Warren, the popular president of the illegal Massachusetts Provincial Congress. Dr. Warren, whose efforts saved John Quincy's finger, and possibly his hand, made an indelible impression.

Outside of Boston, the American forces feared an attack by the better-trained British regulars, and so decided to bring about a confrontation on their own terms. In mid-June, a group of several hundred colonials fortified the Charlestown peninsula across from Boston itself, defying the British to attack. They did. On June 17, the Adamses in Braintree heard the dull thud of distant cannon. Clouds of smoke could be seen to the northeast. Abigail and John Quincy Adams climbed to the top of one of the highest rocks on their farm and saw that the cannon fire came from the British ships at the mouth of the Charles River, and that the smoke came from the burning ruins of Charlestown itself. They were witnessing what the world would call the Battle of Bunker Hill. The next day word came that Dr. Warren, who turned down a command position in order to fight with the rank and file, had been killed.

John Quincy Adams never forgot either the Battle of Bunker Hill or Dr. Warren. Years later, when he was in college, he refused to participate in the ceremonies opening a new bridge over the Charles River because they were to take place near the exact spot where Dr. Warren was thought to have died. In his old age, he could still recall "Britannia's thunders in the Battle of Bunker's Hill," and the family's tears upon learning of "the fall of Warren, a dear friend of my father, and a beloved Physician to me." There would be others. John Quincy's uncle Elihu Adams and his grandmother Elizabeth Quincy

Smith would both be dead by the end of the year, victims of a dysentery epidemic brought on by the unsanitary conditions spread by both armies.

From June 1775 to March 1776 the Continental Army, now commanded by George Washington, laid siege to the British forces in Boston. Then, on March 17, the army sailed away to Nova Scotia. John Quincy promptly wrote to inform his father. "I hope you and your Sister and Brothers will take proper Notice of these great Events," replied the senior Adams. "I hope you will all remember, how many Losses, Dangers, and Inconveniences, have been borne by your Parents, and the Inhabitants of Boston in general for the Sake of preserving Freedom for you and yours—and I hope you will all follow the virtuous Example if, in any future Time, your Countrys Liberties should be in Danger, and suffer every human Evil, rather than Give them up."

In Philadelphia, John Adams had met new members of the Continental Congress, including young Thomas Jefferson of Virginia and old Benjamin Franklin of Pennsylvania. He, Jefferson, and Franklin had been appointed to a committee charged with drafting a declaration in support of complete independence from Great Britain. Not until it was over, did Adams breathe a word to his family. When independence was agreed upon, and the Declaration adopted, he finally broke the news. "I am apt to believe," he predicted of Independence Day, in perhaps his most famous letter to Abigail, "that it will be celebrated, by succeeding Generations, as the great anniversary Festival. It ought to be commemorated, as the Day of Deliverance by solemn Acts of Devotion to God Almighty. It ought to be solemnized with Pomp and Parade, with Shows, Games, Sports, Guns, Bells, Bonfires and Illuminations from one End of this continent to the other, from this Time forward forever more."

By the summer of 1776 nine-year-old John Quincy Adams was making his contribution to the American Revolution by carrying the family mail on horseback from Braintree to Boston and back. Not that his education was being neglected. His mother had discovered a book of lessons entitled *The Renowned History of Giles Gingerbread: A Little Boy Who Lived upon Learning*. It told of little Giles, a baker's son, whose father baked books made of gingerbread. With this for an incentive, Giles literally devoured his lessons. Each was designed to impart both knowledge and values, emphasizing "duty to family and society, unfaltering morality, undogmatic piety, regular industry, and zeal for learning," the same republican ideals the Adamses and other families sought to impress upon their children in the late eighteenth century. As Giles literally devoured his lessons, so John Quincy Adams figuratively consumed his, in the years of his father's absence at Philadelphia.

John Adams' absence resulted in a renewed series of Polonius-like admonitions to his wife about how she should raise the family. "Fix their Attention," he exhorted in 1776, "upon great and glorious Objects, root out every little Thing, weed out every meanness, make them great and manly. Teach them to scorn Injustice, Ingratitude, Cowardice, and Falsehood. Let them revere nothing but Religion, Morality, and Liberty." There were times when Adams struggled with doubts. Who could be sure, in 1776, that the struggle for independence would be worth it? Or that it would succeed at all? What would the world be saying in 1786? Or 1796? Or 1826? What would his own children be saying then of his sacrifices? He needed reassurance. "I believe my Children will think I might as well have thought and laboured, a little, night and Day for their benefit," he told Abigail. But what if they didn't? If not, if they preferred a life of ease and elegance, then "they are not my Children."

He need not have worried. Abigail Adams saw to it that her husband received letters from his children, especially from his eldest son, that told him his sacrifices were not in vain. One of John Quincy's earliest letters to his father, written before his tenth birthday, asked for instructions as to how he should use his time most profitably. Would his father send him a notebook, so that he might "transcribe the most remarkable occurrences I mett with in my reading which will Serve to fix them upon my mind"? A few days later he wrote again of how much he enjoyed "the perusal of history," and assured father that "I am more satisfied with myself when I have applied part of my time to Some useful employment than when I have Idled it away with trifles and play." Back came more instruction from Philadelphia. John Quincy should read Thucydides' history of the Pelopennesian Wars, since "the future circumstances of your

Country, may require other Wars, as well as Councils and Negotiations," John Adams wrote. "I wish to turn your thoughts early to such studies, as will afford you the most solid Instruction and Improvement for the Part which may be allotted to you to act on the Stage of Life."

A few months later an opportunity arose for serious "Instruction and Improvement" for both father and son. John Adams was appointed one of three commissioners to negotiate an alliance with France. If he took the position, it meant an even longer separation from wife and family, further loss of income from his legal practice, a hazardous ocean voyage in time of war, and possible capture and trial followed by a traitor's death. Naturally, Adams accepted the appointment. Not only that, but he resolved to take his ten-year-old eldest son with him. Up to then, the education of John Quincy Adams had been primarily under the eye of his mother. Now, it passed to his father. A voyage to Europe would provide a rare opportunity for instruction in John Quincy's yet undetermined role upon "the Stage of Life."

After weeks of preparation and leave-taking, not without second thoughts and the shedding of tears, father and son embarked for France in February 1778 upon the American frigate *Boston*. The voyage quickly threatened to become a disaster, as the *Boston* was chased by a British frigate. John Adams prepared to throw his papers overboard and the crew prepared for battle, but the British vessel unaccountably lost interest at the last moment. That night the *Boston* was hit by a North Atlantic gale, father and son huddling in their bunk, as John Adams recalled, "our feet against the bed Boards and Bedsteads, to prevent us from having our Brains dashed out against the Planks and Timbers of the Ship." Lightning struck the vessel, mortally wounding one of the crew. With the return of calm weather, the Americans went on the offensive, capturing a British merchantman. While chasing another vessel, a signal gun exploded on deck, wounding an American Lieutenant and necessitating a crude amputation of his leg. Young John Quincy was present during the amputation, and afterwards, when the unfortunate man died of gangrene, watched as his remains were committed to the sea. Over half a century later, John Quincy Adams could recall the event as one of the most "painfully impressive" in his life. Given the dangers to which they had been exposed, John Adams confessed to regrets about bringing his son with him.

When they were not fighting seasickness and the elements, or chasing or being chased by the enemy, father and son studied French with the help of a friendly French army surgeon, although by the end of the voyage neither could as yet speak the language with confidence. John Quincy was also instructed by the ship's crew in the names of all the sails and the points of the mariner's compass. At the end of March, the *Boston* touched safely at the French port of Bordeaux.

Upon their arrival, the two Adamses were greeted effusively by the French authorities, but were told that while they were crossing the Atlantic, a treaty of alliance had already been concluded in Paris. While good news for the Americans, it also suggested that John Adams' voyage was superfluous. He hurried on to Paris to assess the situation and to confer with Benjamin Franklin and Arthur Lee, the other two commissioners. "Doctor" Franklin lived in the suburb of Passy, where John Quincy was placed in Monsieur Le Couer's boarding school, in company with Benjamin Franklin Bache, the Doctor's grandson, and a few other American youths. While the senior Adams was being introduced to the mysteries of European diplomacy, his son continued his study of French and Latin, along with dancing, fencing, music, and drawing—the latter subjects deemed essential to the education of a French gentleman, if not an American one.

John Quincy Adams took to Monsieur Le Couer's academy with alacrity, perhaps because, as his father suggested, "Rewards were given to the best Schollars." He was able to pick up more French in a single day than his father could in a week, which both pleased and mortified the senior Adams. John Quincy spent weekends with his father, diligently turning out letter after letter to his family and friends in Braintree. Not all of them were received, owing to the vicissitudes of wartime communication, but those that did showed the same solemnity demonstrated in his earlier letters to his father in Philadelphia, and a reiteration of the family catechism. "We are Sent into this world for Some end," he told one of his brothers. "It is our duty to discover by Close study what this end is & when we once discover it to pursue it with unconquerable perseverance."

The writing of letters fulfilled several educational purposes important to the Adams family. It improved penmanship in an age when the handwritten word was the principal form of communication. It taught mental discipline and developed the faculties of written expression. And of course it served to convey news, as it did in John Quincy's letter to his mother in April, 1778. "I Suppose before this reaches you," he wrote, "you will hear of the Treaty Concluded between France and america Which I believe will rouse the hearts of the americans exceedingly and also of the desire of the English To make Peace with us and of the Commisioners dispatchd from England for that Purpose." These early letters of John Quincy Adams were written under the close supervision of his father, just as his mother had supervised those written before. Now John Adams was encouraging his son to keep a diary, although for the time being, John Quincy resisted. "A journal Book or letter Book of a lad of Eleven years old, cannot be expected to Contain much of Science, Litterature, arts, wisdom, or wit," he said.

Abigail Adams now took over the role formerly played by her husband in exhorting her son, through letters, to take advantage of the opportunities before him and rise to the highest of moral standards in doing so. "Great Learning and superior abilities, should you ever possess them, will be of little value and small Estimation, unless Virtue, Honor, Truth, and integrity are added to them," she wrote from the Braintree farmhouse. What was true of individuals was also true of nations. One had only to look to England, she said, who had left the paths of virtue and morality in favor of corruption and decadence, and was now sunk into "derision and infamy." Both John and Abigail Adams clung to the conviction that in the long run only the virtuous, the morally sound, deserved success in this world. "Dear as you are to me," Abigail told her son, "I had much rather you should have found your grave in the ocean you have crossed, or any untimely death crop you in your infant years, rather than see you an immoral profligate or a Graceless child."

John Quincy Adams spent less than a year at M. Le Couer's school. His father reluctantly concluded that there was no need for three American commissioners in Paris when one, presumably Franklin, could handle affairs quite as easily if not as efficiently. In fact, the presence of three commissioners had led to dissension and recrimination, mostly between Franklin and Lee, which the American cause could hardly afford. Adams accordingly made plans to return home, but first needed permission from Congress. While waiting to hear from America, both Adamses took full advantage of the allurements of Paris. They climbed the hills of Montmartre, walked silently through the magnificent churches, and patronized the many bookstalls. It was in Paris that John Quincy began to form his lifelong attachment to the theater, which in this case not only improved his fluency in French, but provided the opportunity to observe French society on the stage and in the audiences. His passion for the theater would continue to grow in the coming years, so that no matter where he found himself, in a small town or a big city, the local theater rarely escaped his notice. Yet, like the generations of American tourists that would follow them, the Adamses were uneasy amongst the splendor and sophistication of Paris and Versailles. "I cannot help suspecting," John Adams wrote to Abigail soon after their arrival, "that the more Elegance the less Virtue in all Times and Countries." Americans would have to be on guard against the threats posed by too much luxury and elegance in the future.

Congress agreed with John Adams' suggestion that Benjamin Franklin be named the sole American minister to France, but it was vague regarding its plans for Adams himself. Not content with this, he determined to return to America as soon as possible. In March, just over a year since their departure from Braintree, father and son left for the coastal town of Nantes, where they hoped to catch the first sailing vessel for home. Again, disappointment awaited them. A three-month delay loomed ahead as they were told to await the arrival of the new French minister to the United States.

Time was not completely wasted. Under his father's tutelage John Quincy began serious study of the Latin classics, especially the orations of Cicero, whose denunciations of the tyrannies of Cataline, Julius Caesar, and Mark Anthony were particular favorites of Americans because attacks on a corrupt Rome provided inspiration for attacks on imperial Britain. As the weather grew warmer, young John

Quincy learned to swim under the guidance of French sailors in the harbor at Nantes. And on at least one occasion they were guests of the American-born merchant Joshua Johnson, whose normal residence was in London, but who had taken refuge in France for the duration. Among Johnson's large family was four-year-old Louisa Catherine, whom John Quincy Adams would marry eighteen years later.

At last, the French minister, the Chevalier de la Luzerne, and his secretary, Francois Barbé-Marbois, arrived from Paris. On June 17, 1779, the Adamses and the French delegation sailed from Nantes on *La Sensible*, a French frigate much larger and better armed than the *Boston*. Moreover, they sailed as part of a Franco-American convoy that included the famous Captain John Paul Jones and his ship, the *Bonhomme Richard*. The return voyage was uneventful. John Quincy spent much of the time teaching English to La Luzerne and Barbé-Marbois, whose knowledge of that language was like that of the Adamses' knowledge of French the year before. As a tutor, the twelve-year-old John Quincy Adams was a success. "The Chevalier de la Luzerne, and M. Marbois are in raptures with my Son," John Adams reported proudly to his diary: "I found this Morning the Ambassador, Seating on the Cushing in our State Room, Mr. Marbois in his Cot at his left Hand and my Son stretched out in his at his Right—The Ambassador reading out loud . . . and my Son correcting the Pronunciation of every Word and Syllable and Letter." The two Frenchmen were insistent that John Quincy continue as their teacher throughout the voyage. "He shews us no Mercy and Makes Us no Compliments," they told his father.

La Sensible sailed into Boston Harbor on August 3, 1779, accompanied by a thirteen-gun salute. Much had happened since John Quincy and his father had left eighteen months before. Strengthened by the French alliance, the American war effort had been renewed. George Washington had left Valley Forge, and Spain had entered the war against England. Congress, having been chased out of Philadelphia in 1777, had since returned. It was now sure enough of its position to appoint a new commissioner with full powers to negotiate a treaty of independence and peace—in that order—with Great Britain. The man they chose for the task was John Adams.

At first it seemed unlikely that John Quincy would accompany his father on a second voyage to Europe. He lacked formal schooling, and was at an age when Yankee boys in his social and economic class should be thinking about college. It was the turn of his nine-year-old brother Charles to accompany his father instead. But Abigail Adams, facing what would turn out to be the longest of the separations from her husband, persuaded John Quincy to make a second crossing, both for his own sake, and for his father's. "These are times in which a Genious would wish to live," she reminded him in a letter that would soon follow across the Atlantic. "It is not in the still calm of life, or the repose of a pacific station, that great characters are formed. . . . The habits of a vigorous mind are formed in contending with difficulties." On November 13, 1779, *La Sensible* made its return to Europe, carrying three Adamses. Brother Charles went with John Quincy, as did John Thaxter, a young cousin of Abigail's who would act as tutor and older brother, and Francis Dana, a promising Boston attorney who would act as secretary to the mission. John Quincy would not see his home again for nearly six years.

His second voyage marked the beginning of John Quincy Adams' diary, one of the most remarkable documents in American history. Begun in a childish scrawl that evolved into the mature and legible hand peculiar to several generations of his family, the diary of John Quincy Adams is both a record of the life of its author and a primary source for a good part of the history of the early republic. In the beginning it was little more than a record of day-to-day happenings in the life of its young author. There would be periods during which it was abandoned entirely. But as the boy became a man, the diary became not only a record, but a repository for introspection, self-analysis, and confession. John Quincy Adams came to grips with himself and the world about him through his diary.

Two weeks after her departure from Boston, *La Sensible* sprung a leak, forcing the captain to alter his course and head for land. On December 9, 1779, the Adams party found themselves not in France, but in northwest Spain, in the coastal town of Ferrol. They were over a thousand miles from Paris, with the prospect of a hazardous overland journey ahead of them in the dead of winter. Wasting no time, John Adams promptly bought Spanish grammar books for his sons, chartered three carriages and three mules, hired an appropriate number of Spanish servants, and was on his way.

The portion of Spain over which they travelled contrasted with the grandeur and elegance of Paris. This was the other Europe, the Europe of dingy peasants' hovels that were drafty and cold in winter and intolerably hot in summer. The roads were poor. There were few decent inns, most of them chimneyless with only a hole in the roof through which most but not all of the smoke from the open fireplaces escaped. "They shew us chambers in which any body would think half a dozen hogs had lived there six months," grumbled John Quincy to his new diary. Things improved somewhat when they crossed the border into France. They stopped at Bordeaux, where John and John Quincy had been greeted so effusively two years before, and then travelled directly to Paris, where they arrived exactly two months from the day they set foot in Spain. The Adams brothers were placed in school at Passy, where they settled for several months.

While John Quincy Adams and his brother were studying their lessons, their father was learning the lesson of the pitfalls into which small nations may tumble when they tie their fortunes too closely to large ones. The French foreign minister, the Comte de Vergennes, made it clear to the senior Adams that he preferred that he not reveal the nature of his mission publicly and instead combine American diplomacy with that of the French. In this Vergennes had the support of Benjamin Franklin. Realizing that financial dependence on the French meant political dependence as well, John Adams determined to seek help elsewhere.

Apart from France, the most likely source of funds for the American cause was the Dutch Republic, whose Amsterdam bankers had been financing wars for centuries. Not only that, but the Dutch themselves had once been colonies who had fought for and won their independence; their form of government was similar to that of the Americans, they were overwhelmingly Protestant, and unlike France, were not so powerful as to attempt to dictate American diplomacy. They seemed willing to invest in the American Revolution with no strings attached—provided their interest was paid on time. Against the wishes of Vergennes and Franklin, John Adams left Paris for Amsterdam in July, 1780, taking his two sons with him.

Amsterdam was a bustling commercial center, dependent upon the ocean and international trade. In this it was more like Boston than Paris, which was one reason the Adamses at first found it so congenial. "I am very much pleased with Holland," John Adams told Abigail shortly after their arrival. Unlike the elegant French, the Dutch offered a good example to Americans. "The Frugality, Cleanliness, &c. here, deserve the Imitation of my Countrymen. The Fruit of these Virtues has been immense wealth, and great Prosperity." He he decided to stay, and placed John Quincy and Charles in a "Latin School."

This did not mean that either parent relaxed the supervision of their children's intellectual and moral development. As before, John Quincy received regular instruction, admonition, and criticism; advice on his studies, how much time he should allocate to recreation, what books should be read, and how his handwriting should be improved. Important in John Adams' mind was his sons' grounding in the ancient languages, for only through them could one gain access to the political wisdom of the Greeks and the Roman republic, with whom Americans identified in their struggle against the British empire. Study of these languages—or indeed any language—encouraged mental discipline and the arts of oral and written expression. Science, mathematics, and geography could wait, John Quincy was told, until he returned home. Painting, fencing, dancing, and the "Gentlemanly" arts could wait even longer.

There was a system in these priorities. In a letter to Abigail, John Adams explained: "I must study Politicks and War that my sons may have liberty to study Mathematics and Philosophy. My sons ought to study Mathematics and Philosophy, Geography, natural History, Naval Architecture, navigation, Commerce and Agriculture, in order to give their Children a right to study Painting, Poetry, Musick, Architecture, Statuary, Tapestry and Porcelaine." John Adams believed that Americans would have to postpone dreams of wealth and power until they established their independence and mastered the art of governing themselves. It was up to his generation to point the way.

The Latin School proved to be more authoritarian than the relaxed atmosphere at Passy, and unexpected problems developed. Classes were usually conducted in Dutch, which neither John Quincy nor Charles knew well enough, and the two unhappy Americans were relegated to a separate room. Charles became homesick and John Quincy became "impertinent" (according to the Rector), and was all but expelled before his father withdrew both brothers from the school. John Adams now perceived a different side to the Dutch character. The schoolmasters, he complained to Abigail, were "mean Spirited Writches," and the constant pursuit of wealth often resulted in "Avarice and Stingyness." He would not permit his sons to be educated in such an atmosphere.

Then he learned that the two boys could attend classes at nearby Leyden University, reputed to be one of the finest institutions of higher learning in all Europe. Over a century and a half before, the Reverend John Robinson, William Bradford, William Brewster, and several dozen other English separatists had lived in Leyden prior to their momentous decision to seek a new refuge in North America, which led to the founding of the Plymouth colony in 1620. No New Englander could walk the streets of Leyden without a sense of reverence. His father sought to impress John Quincy with the full scope of opportunity that lay before him. Some of the most outstanding Englishmen and Americans had been students there in the past, and John Adams clearly expected his son to follow in their footsteps. Lectures were to be attended and lessons read. "You will ever remember," he told him, "that all the End of Study is to make you a good Man and a useful Citizen."

Although he had not yet reached his fourteenth birthday, John Quincy Adams' letters to his father from Leyden indicate the struggle between boyhood and manhood. On the one hand he would request the use of his father's set of Alexander Pope's works, ask whether he should read the Latin playwright Terence in translation or the original, ask whether he should buy an obscure essay here or there; and on the other seek permission to buy a pair of ice skates to use on the frozen Leyden canals, or ask if he might have a pen-knife ("I want one very much, and can't get one here").

But for the boy in John Quincy Adams, it was already a lost cause. In the spring of 1781 Congress decided to seek recognition from Catherine the Great of Russia in hopes of further weakening the British position in Europe. Francis Dana, the Massachusetts lawyer who was serving as secretary to the American mission in Paris, was appointed Minister with full powers to negotiate a treaty with the Empress. Understanding little French—the universal language of diplomacy in the eighteenth century—Dana requested of John Adams the loan of his eldest son as interpreter. After the usual hesitation and misgiving, John Adams agreed. John Quincy would spend his fourteenth birthday on the road to Russia and its capital city, St. Petersburg.

AS HE TRAVELLED WITH DANA and a servant through Germany and Poland, the younger Adams recorded the same poverty and the gulf between rich and poor, that he had seen in Spain. Poland in particular, still in the thralls of serfdom, impressed him. "All the Farmers are in the most abject slavery," he wrote back to his father. "They are bought and sold like so many beasts, and are sometimes even chang'd for dogs or horses." That such things also took place in their own country did not, as yet, seem of importance to either Adams.

Upon their arrival in St. Petersburg, he and Dana learned to their dismay that there were no schools available to foreigners. "There is nobody here but Princes and Slaves," John Quincy reported indignantly. The latter were denied any learning at all, and the former sent their children to other countries to be educated. To make matters worse, John Quincy discovered that he had left his Latin-English dictionary behind, which precluded further classical studies for many months. As the Russian winter closed in, he buried himself in his room, occasionally borrowing books from the small English-language library in St. Petersburg. He had already read Voltaire's history of Russia, and supplemented this with other Rus-

These pastel portraits of Abigail Adams and John Adams were made by Benjamin Blyth, a local artist, probably in 1763, four years before the birth of John Quincy Adams. They are the earliest known likenesses of each. *Courtesy of the Massachusetts Historical Society.*

sian histories, usually written in French. By the time the snows had melted from the fields and the ice disappeared from the city's canals, John Quincy had read (or so he claimed in his diary) all eight volumes of Hume's *History of England,* Adam Smith's *Wealth of Nations,* Catharine MacCaulay's *History of England,* Robertson's *History of Charles V,* Watson's *History of Phillip II,* and several books of plays and poems. Under Dana's supervision he continued the study of Cicero's orations, translating them from Latin or French into English.

He had time on his hands because there was little need for his services as interpreter. The Empress, unwilling to risk a rupture with Britain, kept Dana at arm's length. But in France and in America events were moving toward a successful conclusion for the Americans without the help of Russia. While young Adams was translating his Cicero and copying his Shakespeare, George Washington was cornering and defeating Lord Cornwallis in Virginia. When the news of Washington's victory arrived in Europe, the log-jam of diplomacy was broken. By the spring of 1782 John Adams had negotiated diplomatic recognition of the United States by the Dutch government. He decided that it was time for John Quincy to return to Leyden. Brother Charles had already been sent home the summer before. John Adams was lonely, and admitted it. "I want you with me," he told John Quincy in May. He was even more explicit to his wife. "I must go to you or you must come to me. I cannot live, in this horrid Solitude."

It took several more months for John Quincy to make the necessary arrangements to leave St. Petersburg. (Among other things, anyone wishing to depart had to have his name posted three times in the newspapers.) Leaving Dana behind, he left in late October 1782, travelling through Finland (then part of Sweden) to Stockholm and Goteborg. Scandinavians had been generally supportive of the American cause, and John Quincy retained pleasant memories of an otherwise bleak winter in 1782–83 because of the friendliness exhibited towards him in Sweden. "There is no Country in Europe," he told his diary, "where the people are more hospitable and affable to Strangers, or more hospitable among themselves than the Sweeds." From there he went to Denmark, and after nearly a month's sojourn in Copenhagen, sailed to Hamburg in March 1783.

In late April young Adams arrived at the Dutch capital of the Hague and settled in with the family of the Swiss-born Charles William Frederick Dumas, a learned revolutionary who had thrown himself heart and soul into the American cause and was the United States agent in the Netherlands. The Dumas family lived at the Hotel Etat-Unis, the house purchased by Congress for use as an American base of operations. Dumas acted as tutor to John Quincy during his stay in Holland.

While his son travelled, John Adams, along with Franklin and the newly-arrived John Jay, was engaged in the momentous diplomacy that led to British recognition of American independence. His distrust of the French had not lessened with time, and it now included Franklin, whose sunny disposition Adams was convinced only concealed laziness and even senility. Congress had instructed the Americans to defer to the French, but both Adams and Jay chose to ignore the instructions, and came to a preliminary agreement with Britain on their own at the end of November, 1782. They even persuaded Franklin that theirs was the right course.

Delays in signing the final treaty of peace with Great Britain prevented John Adams from retrieving his son from Holland until summer. He took John Quincy back to Paris, where he employed him as his personal secretary. The son's diary recorded the sights and spectacles that interested him, and most everything did. He attended plays at the Bois de Boulogne and the *Comedie Francaise*. He conversed with the scholarly Abbe de Mably about the social system of Poland and with the French Minister to Denmark about future trading prospects between the United States and the Scandinavian countries. He and his father were among the throng in August, 1783, that watched Monsieur Montgolfier's hydrogen balloon ascensions, designed eventually to cross the English Channel.

The stress of European diplomacy took its toll on the senior Adams' health, which only strengthened his determination to reunite as much of his family as possible. With peace declared in September, 1783, and with every expectation of being named the first American Minister to Great Britain, John Adams sent for his wife and daughter to join him in Europe. His two youngest sons would stay behind, probably to be joined by their eldest brother in due course. In late October, father and son crossed the Channel to England, partly with the intent of "taking the waters" at Bath, the famous health spa, but also to investigate the possibilities for an Anglo-American commercial treaty. It was their first visit to the "mother country" so recently their enemy, and they made it with mixed emotions. They spent much of their time as tourists, visiting Westminster Abbey, Buckingham Palace, St. Paul's Cathedral, and the British Museum. John Quincy attended the theaters in Covent Garden and Drury Lane as much as he could, where he saw the famed Mrs. Siddons in a variety of Shakespearian roles. They also visited the homes of several Americans living in London, including the Johnson family, whom they had last seen in Nantes in 1779. When John Adams was recalled to the Netherlands to deal with the Amsterdam bankers early in 1784, John Quincy returned to the Hague, M. Dumas, and his studies.

That spring, John Adams sent John Quincy to meet his mother and sister in London. This first journey proved to be a false start owing to misinformation, but young Adams took advantage of the situation to attend Parliamentary debates and watch the great orators of the era: Charles James Fox, Edmund Burke, Lord North, and William Pitt the Younger. He enjoyed the rivals Pitt and Fox the most, he dutifully reported to his father, but added for good measure that "it is a real misfortune for this country that those talents which were meant to promote the honor and power of the nation should be prostituted to the views of interest and ambition." In late July, 1784, his mother and sister at last arrived. John Quincy met them, armed with a letter from his father describing him as "the greatest Traveller of his age." John Adams then rushed to London, and together the four Adamses made the journey to Paris, where Franklin, Adams, and the newly-arrived Thomas Jefferson had been assigned new diplomatic responsibilities.

Avoiding what he later called the "tainted Atmosphere" of the city, John Quincy's father rented an impressive home in the suburb of Auteuil. Here for nearly a year the Adams family spent what may have been the most pleasant days of their lives together, despite the absence of the two youngest sons. Husband and wife were reunited after five years' separation, and John Quincy took his sister on outings to Paris—including several visits to the theater. He spent most of the evenings plunged in his studies, which now included mathematics. His father was his tutor. "You hear nothing till nine o'clock but of theorems and problems, bisecting and dissecting tangents and segments," Abigail Adams wrote to her sister.

With most of Europe at peace, life in Paris for the ruling classes was at its gayest in the few years that were left to it before the storm of the French Revolution. In late March, 1785, a son, soon to become the ill-fated Dauphin, and briefly Louis XVII, was born to Queen Marie Antoinette. The birth was literally a public event, noted a scandalized John Quincy Adams. "Everybody that pleases" was admitted to the Queen's chamber, "and if there had been time enough, all Paris would have gone *pour voir accoucher la Reine.*" A few days after the birth of the Dauphin, John Quincy attended a dinner party in which the featured guest was America's most popular Frenchman, the Marquis de la Fayette, whose support for the American cause was deemed by many to have been critical to its success. When the Marquis dismissed the upper classes of France as a "parcel of fools," John Quincy Adams was impressed enough to make a note of it in his diary. He thought the Frenchman a bit too free with his words. "Perhaps he thought that among Americans he could speak his mind without any danger."

It was at this time too that John Quincy Adams made the acquaintance of a man whose career was destined to be intertwined with that of the Adams family for the next forty years. "Spent the evening with Mr. Jefferson," he wrote one day in March 1785, "whom I love to be with because he is a man of very extensive learning, and pleasing manners." The Virginian's passion for knowledge and his easy conversation captivated the Adamses. Jefferson represented a different part of the American world from that of Braintree. The land of tobacco plantations, slavery, and rural isolation seemed to vary as much from New England as did Europe itself. But Jefferson saw "his country" as fully typical of American republicanism as Plymouth Rock. He had even written a book about it— *Notes on the State of Virginia*—which had just appeared in print. John Quincy was a frequent guest at Jefferson's house, as well as his companion in visits around Paris. Jefferson even suggested that his young friend consider the College of William and Mary instead of Harvard for his long-delayed college education.

The idea of an Adams not attending Harvard was, of course, unthinkable, and with the approach of spring—John Quincy's eighth in Europe—all agreed it was time for him to return to Massachusetts. He recalled many years later that "by remaining in Europe I saw a danger of an alienation from my own country," and the possibility of contracting European "sentiments, manners, and opinions." Like his father and most Americans, young John Quincy Adams was distrustful of the cosmopolitan Old World, with its convoluted politics, its religious cynicism, and its hierarchical social system. "I thank Almighty God that I was born in a country where any body may get a good living if they Please," he had written as he travelled with his father through northern Spain. No European country, his mother Abigail rhapsodized, could offer its citizens "the inestimable privilege of setting down under their vines, and fig trees, enjoying in peace and security whatever Heaven sent them, having none to make them afraid." And his father's friend Francis Dana reminded him, "Europe remember is a dangerous school."

And yet John Quincy was reluctant to leave. He liked attending, with his father or with Jefferson, the meetings of scientific academies where learned papers were read or discussed. He enjoyed the museums, the galleries, and the theaters of Paris and London. (At home, the theaters in Boston had been closed ever since the departure of the British, who had used Faneuil Hall to stage plays that made fun of George Washington.) He enjoyed the walks about Paris, the conversations with Franklin, and dinners with La Fayette. Whatever its dangers to an innocent American, European civilization had reached levels of achievement in painting, science, music, and literature that Americans clearly had not attained. Now, he reflected, he would have to return home and "spend one or two years in the Pale of a College, subjected to all the rules, which I have been so long freed from."

It is not easy to summarize the impact of his first European experience upon John Quincy Adams, either in terms of his career as a statesman or on his personal character or temperament. There would come a time when his personal and political enemies would point to his lengthy periods of residence abroad and the "contamination" of republicanism that went with them. Yet there is little in his earliest letters and diaries to suggest this was the case. Rather, as his friend John Thaxter put it, "when you return to our dear Country, you will be in a Situation to make Comparisons, and run your Parallels between the Advantages of the old and new World. If your European Travels have produced the same Effects upon you that mine have upon me, You are much more attached to your own Country than when you left it."

But there were practical concerns as well. Although the Adams family lived comfortably, their standard of living was well below that of other diplomats in Paris and London. The American Congress was not known for its generosity in paying the expenses of its representatives, and Jefferson, Franklin, and Adams often had to dip into their own reserves to make ends meet. "My father has been so much taken up all his lifetime with the Interests of the public that his own fortune has suffered by it," wrote John Quincy. There would be little prospect of an inheritance in the future. The most compelling reason for a return lay in his need to strike out on his own, "in an honourable manner." He could not be dependent upon his parents. Like the United States itself, John Quincy Adams was determined to live *"independent and free."*

Often young people seek to break parental ties by leaving home and travelling abroad. For John Quincy Adams it was the reverse. He would cut loose from his family by going home. On May 12, 1785, he said goodbye to his sister and parents, and set off alone for the port city of L'Orient, on the Brittany coast. Ten days later he was at sea, on a French vessel bound for New York.

Chapter Two

"To Serve My Country at its Call"

"THE CHILD WHOM YOU USED to lead out into the Common, to see with detestation the British troops, and with pleasure the Boston militia, will have the honor to deliver this letter," wrote John Adams to his cousin Samuel in 1785. John Quincy Adams carried this along with letters from his father, Jefferson, La Fayette and others when he arrived in New York city just six days after his eighteenth birthday. After spending about a month there, he set off for home, where he was welcomed by his two brothers and a large contingent of cousins, aunts, and uncles.

A century or so later, some historians would refer to the 1780's as "the critical period" of American history. Independence had been gained, to be sure, but with it had come postwar economic dislocation. Inflation was widespread as many state legislatures tried to alleviate the hard times by printing unsupported paper money. American merchants were learning that there had been some advantages to being part of the British Empire, not the least of which had been the commercial opportunities that went with it. The British had shut down the lucrative American trade to the West Indies— Jamaica, Barbados, and other islands in the Caribbean—and were restricting American fishing rights off the Grand Banks of Newfoundland. Mercantile houses were closed, ships lay idle at their wharves, and farmers and planters were unable to find markets for their grain and tobacco. In protest, Massachusetts closed her ports to British vessels. It was the task of John Quincy's father, in London, to negotiate a treaty of commerce with the former enemy that would save as much as he could of the old commercial rights.

At home, the long-range picture was more encouraging. The population in the major cities and towns continued to grow. New York and Philadelphia increased by one-third in the years between 1776 and 1790. Baltimore doubled its numbers. Thousands of settlers were pouring into the river valleys of western Virginia and the Carolinas in the South, and into the unoccupied lands in western Massachusetts, Vermont, and New York in the North. Despite the hard times, pioneers were seeking even newer land beyond the Appalachians. There they threatened the culture and economy of the Native American tribes, some of whom were newcomers themselves, having been pushed there after the Revolution.

Although the American Revolution had been sparked by Parliament's attempt to consolidate power in the British Empire, Americans in the mid-1780's were being asked to consider whether in order to preserve their independence, they might have to consolidate power at home. Men like New York's Alexander Hamilton and Virginia's James Madison were suggesting radical revision of the weak Articles of Confederation in favor of a more nationalized system. The problems of establishing an effective government in such a far-flung nation, already larger in area than France and Great Britain combined, together with postwar economic stress, dominated political dialogue

But in the summer of 1785, John Quincy Adams' main concern was not defects in the Articles of Confederation but defects in his own preparation for college. He had hoped to be admitted as a junior, not a freshman, but in spite of his studies with his father, Dana, Dumas, Thaxter, and others, he was told by Harvard's president Joseph Willard that this would require a few more months' preparation. Notwithstanding the scope of his reading and his familiarity with both classical and modern languages, he lacked training in the rules of grammar and in certain specific works of logic and philosophy. After a few months of study, he was told, he could be admitted as a junior.

Thus John Quincy Adams spent the winter of 1785–86 at the home of his uncle, the Reverend John Shaw, husband of Abigail's sister Elizabeth. The Shaws lived in Haverhill, a small town about thirty miles northwest of Boston. Uncle John was an old-line Calvinist who ran a tight ship, and it was some time before his nephew could adjust from the leisurely pace of life he had known in Paris, to the schedule of a Congregational minister. He chafed against the strict rules and regular hours enforced in the Shaw household. He even argued points of theology with his uncle, who thought him a bit audacious, even for a teenager. That brought a rebuke from his mother in London, who had heard all about it from her sister. At his age, she said, he should not be "too assuming, and too tenacious of your own opinions." This contentiousness was "the only error that I am conscious you possess." His violation of curfews involved late hours of study. "He trims the midnight taper," wrote John Thaxter to the senior Adams. "I have cautioned him against that, as I am confident it will be eventually very injurious." Thaxter may have been right. Later in life John Quincy Adams' vision would sometimes give way completely, and from middle age onward his eyes perpetually watered.

In spite of occasional confrontations, young Adams profited from his uncle's guidance, and the following March presented himself for examination in Cambridge before President Willard, three professors, four tutors, and the college librarian. He answered a series of questions, and was escorted into the next room and given a paragraph in English to translate into Latin. This he did, posted a bond of 200 ounces of silver as a guarantee against his debts, and was at last admitted to Harvard College, as a junior, with advanced standing. His tuition was waived as a gesture of gratitude for his father's service to Massachusetts and the nation.

In many ways, college life in the late eighteenth century would be unrecognizable two centuries later. Only a tiny fraction of the population attended, all of them males. In New England, with few exceptions, a college degree was virtually the only means by which one could achieve social or political influence. John Adams recognized this when he congratulated his son upon his admission to Harvard, where he would be among future "Magistrates and Ministers, Legislators and Heroes, Ambassadors and Generals." Nearly all the subjects studied by Adams and his classmates, whether geometry or Greek, logic or Latin, were aimed at producing accomplished speakers, polished conversationalists, and persuasive reasoners. Much of his time was absorbed with preparation for the regular "forensic disputations" that were at the core of the senior year's curriculum. Topics were assigned by the faculty, as well as the affirmative or negative position to be taken, and it was up to the students to develop the argument. This was, Adams told his sister Nabby in London, "one of the excellent institutions of this University." He joined a small "A.B." club that met regularly to polish their argumentative and oratorical skills.

And yet college life in the 1780's had certain similarities to that of two centuries later. Students were unhappy with rules and regulations imposed from above. Friction existed between students and townspeople, occasionally resulting in fisticuffs and incarceration. Students were late for class, slept through boring lectures, treated unpopular professors with disrespect, and sometimes cribbed on exams and recitations. Freed from parental control, they sometimes engaged in the usual forms of eighteenth-century debauchery: drinking, whoring, and gambling. The night after John Quincy Adams was admitted to Harvard, the sophomore class rioted after a round of serious drinking and broke several tutors' windows. "Such are the achievements of many of the sons of Harvard," noted their newest classmate.

His colleagues scrutinized the new arrival for signs of Old-World affectation or priggishness, but were disappointed. "I find on the contrary that I am the best republican here," he proudly told his mother. By "republican," Adams meant he believed in and practiced an easy-going equalitarian manner that took little or no outward notice of economic or social standing, disdained aristocratic pretensions, and regarded all—or at least all white males—as equals. Yet at the same time he could stuffily assure his father that "I have made it my endeavor to be intimate only with the best characters in my class."

As republicans, Adams and most Americans were proud of the fact that there was no legally constituted or inherited aristocracy in their country, and that each citizen stood equal before the law. At the same time few would deny that certain families had, over the years, accumulated not only a sizable amount of wealth but considerable social standing and prestige as well. Political leadership was almost always drawn from this group. The Adamses, although not part of the elite in the early part of the eighteenth century, clearly counted themselves as part of it by the 1780's. Later historians and sociologists would describe eighteenth-century America as a "deferential society," by which they meant that most citizens willingly "deferred" to this elitist, affluent, educated class of men. Yet there was an inherent contradiction between the ideology of the American Revolution and the foundations of the deferential society. If all men—to say nothing of women—were truly created equal, there were difficult days ahead for those who continued to expect "deference."

In the summer and fall of 1786, Daniel Shays and a group of farmers in western Massachusetts, stung by inflation, debt, and taxes, attempted a redress of grievances through a shutdown of the state's judicial system. Conservatives in America were alarmed. It was one thing to refuse to pay British taxes, to threaten British property, to tar and feather British sympathizers, but to challenge American laws and to refuse to pay American taxes was something else again. Shays and his men got no sympathy from the Adamses. In letters to his family, John Quincy complained of the reluctance of the authorities to quell Shays' Rebellion. In a paper prepared for his "A.B." club, Adams sounded much like the King's ministers in the 1760's, denouncing the Shaysites as promoting "the most detestable of all tyrannies, that of a lawless, and unprincipled rabble." On the other hand, John Quincy's friend Jefferson was unperturbed. "I like a little rebellion now and then," he told Abigail from his perch in Paris. "It is like a storm in the Atmosphere." The differences over Shays' Rebellion were the first hint of greater differences to come.

Most Harvard undergraduates opposed the rebels and some even joined the militia to go out and fight them. John Quincy Adams stayed behind, intent on graduating in 1787. He was accepted into the Phi Beta Kappa society, and for the Commencement exercises was chosen as one the of four "Collectors of Theses," the second highest honor one could receive. This required an oration, and the title assigned to him was "The importance and necessity of public faith, to the well-being of the community." By "public faith" was meant the observance and enforcement of public and private debts and contracts. Adams took the occasion to chastise the Shaysites once again, notwithstanding they had been defeated recently with a minimum of bloodshed. "Although the hand of patriotism, has of late been stretched forth to crop the noxious plant," he cried, "the fatal root, still lies lurking beneath the surface." The "root" was the decline of the spirit of patriotic self-sacrifice that had characterized the Revolution. "What is liberty, what is life, when preserved by the loss of honour?" he asked. Conservatives nodded in approval at Adams' denunciation of any thought of repudiating the Massachu-setts public debt in order to lower taxes and appease the rebels. He concluded by calling upon his classmates to "preserve pure and immaculate the reputation of your Country." Reverend Jeremy Belknap, a well-known New England historian and man of letters, later published the oration in his new *Columbian Magazine*.

NOW ADAMS FACED A DECISION regarding his future occupation. His father assumed that all three of his sons would become lawyers just as he had. John Quincy reluctantly agreed to this, partly because he was a good son, but also because he could not think of anything else. The only remaining question was where and with whom he should prepare for the profession.

In the eighteenth century one prepared for a legal career, not by going to law school, for none existed in the modern sense, but by studying in the office of an established attorney under his supervi-sion, and usually for a fee. It was a form of apprenticeship. Probably Adams would have studied with his own father had that been possible, but in John Adams' absence it was determined that the next best thing would be to "read law" in the Newburyport office of Theophilus Parsons, a thirty-seven-year-old legal scholar of the post-

Revolutionary generation and a future Chief Justice of the Massachusetts Supreme Court. In September, 1787, Adams joined four other students in Parsons' office.

Parsons prescribed a course of study that went well beyond the law: into history, government, the classics, and science as well. His students were often left on their own, for he was frequently in Boston. In his first year, Adams read the usual treatises on English common law, as well as Gibbon's *Decline and Fall of the Roman Empire*, and even Jefferson's *Notes on Virginia*. In science he read Buffon's *Natural History* and Priestley's *History and General Policy*. He also read novels, although it is not clear whether they were part of Parsons' regimen: Fielding's *Tom Jones*, Voltaire's *Tales*, Sterne's *Tristam Shandy*, Shakespeare's plays (several times) and Rousseau's *Confessions* ("the most extraordinary book I have ever read in my life").

During the three years in Newburyport, Adams became part of a "set" of young people who participated in the usual parties, dances, and sleighrides typical of small-town New England life. He became romantically attached to a series of Newburyport girls whose charms he would often describe in poems, some of which appeared in the local newspapers. But in spite of his impressive intellectual diet and his burgeoning social schedule, he was haunted by the conviction that his life was slipping away. "My time flies from me with the rapidity of a whirlwind," he told his diary. "Every hour is precious, and every moment unemployed becomes a subject of regret." He studied more than his fellow students but became increasingly uncertain as to the purpose of it all. He had not inherited his father's enthusiasm for Coke and Blackstone, and he began to wonder if a career before the Bar was indeed his "calling," or his role in the "Stage of Life." His eyes bothered him. More than once he suffered a nervous collapse and retreated to the old family farm in Braintree.

While John Quincy fitfully pursued his legal studies, the nation was inching toward the adoption of a new Constitution. Having worked throughout the summer of 1787, Hamilton, Madison, and delegates from twelve of the thirteen states were ready with a proposed substitute for the Articles of Confederation. Ratification by Massachusetts, the largest state in the North and the third largest in the Union, was essential to the Constitution's success. But there was strong "anti-federalist" opposition, which for awhile included John Quincy Adams. "If the Constitution be adopted," he told his diary in October, 1787, "it will be a grand point gained in favor of the aristocratic party: there are to be no titles of nobility; but there will be great distinctions; and these distinctions will soon be hereditary, and we shall consequently have nobles but no titles." This was standard anti-federalist rhetoric, and the young law student stuck to his position, notwithstanding the fact that his mentor Parsons was a leading advocate of the Constitution and was chosen to represent Newburyport in the Massachusetts ratification convention in Boston. There he played a key role in engineering its success.

"I am converted, though not convinced," he wrote cautiously after Parsons and his fellow delegates returned in triumph in February, 1788. John Quincy and some friends journeyed north to Exeter, New Hampshire, to watch the ratification debates in that state, and saw the federalist cause triumph there as well. Then he learned that his own father in London had published *A Defence of the Constitutions of Government of the United States of America*, which concluded with an endorsement of the new Constitution. "I am glad to learn I was mistaken," wrote the son contritely. Years later, when he was president of the United States, John Quincy Adams would look back upon his youthful antifederalism as a "monumental" error.

That spring, John and Abigail Adams returned from England to occupy a new home that would become the Adams family seat for more than a century. John Quincy rode all the way from Newburyport to greet them. Their arrival gave him an excuse to stay away from his studies for most of the remainder of the year.

His father's return coincided with the final stages of ratification of the Constitution. Unlike the Articles of Confederation, the new document provided for an executive branch, with a President and a Vice President. Most assumed that if the Constitution were adopted, the presidency would go to George Washington, if he wanted it. Political reality dictated that the second position would then go to a northerner. No northerner had a better claim than John Adams. It was not long after his return before he was importuned by friends and admirers from all over the country to be a candidate for the vice presidency.

One of the rules of political behavior in a deferential society was that one never "campaigned" or "electioneered" for public office, even if he wanted it desperately. Much later, John Quincy Adams likened the family's attitude toward public service to its attitude toward death: "never to be desired, never to be avoided." This was not quite accurate for either himself or his father. In truth, once his interest was piqued, John Adams would have been bitterly disappointed if the office had not come to him. Although many had doubts about his temperament, no one else had enough support, and in 1789 Adams took the oath of office as the nation's first vice president.

His parents' return and his father's success did little to satisfy John Quincy Adams' discontent. He bounced about from Braintree to Cambridge to Newburyport, and then back to Braintree, again on the verge of nervous collapse. He discontinued his diary, confining himself to one-line entries in an almanac for most of the next five years. In the spring of 1789, he returned to Newburyport. He eased up on his studies, and spent more time in society. In September he journeyed to New York, still the national capital until its removal to Philadelphia a few months later. He visited his family and inspected the new government. He met George Washington and several members of his cabinet, and attended the debates in the House of Representatives. He was not impressed. "I did not perceive any extraordinary powers of oratory displayed by any of these gentlemen," he remarked in one of his rare diary entries for this period. He who had watched Burke, Fox, and Pitt was not about to be swept off his feet by a Jonathan Dayton or even a James Madison. But he was impressed, as were most people, with the impassive dignity of George Washington, the man who, next to his own father, would become the model for his life and career. Six weeks later, when the Great Man passed through Newburyport on a national tour, John Quincy was selected to deliver a brief address of welcome.

As his apprenticeship came to an end he did not look forward to the future. Where should he set up his practice? Most ambitious attorneys headed for Boston, where the fees were greatest but the competition stiffest. A return to Braintree might be desirable, but there he would have to compete with his own cousin, the affable

Billy Cranch, son of Abigail's sister Mary. Then there was Newburyport itself, where, he explained to his father, "an agreeable circle of acquaintance would render the situation particularly pleasing." But there he would be thrown into rivalry with his own mentor, Parsons. In the end he opted for Boston. If the competition was greater, so was the opportunity. Moreover, if his role on the "Stage of Life" included public service, as his parents always assumed, it would be best to be near the center of power and decision-making. And he could live rent-free in the family townhouse. Accordingly, in the summer of 1790 he was sworn into practice, and John Quincy Adams, Esq., opened his office and awaited clients.

Few came. If he needed confirmation of his doubts about the law, the thin business that greeted him provided just that. Many years later he would refer to this period as "four of the most trying years of my life." Having to rely on subsidies from his family was particularly galling. This was hardly living "*independent* and *free*." The Vice President was not concerned. "Your Anxiety is too great," he wrote from New York. "You have no right to expect and no reason to hope for more Business than you have. Remember, your Reputation is not formed, but to form. . . . Your Name can as yet be no more than that of a promising youth." He urged his son to become visible, attend and take part in Boston town meetings, and to report to him regularly on local politics.

His attendance at the Boston town meetings only served to strengthen the conservatism that had been sparked by Shays' Rebellion. Often more than a thousand people came to watch and participate, and the disorderly nature of the meetings disturbed him. They were hardly the occasion for sober deliberation. To his youngest brother Tom, also a struggling attorney in Philadelphia, he declared his "abhorrence and contempt of simple democracy as a Government." Moreover, town meetings dealt only with local issues. There was nothing there to inspire the imagination of anyone who imagined a larger role in the "Stage of Life."

In New York there was dissension within the new federal government over the economic reforms of Treasury Secretary Alexander Hamilton and his friends. Congressman James Madison, later joined by Secretary of State Jefferson, were increasingly disturbed by the

implications of Hamilton's Report on Public Credit and his proposed new Bank of the United States. In time, the disagreements
would divide Congress into the "Federalist" supporters of Hamilton
and the Washington administration, and the "Republican" critics,
led by Madison and Jefferson. But few as yet outside the capital paid
much attention to the controversy.

Foreign affairs were another matter. Since 1789, the French
Revolution, and its transition from its "moderate" to its "radical"
phase, commanded increased attention in America. Initially most
Americans gave it their hearty approval, since the French revolutionaries proclaimed themselves "republicans" and invoked memories of the American Revolution and its Declaration of Independence.
Thomas Jefferson, before he returned to America to become the
nation's first Secretary of State in 1790, had even provided advice
and counsel to the Revolution's leaders.

But by 1793 two developments served to dampen the enthusiasm of many Americans. As the Revolution moved away from its
earlier constitutionalism, the moderate elements with whom Jefferson
had worked were replaced by the increasingly radical "Jacobins,"
who proceeded to arrest, try, convict, and execute King Louis XVI,
the very same monarch who had aided the Americans in their own
revolution. Following this, France and Great Britain went to war.
With one or two interludes, they would not cease fighting until 1815.

The French Revolution and the war that followed drove a wedge
into American politics far more serious than any issue since the War
for Independence. Men of conservative temperament quickly lost
what little enthusiasm they had for the French Revolution and
criticized it privately and publicly. As early as 1790, John Quincy had
feared that the French republicans, "in tearing the lace from the
garb of government, will tear the coat itself into a thousand rags."
They were particularly dismayed when Jefferson and others insisted
on linking the French Revolution, with its increasing bloodshed,
with the revolt of the colonies in 1776. Most conservatives too,
although not the Adamses, sympathized with Great Britain in the
Anglo-French war. Jefferson and others identified with the French,
seeing them as defending the "republican" principles of 1776 against
a host of reactionary monarchies and their supporters. The critics of

the Revolution were most often found among the Federalists, while the Jeffersonian Republicans continued to defend it. Federalists attacked their opponents as "anti-Federalists" and "Jacobins," while Republicans retaliated by calling their rivals "monarchists," and "tories."

But the disagreement over the French Revolution and its consequences was more than a simple philosophical debate; it carried cultural and religious overtones as well. Those who lived in New England, in spite of Concord, Lexington, and Bunker Hill, still tended to see themselves as extensions of English culture. Abigail Adams revelled in the language and literature of Shakespeare, Milton, and Pope, while her husband John was always an enthusiast for the English Common Law and all its authorities. In rejecting British rule, they had no intention of rejecting the English language, English religious practice (or at least not the Congregational version thereof), or the notions of English "liberty" that had caused them to revolt in the first place.

But it was precisely this prospect of an Anglicized America that caused the Republicans to rally in opposition. To them, Hamilton, Adams, and the Federalist party seemed bent upon making the new nation simply a modified version of Great Britain, with all the implications of the class society, established religion, and monarchical institutions that "republicanism" rejected. Many Americans of non-English background, particularly Irish Catholics, tended to gravitate to the Republicans, as did the majority of the more secular-minded protestants outside of New England. Southerners, particularly those who lived away from the tidewater plantations of Virginia and the Carolinas, distrusted both New England religion and Yankee merchants.

At this stage of his life, John Quincy Adams may be compared to a young and inexperienced athlete, watching the political game from the sidelines as it unfolded in the early 1790's and itching to get into the fray. He entered through a series of essays and letters dealing mostly with foreign affairs and published between 1791 and 1794. They had the effect of establishing him not only as a loyal supporter of the Federalists and the Washington-Adams administration, but an articulate one as well.

His initial appearance in the arena came in the spring of 1791, following the publication of the American edition of Thomas Paine's *The Rights of Man*. The pamphlet was a response to Edmund Burke's *Reflections on the Revolution in France*, a wholesale attack on the Revolution published the year before. Secretary of State Jefferson had praised Paine's work, hoping that it would work as an antidote to certain "political heresies" that he claimed had cropped up recently in his own country. No one could say for sure, but many suspected that the "heresies" were a series of essays written by Vice President Adams, criticizing the French for not adopting a "balanced" government similar to that of Great Britain, or, for that matter, the United States. Although Jefferson had made a similar recommendation to the French when he was in Paris, positions had hardened by 1791 to the point where John Adams now appeared to be a defender of the old order, even a closet monarchist. Relations between Jefferson and the Adams family would never be the same again.

A few weeks later, a series of essays appeared in a Boston newspaper under the pen-name "Publicola," and were widely reprinted. The author jumped on the supposedly open-minded Secretary of State for using the word "heresy" to describe ideas with which he disagreed. Did Jefferson really consider "this pamphlet of Mr. Paine's as the canonical book of political scripture?" Publicola wondered. "As containing the true doctrine of popular infallibility, from which it would be heretical to depart on one single point?" Nearly all who read the essays assumed that "Publicola" was John Adams, but they were mistaken. "Publicola" was his son. Although rambling and not particularly well organized, the essays expressed principles that would guide the diplomacy and statesmanship of John Quincy Adams over the next thirty years.

He was very careful not to side with the increasingly reactionary Burke, nor to attack Paine or Jefferson directly: "Both of these gentlemen are entitled to the gratitude of their countrymen; the latter still renders important service in a very dignified station," he said at the outset. Instead he used Jefferson's rhetoric to show how inconsistent Paine's latest pamphlet was with the republican theory of natural rights contained within the Virginian's own Declaration of Independence. As a radical, Paine believed that there was no limit to what majorities could legitimately do to change their government. "That which a nation chooses to do, it has a right to do," he said. But if this were true, replied John Quincy Adams, what protection was there for the individual? "What possible security can any citizen have for the protection of his unalienable rights?" Paine had confused the "right" of governments with their "power." If, as the Declaration of Independence stated, governments were created to protect individual rights, there had to be limits. Certainly "the venerable character who drew up this declaration never could believe that the rights of a nation have no other limits than their powers."

As for the two Revolutions, the differences between the American and the French were as great as the differences between America and Europe, Adams continued. Republican equality, so far as it existed, was the natural product of America's colonial past, where the availability of land prevented the establishment of any hereditary aristocracy. American society was the result of history, not revolution. In Europe, including France and Britain, inequality, venality, and corruption were part of the "natural order of things," and to expect them to abolish centuries of custom and tradition overnight was an exercise in foolishness. "Mr. Paine seems to think it is as easy for a nation to change its government, as for a man to change his coat." Social conditions, not philosophers, determined the outcome of revolutions. Should the French attempt to export their revolution to other European nations, Americans should stand aside, for the result would be a ghastly European war between European powers for European objectives in which Americans had no stake.

Far from defending the hereditary aristocracy and the inequality he had witnessed in Europe, John Quincy Adams praised Americans for having achieved a republican society without having to fight a revolution to get it. "Happy, thrice happy the people of America!" he rhapsodized, "Whose gentleness of manners and habits of virtue are still sufficient to reconcile the enjoyment of their natural rights, with the peace and tranquillity of their country; whose principles of religious liberty did not result from an indiscriminate contempt of all religion whatever, and whose equal representation in their legislative councils was founded on an equality really existing among them, and not upon the metaphysical speculations of fanciful politicians."

By asserting differences between American and European society, and in affirming the immutability of certain "inalienable rights," Adams was doing no more than repeating ideas that other American leaders, including both Jefferson and his own father, had been offering for years. But the charged political atmosphere of the 1790's caused the Republicans to swoop down on the Publicola letters as defenses of aristocracy, privilege, and Great Britain. Sensing that he may have caused problems for his father, Adams abruptly ended the series, with some essays left unpublished.

The notoriety of the essays did little to alleviate the personal discontent that had first emerged during Adams' Newburyport years. Although his legal practice was slowly improving, he took little pleasure in it. He attended town meetings, but was almost always on the losing side, or so it seemed. He did help draw up the ordinance by which the precinct of North Braintree was re-named "Quincy," but that was about all he could point to by way of solid achievement. He and a group of young attorneys formed what they called the "Crackbrain Club," dedicated, it would seem, to little more than weekend carousing and trying to impress the eligible young women of the town. Occasionally he descended into self-pity. "I am not satisfied with the manner in which I employ my time," he wrote a year after the Publicola essays: "It is calculated to keep me forever fixed in that state of useless and disgraceful insignificancy, which has been my lot for some years past. At an age bearing close upon twenty-five . . . I still find myself as obscure, as unknown to the world, as the most indolent, or the most stupid of human beings. In the walks of active life I have done nothing. Fortune, indeed . . . has not hitherto been indulgent to me."

Events would again provide him with opportunity. Following the outbreak of the Anglo-French war in 1793, the domestic political scene deteriorated as both Britain and France violated the principle of neutral rights, or "free ships, free goods," which most American held to be vital to their sovereignty and economic well-being. Feelings ran more strongly against the British, who with their larger navy were in a position to disrupt American commerce more than the French. The British also claimed the right of "impressment," that is, to search American merchant vessels on the high seas and in foreign ports for alleged deserters from the Royal Navy and force them back into service. Moreover, they refused to return American slaves who had fled to their armies during the Revolution, and refused to evacuate their former forts along the Great Lakes until Americans (most of them southerners) paid their pre-war debts to British merchants.

Feelings, then, ran high against Britain in 1793, further aggravated by the antics of the flamboyant "Citizen" Edmond Genet, the new French Minister to the United States. Arriving at Charleston, South Carolina, Genet paraded northward to Philadelphia, wined and dined by Republicans at every stop. Along the way he issued permits to American "privateers" to attack British vessels on the high seas. His violation of American neutrality eventually led to his recall (he remained in America as an immigrant), but his mission further inflamed party feelings. So long as France and Britain remained at war, Republicans and Federalists would sympathize with one side or the other, and so long as Americans were tempted to choose sides, there would be the danger of them slipping into war themselves.

At last John Quincy Adams had issues for which he was well-prepared. In two letters published in the spring of 1793, signed "Marcellus," Adams defended Washington's policy of strict neutrality and denounced privateering against Britain or any other nation. Not only was this "buccaneering plan of piratical plunder" degrading to a free and independent people, it was a sure formula for eventual war, a war the United States could ill afford. The United States, he said, was "a nation whose happiness consists of real independence, disconnected from all European interests and European politics." This was not isolationism; he did not want Americans to withdraw from the world. On the contrary, their commerce stood to benefit from the war between the two superpowers. If Americans would stay neutral and concentrate on supplying the needs of the belligerents, the returns "can have no other limitation than the extent of our own capacity to provide for them."

Later in the year, this time as "Columbus," Adams poured ridicule on Genet himself. Possessing little information on the true state of American public opinion, and overestimating the patience and sympathy of Republicans like Jefferson and James Madison, Genet had tried to rally the American people against Britain, even if it meant organizing opposition to President Washington. Adams, whose admiration for Washington knew no bounds, denounced the "petulant stripling," the "beardless foreigner," and the "hair-brained Hotspur of an Envoy." He condemned French interference in American politics, reminding Genet of the law of ancient Athens that put to death any foreigner caught meddling in its legislative affairs. A contributing cause to the death of liberty in any society, he warned, was "the association of internal faction, and external power."

That year the Boston town fathers invited Adams to deliver the annual Independence Day oration. It was an important honor, an occasion for recalling the sacrifices of the revolutionary generation and denouncing the folly and misdeeds of Great Britain. He spent many weeks preparing his speech. It was also an opportunity to offset the charge that he and his family had grown soft on the former Mother Country. He did not disappoint the audience. Not only did he condemn the "obstinancy and cruelty" of the British, he paid tribute to the French who had helped the Americans in their struggle for freedom. Sounding more like Thomas Paine than Edmund Burke, he looked forward to the day "when all the nations of Europe shall partake in the blessings of equal liberty and universal peace." That day was inevitable, he said, when "the governments of Europe must fall; and the only remaining expedient in their power, is to gather up their garments and fall with decency."

The "Marcellus" and "Columbus" essays, together with the Independence Day oration, developed further the ideas first expressed by "Publicola" in 1791. America and Europe were separated not only by an ocean but by fundamentally different social and political institutions. This separateness demanded American neutrality in the current war between Britain and France, or between any European powers. Privately, Adams was more critical of Great Britain and its hostile attitude toward neutral rights than most Federalists. "If the principle upon which the British have lately proceeded to seize our ships be persisted in," he warned his father in early 1794, "I fear we shall have no alternative but war." He acknowledged that "the general disposition of French ruling powers has been constantly favorable to us," but that the British had been "acrimonious, jealous, and under guise of fair pretensions, deeply malignant." His commitment to neutrality therefore was not unlimited, and he could foresee circumstances that might justify war with either Britain or France.

In Philadelphia, the Vice President saw to it that everyone, from George Washington on down, knew that "Publicola," "Marcellus," and "Columbus" were the same person. "His Talents, his Virtues, his Studies and his Writings are not unknown," he wrote cryptically to Abigail, "nor will they go without their Recompence." The President had been making inquiries about him, "his Age, his Practice, his Character, &c, &c, &c." A few months later the senior Adams again hinted that "His Writings have given him a greater Consideration in this Place than he is aware of."

The President's inquiries were the result of cabinet discussions concerning the Dutch loans to the United States, and the need to have a full-time minister at the Hague. John Quincy Adams was one of the few Americans fluent in French who had ever visited the Netherlands. His writings had demonstrated both moderation and loyalty to the Washington administration's policy of determined neutrality in the face of provocation by both the British and the French. Even Thomas Jefferson, who had resigned as Secretary of State, was said to have put in a good word for his former walking companion in Paris—Publicola notwithstanding.

In late May the Vice President informed his son of his appointment as Minister to the Netherlands. The primary mission was financial: to ensure that the Amsterdam bankers were paid their interest on time, and that any new loans were obtained at the best possible rates. Beyond this, John Quincy Adams was expected to keep an eye on European political and military developments and report them regularly to the State Department. The appointment was proof, his father wrote triumphantly, "that sound Principles in Morals and Government, are cherished by the Executive of the United States and that Study, Science, and Literature are recommendations which will not be overlooked."

The news took John Quincy Adams by surprise. At first he

pretended he did not want the post. He was now making money in his law practice, so much so that he would not need his father's subsidy in the future. Were he to leave it would mean lost clients that would take years to replace should he return. People would no doubt whisper that he owed his appointment to his father's influence. Yet, Adams-like, the more inconvenience accepting the offer would entail, the more attractive it looked. He could never be accused of undue ambition if taking the appointment involved financial loss. With that settled, he notified Secretary of State Edmund Randolph that he would accept, and, significantly, went out and bought a notebook with which to renew his diary.

He spent July in Philadelphia, lodging with his brother Thomas and studying the diplomatic records of the 1780's. Here he read for the first time the details of his father's resistance to the French attempts to control American diplomacy, and of his differences with Benjamin Franklin. Having won their independence from Britain in the 1780's, the Americans had had to struggle to avoid becoming a satellite of the French. Now France and Britain were at war again, each attempting to draw the United States into its orbit.

Before leaving, Adams reflected on his future. His father was certain this was only the beginning of an illustrious career. After "a few years spent in the present Grade," the Vice President confidently assured him, he would be ready for "Advancement to higher stages and larger spheres." But the son was not so certain. The distance from home, the slowness of communication, and the lost legal practice, all suggested that it would not be wise to stay long. And there was the old fear of contamination by the Old World. It was hardly possible, Adams told his father, "for an American to be long in Europe without losing in some measure his national character." After too long a stay, "he gradually takes an European disposition, becomes a stranger to his own Country, and when at length he returns finds himself an alien in the midst of his own fellow citizens." They finally agreed that he should not stay away for more than three years, the normal tour of duty for a Minister abroad. He managed to persuade his brother Thomas to accompany him as his secretary, and after a round of goodbyes from family and friends, the two Adamses sailed from Boston on September 17, 1794.

THEY HEADED FIRST FOR LONDON, where Adams met with Chief Justice John Jay, sent by President Washington months before in an attempt to resolve the differences between the United States and His Majesty's Government. The Chief Justice had just completed the series of agreements that would soon be called Jay's Treaty. The result was disappointing. The British still refused to accept the concept of "free ships, free goods" in wartime, still claimed the right of impressment, and still refused compensation for slaves taken during the war for independence. The only real breakthroughs were concessions to American trade with the British West Indies, and an agreement finally to give up the forts on American territory that they had agreed to vacate eleven years before. Adams dutifully supported the treaty as the best means to avoid war, but admitted it was "much below the standard which I think would be advantageous to this country."

He spent about two weeks in London, re-visiting the theaters he had seen a decade before as a teenager, reluctantly standing as they played "God Save the King" at each performance. "Neither the Government, nor the people of this Country, have any real friendship for America," he declared in a letter to a friend in Boston. After borrowing some money from Jay, the Adams party crossed the Channel to the continent and hurried on to the Hague. In due course Minister Adams was presented to the Dutch ruler, known as the *stadtholder*, and to the ruling council, known as their High Mightinesses. Adams then proceeded to organize his office, opening correspondence with American consuls in Amsterdam, Hamburg, and other north European ports.

Like most western Europeans, the Dutch were caught in the struggle between the old aristocracy, increasingly aligned with the British, and the new republicanism, supported by the French. The Dutch were divided into pro-British and pro-French factions, and each welcomed the humiliation of the other. The pro-British faction supported the *stadtholder*, who was related to the British royal family, and whose government was propped up by British troops. But most of those who had previously supported American independence, like his old tutor Charles W. F. Dumas and many of the Amsterdam bankers, were openly pro-French. To the south, a French army was massing on the border, promising to free the Dutch people from British subjection and create a new republican order.

In January 1795 the French invaded the Netherlands, having no trouble crossing its frozen canals. There was little resistance. The supporters of the *stadtholder* either went into hiding or joined him and his family in England. "The national sentiment in this country is universally subordinate to the spirit of party," Adams reported. There was no concept of the public interest except as it served private interest or partisan gain. He saw a disturbing parallel between Dutch disunity and the divisions between pro-British Federalists and pro-French Republicans in his own country. It strengthened Adams' hostility to political parties, particularly when they were attached to foreign interests. Internal divisions were so great, he reported to the Secretary of State, that the people were no longer capable of self-government. The choice lay between rule by the French or civil war. The once independent Dutch Republic was "irretrievably ruined."

With the arrival of spring he read with dismay the reports from America of increased dissension and partisanship over Jay's Treaty. Republicans denounced it as a sellout to Great Britain and rallied public opinion through meetings up and down the East Coast. Jefferson and Madison orchestrated the outcry, abetted by Samuel Adams in New England. After it was approved by the Senate with no votes to spare, the French warned of serious consequences if the President ratified it. Federalists swallowed their misgivings and rallied to its support. John Quincy Adams, well aware of its weaknesses, agreed that the Treaty was the only way to preserve neutrality and avoid war. If there was any American who doubted the wisdom of neutrality, he told his cousin William Cranch, "let him come to Europe. Let him look at the misery which war has brought upon every nation that has been involved in it. . . ."

After the President signed the Treaty, it fell to Adams to go to London to arrange for the exchange of ratifications in the absence of the regular American Minister there. He did not look forward to the assignment, not wishing to be identified with an unpopular treaty and not caring for the arrogance and condescension he detected in British society. Adams found French company more pleasant and easier to deal with. No matter what they thought privately, he explained in a letter to his father, the French at least pretended to like and admire Americans. "In the general treatment of strangers [i.e., foreigners] the French manners are captivating, the English are repulsive. In the particular sentiments towards Americans . . . those of the French are amicable and attractive, those of England always cold and distant, generally insolent and overbearing, and not infrequently contemptuous and malignant." He doubted whether between the United States and Great Britain any "*cordiality*" could exist. In fact, "I do not think it is on our part to be desired." But he kept his Anglophobia to himself.

As it turned out, Adams was held up by contrary winds so long at the Channel that he arrived after the deadline for the exchange had passed, leaving it to be performed by someone else. Thomas Pinckney, the regular Minister, was on a mission to Spain, which made Adams the only accredited American diplomat in Britain. Uncertain as to what he should do, he wrote to the Secretary of State for instructions and settled down to await a reply. When it came, it was from a new Secretary of State, Timothy Pickering, who had replaced Edmund Randolph after the latter had been forced to resign in the wake of accusations of improper dealings with French agents. More evidence, Adams thought, of the dangers of "the association of internal faction, and external power."

In London, he found himself caught between extremes. Americans with whom he associated either wished to see the United States enlisted in the cause of worldwide revolution, even if it meant risking war with Britain, or were staunch supporters of the old order. "I cannot find a single American who appears to have common sense upon the affairs of his nation," Adams complained. His conduct, he told his father, "will not suit the views of any *partizans* either of France or Britain."

While awaiting Pinckney's return, Adams managed to enjoy himself in London as much as conditions permitted. He reported home on the operations of His Majesty's Government, had an audience with his father's old enemy George III, and sat for a portrait by the American emigré artist John Singleton Copley, which he sent home as a surprise gift to his mother. He also attended the

While in London in 1795, John Quincy Adams had his portrait painted by John Singleton Copley, the American-born artist then living in England. It was done as a surprise present for his mother, Abigail Adams. *Courtesy, Museum of Fine Arts, Boston. Bequest of Charles Francis Adams.*

theater as often as he could. "Shakespear's attractions are irresistible," he wrote.

Shakespeare's plays were not the only "irresistible" attraction for Adams in the winter of 1795–96. He spent more and more time at the home of the American consul in London, Joshua Johnson, whose family he had first visited as a youngster in France in 1779. Johnson and his English-born wife now had a bevy of daughters of varying ages who were "pretty and agreeable," according to the young diplomat. "The eldest performs remarkably well on the pianoforte. The second, Louisa, sings. The third plays on the harp." It was Louisa to whom he found himself attracted, and by the time of his return to the Hague in the following spring, the two were engaged. The date of the wedding had yet to be set.

Louisa Catherine Johnson was not the first love of John Quincy Adams' life. He had been smitten from time to time during his Harvard and Newburyport years, but with one exception the infatuations were short-lived. The exception was Mary Frazier, a sixteen-year-old Newburyport girl with whom Adams fell in love shortly before his move to Boston in 1790. He hoped to continue the relationship, but in due course his mother found out about it and moved quickly to end it. Already a witness to the unhappy marriage of her daughter Nabby, who had wedded on the rebound from a broken love affair and was burdened with a surfeit of children and debts, Abigail warned that her son's financial position put marriage out of the question. Dutifully, Adams had bowed to this mixture of sound advice and maternal possessiveness. The relationship ended, but the memory did not.

He was nevertheless in no hurry to get married, even in 1796. His stay in London had disrupted his regular routine, and he longed to get back to it. "I was not formed to shine in society, nor to be delighted with it," he admitted. He recorded his regimen: "Rise and dress at six. Read works of *instruction* from thence till nine. Read the papers and translate from the Dutch till eleven or twelve. Then dress for the day. Write letters or attend to other business that occurs till between two and three. Walk till half-past three. Dine and sit till five. Read works of *amusement* till between eight and nine. Walk again about an hour. Then take a slight supper and my segar, and retire to bed at eleven." He was, as he told his brother Charles, "a great lover of order and method in all things."

Originally, Adams intended to serve the remainder of his three-year appointment at the Hague and return to America to be married, but complications arose, not the least of which was George Washington's decision not to serve a third term. This meant that John Adams, the Vice President, would be a candidate to succeed him in the election of 1796. Then John Quincy Adams learned that Washington had promoted him to Minister to Portugal, with a doubling of his salary. If he accepted, it would conflict with Joshua Johnson's plans to return to America with his family, forcing Adams to choose between an earlier marriage or a three-year postponement. At first he opted for the latter, breezily informing his fiancée that the delay was "one of those counter-checks in the affairs of life which happen to all, which all must endure whether they will or not. . . ." When Louisa not unreasonably suggested that he might place their mutual happiness ahead of his career plans, she received an ominous rebuke: "To serve my country at its call," he wrote, "is not merely an ambition, but a duty. . . . I have repeatedly talked to you of my country; of my unlimited attachment and devotion to it. . . . My duty to my country is in my mind the first and most imperious of all obligations; before which every interest and every feeling inconsistent with it must forever disappear."

No one could say that Louisa had not been warned.

Then his future father-in-law made an offer that Adams could not refuse: if he would come to London and be married on his way to Portugal, Johnson would provide a private vessel to take the couple to Lisbon. It only remained to be seen whether he would go to Lisbon as an ordinary diplomat, or as son of the President of the United States.

As an official representative of his country, Adams was bound to be non-partisan regarding the presidential contest at home. Privately, he believed the Federalists were the more responsible party and had the better of the argument over foreign policy. If the Republicans accused John Adams and the Federalists of submitting to the "English yoke," he told an fellow diplomat, "I hope and trust in

God that we shall teach both France and Britain, that we are not inclined to bear the yoke of either." But the fact that his father's opponent was Thomas Jefferson complicated matters. John Adams and Jefferson had drifted apart politically and socially over the years, and John Quincy Adams regarded Jefferson as naive on matters of foreign policy and the role of the United States in European affairs. But he professed to be unconcerned about a Jefferson presidency. "I speak with confidence in saying that he will inflexibly pursue the same general system of policy which is now established," he told a staunch Federalist. If the French thought they could manipulate him, they were wrong. "Mr. Jefferson is not the man who will make himself the instrument of any such designs." To a fellow New Englander he asked "Is the devil to be raised, or are we to be set all by the ears, for having a Virginian instead of a New England man for President? One honest and able man instead of another?"

Of course, should Jefferson win, it would not be wise to be on record as having criticized him as a candidate. But he brooded over the outcome. "A profound anxiety has taken possession of my mind," he admitted at the end of January, when no word had arrived. "The two objects nearest to my heart, my country and my father, press continually upon my reflections." (No mention of his fiancée.) Not until the end of March, 1797, three weeks after his father had been sworn in, did Adams learn of his father's narrow victory. Under the Constitution, Thomas Jefferson, with the second highest number of electoral votes, became Vice President.

As he packed up his books, furniture, and other personal possessions, and made preparations to leave the Hague, Adams could take satisfaction in the previous three years. There had been no serious crises to contend with, and his regular dispatches on European affairs had been well received. "Your son," George Washington had written to John Adams, "must not think of retiring from the walk of life he is in. . . . . I shall be much mistaken if, in as short a period of time as can well be expected, he is not found at the head of the diplomatic corps, let the government be administered by whomsoever the people may choose." As President, John Adams was in complete agreement, so much so that one of his first acts was to change his son's appointment from Minister to Portugal to Minister to Prussia. His new place of residence would not be Lisbon after all, but Berlin.

When John Quincy Adams learned of the reassignment, he was not pleased. All of his mature life he had struggled for "independence," avoiding as much as possible the slightest hint that he had benefitted from his father's status. The appointments to the Hague and to Lisbon had come to him honestly, or so he believed. But his father's decision, he told his mother heatedly, destroyed "all the satisfaction which I have enjoyed hitherto in considering myself a public servant." This was the closest Adams ever came to a quarrel with his parents. When he learned of his son's reaction, the President responded with equal heat. His objection was "the worst opinion I ever knew you to conceive." There was no promotion, no additional salary, and no favoritism. The national interest required his presence in Berlin, closer to the center of European affairs, than in Lisbon, where "there will be little to do, that I can see, besides sleeping *siestas*." Besides, he added, there would be no objection to the transfer if he had been anyone else's son. Sons of presidents should not be discriminated against. They had "the same claim to liberty, equality, and the benefit of the laws with all other citizens."

His father's logic reached the thirty-year-old John Quincy Adams as a newly married man. He and Louisa Catherine Johnson were married on July 26, 1797 at a church near the Tower of London, with his brother Thomas and the Johnson clan in attendance. Upon learning of the marriage, an irreverent Republican newspaper in Boston reported that "Young John Adams' Negotiations, have terminated in a Marriage Treaty with an English lady. . . . It is a happy circumstance that he made no other Treaty." Years later, his wife's "English" status—although she was an American citizen by virtue of her father's citizenship—would be used against Adams by various opponents. As for the "Marriage Treaty," it would endure, not without hardships, for more than half a century.

ADAMS SPENT THE NEXT THREE months in London, waiting for confirmation of his new assignment by the U. S. Senate. Parsimonious Republicans were objecting to the expansion of the diplomatic corps to include Prussia, not at the time considered to be a nation deemed significant enough to have an American Minister. In the meantime, Adams reconciled himself to the assignment in the time-honored family manner. He had already spent a considerable sum of money shipping his goods to Lisbon; he had even rented a house there. He would not be able to recover the financial loss. Since he was making a considerable sacrifice in accepting the new assignment, he told his mother, no one could accuse him of benefiting personally from his father's election. At home, others were not convinced. His old schoolmate Benny Bache, now a Republican newspaper editor, ungenerously insisted that the mission had been created in order to put additional money into the Adams family pockets.

The Federalist-controlled Senate nevertheless approved his appointment, and Adams, his wife, brother Thomas, and some servants sailed for Prussia and the port of Hamburg in October, 1797. After the journey from Hamburg to Berlin, they presented themselves at the city gates on the 7th of November. "Questioned at the gate by a dapper lieutenant," Adams noted in his diary, "who did not know, until one of his private soldiers explained to him, who the United States were."

His major assignment in Berlin was to renew and revise certain treaties of commerce and amity with Prussia and nearby Sweden that were about to expire, and bring them into harmony with the principles of Jay's Treaty, which meant abandoning insistence on "free ships, free goods." This Adams did, reluctantly. The new treaty with Prussia took a year and a half to complete, and was signed on his thirty-second birthday, July 11, 1799. The treaty with Sweden never materialized, owing to that nation's close ties with France, and the deterioration of Franco-American relations that set in after the approval of Jay's Treaty. Beyond these official responsibilities he was to act as an unofficial listening-post for his father. "Send us all the information you can collect," wrote the President. "I wish you to continue the practice of writing freely to me, and cautiously to the Office of State."

During most of Adams' stay in Berlin, the United States was engaged in what has been called a "quasi-war" with France. It was a shooting war, taking place entirely at sea and with casualties on both sides, but it was never formally declared. The root cause of the difficulties lay in the conviction of the French government that by acquiescing in Jay's Treaty and abandoning the principle of "free ships, free goods," the United States had accepted Britain's mastery of the seas and had in effect re-joined the British Empire. If "free ships, free goods" did not apply to Britain, they argued, then it should not apply to France. She too would have the right to stop and confiscate neutral commerce intended for her enemy. Indeed, France did more than that. Beginning in early 1798, she proceeded to confiscate all American vessels that carried anything of British derivation, including clothing or personal effects of passengers and crew.

President Adams had already sent a three-person delegation to Paris, similar to the Jay mission to London three years earlier, in hopes of achieving a settlement. But they were rudely treated by mysterious French agents, who demanded bribes and a loan before matters could proceed. When the details of the treatment given to the three American ministers emerged in the following year—the so-called "XYZ" scandal—a wave of anti-French feeling swept the United States. Congress appropriated money for a new army, created a new department of the Navy, and passed the notorious Alien and Sedition Acts. Where once Republicans had thundered against Great Britain and her depredations, now Federalists urged mobilization against France. Republicans were in full retreat. Abigail Adams thought that Benny Bache and his newspaper should be "seized." Charleston, South Carolina, which had greeted Citizen Genet so enthusiastically in 1793, now raised $100,000 for build a warship to be used against France, which was to be named the *John Adams*. For his part, President Adams angrily proclaimed that he would never send a representative to France until she gave assurances that he would be treated as "the representative of a great, free, powerful, and independent nation." For the first and only time in his career, John Adams was a popular hero.

In Berlin, his son likewise breathed fire against the French and their Republican sympathizers at home. Every third man in the House of Representatives, he now declared, "is at the bottom of his heart at war with every two others. In that war his countrymen are his enemies, and France is his ally." Gone were the anti-war strictures of "Marcellus" and "Columbus." We must become a *warlike people*," he told his friend William Vans Murray, who had succeeded him at the Hague. Gone too were his praises of French culture and manners. They were "no more an object of reasoning than a hurricane, a thunderbolt, or an earthquake. Talk of justice to a boiling lava," he declared, "and you will sooner meet with success." The conflict taught Adams that neutrality cannot always be maintained, nor war avoided, merely by wishful thinking.

For France, the results of its policy were disastrous. Unlike the British, whose mammoth Royal Navy and merchant marine made it possible for them indeed to "rule the waves," the French were dependent upon the commerce of neutral nations like the United States to feed their Grand Army, who dominated the continent of Europe almost as thoroughly as the Royal Navy dominated the ocean around it. The British could afford to alienate the Americans; the French could not.

French foreign policy at this time was directed by Charles Maurice de Talleyrand-Perigord, the legendary ex-bishop who was then beginning his rise to power as the genius behind French diplomacy for the next twenty years. Talleyrand had scant use for Americans, whom he regarded for the most part as transplanted Englishmen with all the faults of that particular race. But with the drying up of American commerce, the errors of French policy became obvious. Talleyrand now made known his desire for peace in several ways, including a quiet approach to Adams' friend Murray at the Hague.

As soon as he learned of it, Minister Adams lost no time in encouraging Murray to pursue the opportunity, and notified his father and Secretary Pickering. In France, he said, there was "a great and important change in her conduct toward us." For his part, Murray reminded the French of President Adams' condition for a resumption of relations: that the United States be recognized by them in advance as a "great, free, powerful and independent nation." After some twisting and turning, Talleyrand produced almost the exact words required by the president. It was an important diplomatic triumph, but ironically one that contained within it the seeds of John Adams' defeat in the presidential election of 1800, and the termination of John Quincy Adams' first diplomatic career.

Unbeknownst to the President, most of his cabinet, including his Secretary of State, was receiving advice and direction from former Treasury Secretary Alexander Hamilton, leader of the so-called "High Federalists," who wished to see the crisis with France prolonged even if it meant a real war. They could be counted on to resist any attempt to renew and normalize relations. The president, however, in spite of his reputation as an Anglophile, was determined to walk the line between the two superpowers. "We will have neither John Bull nor Louis Baboon," he had told his wife.

While he pondered the alternatives in January, 1799, Thomas Boylston Adams, fresh from his five-year stint as his brother's secretary and confidant, returned home to Quincy. He made it clear that both John Quincy Adams and William Vans Murray favored one more mission to France in hopes of avoiding war. No single opinion counted for more with the President than that of his eldest son. After some further reflection, John Adams nominated Murray as a special envoy to Paris.

Hamilton, Pickering, and the other High Federalists succeeded in delaying the Murray mission, first through inaction and then by insisting on two other appointees. The Republicans now gained a political reprieve, as the Federalists split between the supporters of President Adams and the High Federalists. With conciliatory gestures from the French, the martial spirit of the previous year died down, and the hopes of the Republicans rose. In Berlin, John Quincy could only lament to his mother that "the spirit of party has indeed done so much injury among us in various shapes." When he learned of Federalist attempts to provoke war with France and thus sabotage the Murray mission, he declared he should have no hesitation in abandoning that party, "be the consequences what they may." His father evidently agreed, for in the spring of 1800, as the mission finally was underway, he summarily fired the obstructionist Pickering from his cabinet, along with James McHenry, the Secretary of War, and replaced them with more congenial Federalists. With that, the split in the Federalist party was out in the open. With the united Republicans planning to run Thomas Jefferson again for president, John Adams' chances for re-election were seriously damaged.

But as the President's position deteriorated at home, diplomatic prospects improved abroad. In France, the five-man Directory, under whose regime most of the difficulties with the United States had occurred, was ousted by a *coup d'etat* led by the young Corsican General Napoleon Bonaparte, who expressed nothing but the friendliest of sentiments toward America. At his side stood the smiling Talleyrand, who had survived this *coup*, as he would others. With this change, the prospects for Franco-American accommodation took another leap forward. But owing to the High Federalist delay, it would not be until October 1, 1800, that a convention was signed, too late for it to have any effect on the presidential election. John Adams was defeated by Thomas Jefferson by almost as narrow a margin as he had won with four years earlier.

At the end of his first full year in Berlin, John Quincy Adams wrote that it had not "in any respect been a profitable one to me." Notwithstanding his role in encouraging his father to reopen communication to France, he found himself frustrated by his isolation from European affairs and the limited nature of his responsibilities. To absorb the empty hours, he took up the study of German, a language which at that time few of his countrymen had bothered to learn. He immersed himself in it, perhaps as a way of re-enforcing his neutrality. "The flimsy prejudices of the French and English nations against the German language," he told a friend, "have long blinded them to the excellencies of its literature." To sharpen his skills, he translated German works into English, some of which were later published. (One of them was a lengthy essay by the Prussian conservative Friedrich Gentz entitled *Origin and Principles of the American Revolution, compared with the French Revolution*, which, as Adams explained in his preface, rescued the American revolution "from the disgraceful imputation of having proceeded from the same principles as that of France.") In later years, he continued to encourage the study of German, and in the opinion of some, became "the father of German studies in America."

It was well that his diplomatic responsibilities rested lightly on his shoulders, for his domestic responsibilities turned out to be more than he had bargained for. The Adamses had difficulty finding adequate housing and servants appropriate to their status, complicated by their initially inadequate command of the language. Louisa Adams' health turned out to be fragile, no doubt aggravated by at least four miscarriages suffered while in Berlin. She required frequent medical attention and was often in excruciating pain. In an age in which death in childbirth was an ever-present possibility, Adams was continually apprehensive, often fatalist. "It is neither wise nor good to murmur at the ways of Providence," he remarked laconically to his diary. "I have been highly favoured: beyond my deserts and even beyond my wishes. Shall I receive good, and shall I not receive evil? The mind at least submits, however the heart will rebel."

As soon as the Prussian treaty was signed in July, 1799, Adams arranged for a summer vacation near the city of Dresden in hopes that Louisa's health would be improved by the medicinal baths there. It improved so much that they took an even longer vacation the following summer, touring the Prussian province of Silesia. The Adamses inspected castles, visited museums and galleries, attended theaters, and even climbed a mountain or two. The American Minister mixed business with pleasure, noting the Silesian manufacture of linen and glass, and the opportunities for American trade that lay therein. He wrote lengthy letters describing Silesia to his brother Thomas in America, who arranged to have them published. They were a great source of pride to their author, who now gave thought to becoming a man of letters, rather than returning to the law, should his public career be terminated.

When he returned to Berlin, Adams realized that his father's defeat for re-election was imminent. He was angered at his countrymen. He was contemptuous of the Republicans, whose sloganeering and partisanship put their loyalty to their country in doubt, and whose victory had been bought by "pimping to the popular passions." He was dismayed by Vice President Jefferson, who had sided with the opposition against his former friend. Jefferson's writings, he told his mother, revealed either "a mind full of error or a heart full of falsehood." But the blame for his father's defeat lay as much with Hamilton and the High Federalists, who placed their partisan need to maintain anti-French hysteria ahead of the general need to restore peace.

When the result was certain, he wrote a long letter home to his father, emphasizing the theme of public service and private sacrifice familiar to them both. Whereas "the common and vulgar herd of statesmen and warriors" might follow their own private and personal interests, he said, "it will be a great and glorious pre-eminence for you to have exhibited an example of the contrary, a statesman who made the sacrifice of his own interest and influence to the real and unquestionable benefit of his country." His father had, Adams concluded, "given the most decisive proof that in your administration you were not the man of any party, but the man of the whole nation."

As for John Quincy, he had learned much since his departure from Boston in 1794. He had seen how the Dutch, as a result of their partisan divisions, had become first a British, and then a French satellite. He believed too, that partisanship at home, when foolishly attached to foreign interests, had threatened national survival. Nations, like individuals, could not be truly free unless they were truly independent at the same time. Now his personal future depended upon Thomas Jefferson. He abstained from further criticism, hopeful perhaps that Jefferson would retain his services. "I know him," he told William Murray, "know he has long estimated me beyond my deserts, and I have reason to believe contributed much by his testimony, if not by his recommendation to the first President, to introduce me into the public service." On the other hand, the three years he had originally planned to spend abroad were turning into seven. Another appointment would add another three years. Perhaps it would be better to return home and recover his personal independence, even if it meant returning to the hated practice of law.

In any event, the Adamses were temporarily immobilized in Berlin, for Louisa was again pregnant, and her past history dictated

complete rest. The entire diplomatic community awaited the outcome, and the King of Prussia banned all traffic from the street in
front of the Adams home. This time Louisa gave birth to a healthy
baby boy, who was christened George Washington Adams. There
never was any question about the name. "President Washington was
next to my own father the man upon earth to whom I was indebted
for the greatest of personal obligations," he wrote to his brother. It
was Washington—who had died in December 1799—who had
plucked Adams from his unhappy law practice, who had sent him
abroad, and who had promoted him in more ways than one. For all
his life, he would remain Adams' model of the ideal statesman.

Two weeks after the birth of his son, Adams received his letter of
recall. It came, not from Jefferson, but from his own father, who had
decided to spare his son's feelings in the event that the new President did not want him, or perhaps to pre-empt the decision from
Jefferson. In any event, there was now nothing to do but proceed
with the formalities of leave-taking. The three Adamses left Berlin
in mid-June, and three weeks later boarded the ship *America* at
Hamburg. Contrary winds delayed their arrival at Philadelphia until
mid-September, where they were met by the faithful brother Thomas. Here the Adamses separated for the first time since their
marriage, Louisa and George going south to the family in Maryland,
while her husband headed north for Quincy, where he "had the
inexpressible delight of finding once more my parents, after an
absence of seven years."

Chapter Three

───────○───────

"Hitherto My Conduct has Given Satisfaction to Neither Side"

EVERYWHERE IN AMERICA, wrote John Quincy Adams in 1801, there were signs of "peace within our walls, and prosperity within our palaces." The words, taken from the Old Testament, seemed no exaggeration. Even "palace" was appropriate, he thought, for those "splendid and costly mansions which since my departure seem to have shot up from the earth by enchantment." As he travelled northward to Quincy, as he inspected the new homes going up on Boston's Beacon Hill, and as he surveyed from his father's farm the scores of sailing vessels spread out across the harbor, the signs of "peace and prosperity" were all around him. At age thirty-four, John Quincy Adams now showed both a receding hairline and an expanding waistline.

Not everyone he left behind in 1794 was there in 1801. His brother Charles, whom many had regarded as the most engaging of the three Adams brothers, had died the year before, a victim of alcoholism. His death was grim evidence that the republican exhortations showered upon all the Adams children were no guarantee of success. The marriage of his sister Abigail to the dashing William Stephens Smith had not gone well either. Smith was absent for months at a time in search of a quick killing in real estate, which never materialized. His mounting debts would eventually land him in prison. "My children give me more pain than my enemies," growled old John Adams at one point. He was not thinking of his eldest son. "I have many projects in my head to communicate to you," the ex-President wrote upon John Quincy's arrival in Philadelphia.

But his parents were in good health and generally good spirits as they recovered from the twin hurts of political defeat and the loss of their son. Adams and his father walked once again along the shore from which they departed for France nearly a quarter of a century before, climbed the rocks of the family farm, talking of the past and the future. John Quincy had given thought to pulling up stakes and relocating elsewhere, perhaps in the South or in western New York state. His father would have none of this. "For the sake of peace, and for the want of better employment," John Quincy later explained to his brother, he would stay in Boston and resume his legal practice. But, he added, "I confirm myself more and more in the determination to have no concern whatever in politics. There is not a political party in this country with which an honest man can act without blushing. . . ." After spending a month with his parents and making arrangements for buying a house, Adams left for Washington, the new "federal city," to collect his wife and son.

"Never did hermit or saint condemn himself to solitude more consciously than Congress and the Executive in removing the government from Philadelphia to Washington," wrote Henry Adams, John Quincy's historian grandson, eighty years later. Built on a swamp next to the Potomac, Washington in 1801 was little more than a forlorn village. But John Quincy Adams made no complaint as he wandered about the town, paying courtesy calls on President Jefferson, Secretary of State Madison, and Treasury Secretary Gallatin. He took his wife and infant son across the Potomac to Mount Vernon, where he introduced Martha Washington to her late husband's namesake. President Jefferson, always gracious and anxious to mend relations as best he could, invited the Adamses and the Johnson family to dinner. But the meal, Adams noted, was of "chilling frigidity."

He brought the family to Quincy in time for Thanksgiving. Louisa Catherine Adams, new to this part of the world, never forgot her introduction to the Adams family, particularly to her formidable mother-in-law, with whom she never would be comfortable. Disappointed that her eldest son had not married a home-grown Yankee, Abigail doubted whether her daughter-in-law's fragile health would survive the stormy blasts of a New England winter. But Louisa quickly won the heart of old John Adams, with whom she became a fast friend for the rest of his life. As she herself admitted years later, her background as the somewhat spoiled daughter of a London merchant had not prepared her for the duties of an American housewife. The ordinary responsibilities of household maintenance were unfamiliar to her, and for many years her husband kept the family accounts. With no friends of her own, Louisa felt isolated in Boston and Quincy. To compensate, she often invited one of her younger sisters to live with them. It was not long before she became an effective hostess for her husband, and after a few years, he even let her take over the household finances.

Although a dutiful, caring, and at times affectionate husband and father, the compulsive Adams nonetheless was often remote as he buried himself in his books, writings, and professional responsibilities. His letters to Louisa, from the days of their engagement in 1796 to their old age, are businesslike, informative, and occasionally humorous, but on the whole show less sparkle and playfulness than his father's letters to Abigail. Yet, in contrast to the predictions of her mother-in-law, the northern climate agreed with Louisa Adams. Her health improved, and a pregnancy in 1803 was unaccompanied by any of the danger signals experienced in Berlin. That summer she and her husband celebrated the arrival of John Adams II, born on the Fourth of July.

IN BOSTON, JOHN QUINCY ADAMS re-established as many of his old social and professional contacts as he could. He rented an office from John Lowell, a well-to-do fellow attorney, purchased books and furniture, re-read Blackstone's *Commentaries*, and once again awaited clients. He joined a group of young Bostonians who tinkered with scientific apparatus and performed experiments for mutual entertainment and edification. He wrote articles and translated German fables for the Philadelphia *Port Folio*, a Federalist literary journal edited by his brother's friend Joseph Dennie. The *Port Folio* had published his letters from Silesia, and Adams continued to contribute to it in hopes, he said, of removing "that foul stain of literary barbarism which has long exposed our country to the reproach of strangers, and to the derision of her enemies." His patriotism did not leave him insensitive to America's modest achievements in the fine arts. Privately, he hoped to establish a reputation as a man of letters, as a leader in the crusade to elevate America's taste for good literature.

At the end of January, 1802, Adams described his routine. He spent the mornings reading or writing. Then he went to the office from about eleven in the morning until two in the afternoon. Then home again for lunch ("dinner" in the early nineteenth century), and then back to the office until dark, after which he went for a walk before returning home. Evenings he spent with his friends at the scientific society, or at home, reading Shakespeare or Milton to "the ladies." Weekends he spent with his parents in Quincy, sometimes with Louisa, sometimes not. He resolved upon a course of self-improvement. "During the course of the present year," he wrote not long after he had settled in, "I shall undertake to *do* little or nothing. My object will be to *learn*. It is late in the progress of my life to complete my education, and perhaps after my age, a man can learn but little. Yet I must not despair." Above all, he resolved to overcome his distaste for the law, but it would not be easy. "The commencement of my old profession again is attended with difficulties somewhat embarrassing," he told his diary at the beginning of the new year. "But I thank God," he proclaimed, "I can yet struggle with the ills of life allotted to me."

He did not struggle very long. Three weeks later he wrote "I feel strong temptation, and have had great provocation to plunge into political controversy." Just what the "great provocation" was is not clear. That winter he could be seen in a number of high-profile capacities that make it hard to avoid the conclusion that he was deliberately placing himself in the public view. He let it be known that he would accept the relatively low-level federal appointment as a Commissioner of Bankruptcy (from which he was later removed when the Republicans made the office a presidential rather than a judicial appointment). He joined the volunteer firemen, patrolling the streets of Boston with other young men, even assisting in dousing one or two fires in the still largely wooden-built town. He purchased a pew in the Old Brick Meeting House, where his Harvard classmate William Emerson (father of the more famous Ralph Waldo) preached. He accepted invitations to speak. And in April he was a Federalist candidate for the Massachusetts state senate, winning easily.

Barely six months earlier he had proclaimed that there were no political parties in America with which an honest man could associate without blushing. Now, blushing or not, Adams modified his views. In Massachusetts, Republicans and Federalists confronted one another throughout the entire range of public offices. Alliance with one or the other was the price of entry, and John Quincy Adams was now willing to pay it, albeit reluctantly. "A politician in this country must be a man of a party," he acknowledged. "I would fain be the man of my whole country." The words he first applied to his father he now claimed for himself.

This was a problem that would nag Adams throughout his life. As a diplomat abroad, he was necessarily detached from partisanship, committed to the loftier perspective of national interest. But at home, he believed, "the spirit of party" resulted in the subordination of the general interest to the party interest or to personal ambition. It led, as he put it years later, to "the perverted axiom that a part is greater than the whole." His antiparty feelings were shaped in part by his experience abroad, but also by his own situation. Like his father, Adams had a burning ambition to serve the public, always expressed in the familiar Adams rhetoric of duty and sacrifice. His "calling" was to serve the nation, even humanity itself. But organized political parties, with their strategies, their caucuses, their staged management of the nation's business, were to him artificial devices designed not to promote the public welfare but to manipulate the public's passions.

Having nevertheless to choose, Adams did not hesitate to ally himself with the Federalists. They were a minority in the nation, but dominant in Massachusetts. Most of his friends and colleagues, including John Lowell, from whom he rented his office, Harrison Gray Otis, one of the old "Crackbrain Club," Theophilus Parsons, his old mentor, and Josiah Quincy, his distant cousin, were all Federalists. They were the party of the "host culture," led by descendents of the old colonial elite, reflecting social and political conservatism, religious orthodoxy, Anglo-Saxon descent, and a pro-British, anti-French foreign policy. The last item had created the difficulties in 1800, when extreme Anglophiles like Timothy Pickering and others challenged President John Adams' normalization of Franco-American relations. But now, two years later, the son was willing to allow these wounds to heal.

The Jeffersonian Republicans, on the ascendant elsewhere, were still a minority in Massachusetts. Of the old Revolutionary leaders, only the aging Samuel Adams figured prominently in their ranks. They were more often the "outsiders," often without college education, belonging to the "dissenting" religious sects: Baptist, Methodists, Quakers, even Catholics. Republican leaders paid more attention to public opinion in fashioning their appeals, which, in the view of most Federalists, was like abandoning the helm of a ship and letting it be carried by the winds and current to inevitable disaster. It was one thing to maintain, as did nearly all Americans, that the people should choose their leaders. It was quite another to assert, as did many Republicans, that the people should control their leaders after they had been chosen. Put another way, the Federalists still clung to the broad features of the "deferential society" of the eighteenth century, while the rise of the Republicans was evidence of its steady weakening. John Quincy Adams, who throughout his life would oppose what he called "electioneering," was more content with the elitist Federalist approach.

But no sooner had Adams been sworn into office than it became evident to the Massachusetts Federalists that he might be a problem. Since Federalists controlled the state senate, they planned on appointing all five of the Governor's Councilors, an advisory board. Adams proposed, unsuccessfully, that two of the five be Republicans, thus making the group more representative of the entire legislature. Later, when wealthy Federalists like Harrison Gray Otis wanted a charter for a new banking corporation, but declined to reveal the names of the stockholders, he opposed the project. The following year he voted against a Federalist attempt to remove two Republican state judges, defending the principle of judicial independence. Word quickly went around that John Quincy Adams, like his father, was "too unmanageable."

Perhaps as a means of getting him out of the way, Adams' name was placed on the Federalist ballot for the Boston Congressional seat in the fall elections. Although he did not "electioneer" for the post, he carried the town of Boston by 66 votes out of a total of about 3000. But too many Federalists stayed home in the suburban towns, where the Republicans had greater strength, and Adams lost in the total count. The opposition, he noted, were "more sure, more earnest," when it came to politics. He persuaded himself that he did not want the job anyway.

In spite of his defeat and his maverick voting record, Adams was still high on the list of possible Federalist successors to an open United States Senate seat in 1803. Prior to the twentieth century, national senators were chosen by the state legislatures instead of by the public, which meant that in nearly every instance the political party that controlled the legislature controlled the choice of senator. With the Federalists in control, it remained only for them to agree on a name. Party unity was threatened, however, as many Federalists, distrusting Adams, favored the crusty former Secretary of State Timothy Pickering. On the other hand, moderate Federalists, friends of the Adamses, did not want to see Pickering rewarded in 1803 for his treachery in 1800.

Adams, anxious to avoid any appearance of vindictiveness, now revealed himself as something more than the political innocent he always claimed to be. He let it be known that he had no objection to Pickering provided a majority of the Federalist legislators agreed to support him. He thus avoided alienating the so-called High Federalists, while not removing himself from consideration. It was finally agreed that Pickering, as the older man, would have two chances to gain his majority in the legislature, but failing that, unanimous

Federalist support would go to Adams. As it turned out, there was enough hostility to stop Pickering, after which Adams was elected. But then the other Massachusetts Senator suddenly decided to resign, and Pickering was chosen to succeed him. Thus the division in the Federalist party between the High Federalists and the Adamsites was reflected in the Massachusetts senatorial delegation.

Shortly after his election, Adams learned of the failure of the London banking firm of Bird, Savage, and Bird, where both he and his father had deposited a considerable portion of their personal funds: some 3500 pounds sterling. Promissory notes that John Quincy had written against these funds had "bounced," and the new Senator was forced to sell some of his Boston property in order to cover the losses. Eventually the damage was repaired, but to make ends meet, Senator Adams and his wife made plans to board at the Washington home of his wife's older sister Nancy and her husband.

IN THE YEARS AFTER HIS retirement from the presidency, Thomas Jefferson liked to refer to his election and the defeat of the Federalists as "the Revolution of 1800." By then he had convinced himself that the changes brought about by his administration were fully as important as those of 1776. Although party platforms did not exist as such, and would not appear for more than a generation, Republicans had promised lower taxes, the elimination of the national debt, a reduction of the role of the federal government in domestic affairs, and a more even-handed policy toward the two superpowers in foreign affairs. And they were true to their word, at least in the early years of Jefferson's first administration. They abolished all internal taxes, slashed appropriations for the army and navy, and lowered the national profile abroad by closing the American legations in the Netherlands and Prussia. Whether these measures constituted a "revolution" may be doubted, but they proved to be extremely popular.

In fact, it was his Federalist opponents, rather than Jefferson himself, who spoke of revolution in 1800 and thereafter. Nervous conservatives like Pickering and his friend, former Congressman

Perhaps the best-known of all the portraits of Jefferson, this one was painted by Rembrandt Peale in 1800, the year he defeated John Quincy Adams' father, John Adams, for the Presidency. *Courtesy of the White House.*

Fisher Ames, were convinced that Jefferson was an anarchist in politics, an atheist in religion, and a libertine in personal morals. Recalling Jefferson's earlier enthusiasm for the French Revolution, they fully expected an American version to follow in 1801. "Our days are made heavy with the pressure of anxiety," moaned Ames, "and our nights restless with visions of horror. We listen to the clank of chains, and overhear the whispers of assassins."

Ames was an extremist, as events would prove. There were no chains or assassins to be seen during Jefferson's administration. "We are all republicans, we are all federalists," the new President had said during his inaugural. But the Federalists, victims of the first peaceful overthrow of an administration in American history, can be forgiven for not knowing what to expect. Some simply gave up in despair, while others waited confidently for the people to return to their senses.

But, as John Quincy Adams noted, the nation seemed to prosper. Revenues increased in spite of the elimination of internal taxes. John Adams' agreement with France had been followed by a truce in the Anglo-French war, and so long as peace prevailed, there would be no grounds for conflict over the issues of impressment or of neutral rights. During most of Jefferson's first term, there was a tranquillity in both foreign and domestic affairs that the new nation had not known for a long time. The Louisiana Purchase would prove to be the icing on the cake.

The Louisiana Territory had belonged to the decaying Spanish empire since 1763, when they received it from the French following the Seven Year's War. Spanish rule had been notoriously ineffective among the white inhabitants, most of whom were either English- or French-speaking, and had little or no loyalty to Madrid. But after Bonaparte's rise to power, Louisiana had passed back to France, whose ability to enforce its rule was considerably greater. With the vital port city of New Orleans about to fall into French hands, Jefferson authorized his negotiators in Paris to offer to buy the city and its environs from Napoleon for $5,000,000. Instead they were confronted with an offer from the ubiquitous foreign minister Talleyrand to sell the entire territory for $15,000,000. Wisely laying aside any constitutional scruples arising from his limited-government views, Jefferson had accepted the offer and called a special meeting of the Senate for October, 1803.

A delay in his departure from Quincy prevented Senator Adams from arriving in time to vote on the Treaty. He fully intended to support it, which would have made him the only Federalist in Congress to do so. His colleague Pickering and the others believed that by nearly doubling the territory of the United States, New England's influence—which they identified with sound government—would be engulfed by waves of uncouth frontiersmen who would eventually populate the Mississippi Valley and demand representation in Congress.

No one valued New England and her institutions—the town meeting, the Congregational church, public education—more than John Quincy Adams. But his knowledge of the jealousy with which Old World powers regarded America's expansion overcame whatever reservations he might have had against the treaty. The removal of French and Spanish influence from the heart of North America was well worth the sacrifice. Besides, the potential wealth of the Mississippi Valley might someday be carried abroad in Yankee sailing ships, and its farmlands populated by Yankee sons and daughters. Already, in an oration delivered at Plymouth the year before on the anniversary the landing of the Pilgrim Fathers, Adams had looked forward to continued American expansion. Someday, he thought, there would be more Americans than Europeans. "The destinies of this empire," he said, ". . . disdain the powers of human calculation." He closed his speech by quoting the spirit, if not the exact words, of Bishop Berkeley's famous lines: "Westward the Star of Empire takes its way." In 1803 John Quincy Adams would not be found among those who wished to restrict the growth of the United States.

Washington was still the "city of magnificent distances." The same muddy streets, unfinished buildings, and seedy boardinghouses that Adams had noticed two years before greeted him upon his arrival. When he walked into the Senate chamber for the first time in his official capacity, the roof still leaked. With only one theater in town, Congress was often the only place to go for entertainment. Signs warned visitors not to place their feet on the rails in front of the gallery, lest dirt fall on the Senators. Spectators consumed popcorn and candy, often sent from the floor in packets attached to fishing poles. The Senate consisted of just thirty-four members, representing seventeen states. Although the Republicans had a majority in both houses of Congress, there were no official "majority leaders" in the twentieth-century sense. President Jefferson and his Vice President Aaron Burr had parted company, and there was already friction between the more equalitarian Republicans from the North and the occasionally imperious slaveholders from Virginia and South Carolina. No one spoke for the Federalists.

The home of Nancy and Walter Hellen, Adams' sister-in-law and her husband, was about two-and-a-half miles from the Capitol building. Mindful of his weight, Adams walked the distance whenever he could, timing himself as he went. At sixteen minutes per mile, he was able to make it to the Senate in less than forty-five minutes.

He lost no time in establishing his presence, notwithstanding his freshman status. Adams was not always astute in his choice of topic. Soon after his arrival, a routine resolution came before the body calling for the wearing of black crepe by Senators in mourning for the recent deaths of Samuel Adams of Massachusetts, and two prominent Virginians, Senator Stevens T. Mason, and Edmund Pendleton. Adams rose to object. Wearing crepe for non-Senators, the new Senator said, would lead to "unsuitable discussions of character, and . . . debates altogether foreign to the subjects which properly belong to them." He had a point, but to many it seemed unnecessary nitpicking, and ungenerous toward his late kinsman, who had sided with the Republicans in his old age. It touched off a three-hour debate, resulting in the separation of Mason from the others. All three were eventually approved, but Adams pointedly voted against any official mourning for Pendleton and Samuel Adams.

He succeeded in creating confusion again when he argued that although the Louisiana Purchase was constitutional, the Constitution still needed to be amended before the federal government could extend its powers over the territory. Moreover, the citizens of Louisiana should be allowed to give their assent to the new government. Otherwise, he contended, the "first principles of the social contract," as well as those of the Declaration of Independence, that legitimate government exists only by consent of the governed, would be violated. The present citizens of Louisiana, he added, were a people "whose language we do not understand, whose manners, opinions, and prejudices are totally variant from our own, and of whom we know nothing more than could be collected from a couple of small pamphlets." While many Republicans said privately that they agreed with him, neither Congress nor the President were in a mood for delay, and his objection received little public support. His efforts were, he remarked to his diary, like a "feather against a whirlwind."

In the debates over the future of Louisiana, Adams had the first of many opportunities to consider the future of slavery as well. In this he was ambivalent, even inconsistent. He resisted the attempts to limit the importation of slaves into the new territory. "Slavery in a moral sense is an evil," he declared, but "as connected with commerce, it has its uses." Any limitations on the citizens of Louisiana enacted by Congress were illegitimate, he believed, including this one. In 1805, when a group of Quakers petitioned Congress calling for restraints on slavery's growth, Adams joined with those advocating the right of the petitioners to at least be heard. The issue, he noted in his diary, was "very warmly debated" for three hours. Yet that same year, when a Republican senator proposed to outlaw the importation of slaves into the United States beginning in 1808—as provided for in the Constitution—Adams joined those who argued that the measure was premature. During his years in the Senate slavery was not an issue to which he devoted much consideration one way or the other.

Other items before the Senate in the 1803–04 Congressional session included a proposed treaty that attempted to resolve the boundaries between the United States and British North America, the impeachment and subsequent trial of Federalist district Judge John Pickering, and a proposed constitutional amendment requiring separate balloting in the electoral college for President and Vice President.

Recognizing that the senior Senator from Massachusetts, although only thirty-six years old, was one of the few of their number who had ever been abroad, let alone serve in the diplomatic corps, the Senate appointed him chairman of an *ad hoc* committee created to report on the boundary treaty. The agreement fixed the line between Maine and New Brunswick in the Northeast on terms favorable to the Americans, and attempted to draw a line in the Northwest, where knowledge of the area was much less certain. But here the new Louisiana Treaty complicated matters, since the former French claims to the territory, now in American hands, might well extend into land claimed by Britain. To be safe, the Senate, over the objections of Adams and most New Englanders, voted to delete the article dealing with the Northwest boundary until the limits of Louisiana could be determined. This did not suit the British, who rejected the amended treaty, leaving the matter to be settled at a later date. As it was, John Quincy Adams would be Secretary of State when that occurred, and he would have good reason to be grateful for the Senate's action.

Although Jefferson as President did not remove as many Federalist appointees from office as many had feared and others had hoped, he was determined to weaken the Federalist grip on the judiciary, where appointments were held for life. The Constitution, however, stipulated that judges and other federal official could be removed by Congress only after impeachment and conviction for "high crimes and other misdemeanours." Unless those words were interpreted liberally, the Federalist grip was bound to last for a long time. Before Adams' arrival in the Senate, an opportunity had presented itself to the Republicans in the form of Judge John Pickering, a New Hampshire Federalist who over the years had lapsed into alcoholism and insanity. His removal could establish a precedent for the removal of others. Now Adams and his colleagues had the painful responsibility of sitting as judges in the case of a man who clearly had committed no "high crime or misdemeanour" and who was equally clearly incapable of defending himself. He joined with the other Federalists in an unsuccessful protest against Pickering's trial, conviction, and removal. For Adams, the independence of the judiciary, a principle that he had first defended in Massachusetts when it had been Republican judges under fire from Federalists, was at stake. The next target would be arch-Federalist

Supreme Court Justice Samuel Chase, who would be brought to trial by the Jeffersonians in the following year.

The Twelfth Amendment, as it was to become known, was a recognition by Congress and the states of the reality of organized political parties. Originally the Founders had hoped that the members of the "Electoral College," each with two votes to cast for President, would somehow agree on a small number of qualified persons, even though the "College" would never meet in one place as a single body. The system had worked with the selection of George Washington, but with no one else. By 1796, Federalists and Republicans were running geographically balanced tickets for President and Vice President, and in 1800 the disciplined Republican electors each dutifully voted for Thomas Jefferson and Aaron Burr, resulting in an embarrassing but potentially dangerous tie. The proposed Twelfth Amendment specified separate votes for President and Vice President and reduced the number of finalists in the event of a non-majority from five to three. John Quincy Adams grudgingly accepted the need for separating the two votes, but balked at the reduction. It discriminated, he said, against the smaller states whose candidates might not be as well known. He dubbed the Twelfth Amendment the "electioneering amendment," and hoped, unsuccessfully, that Massachusetts would reject it. As many have since pointed out, the reduction of the number of finalists from five to three made possible Adams' own election to the presidency some twenty-two years later, in 1825.

"Hitherto my conduct has given satisfaction to neither side," he proudly told his mother after two months in Washington, "and both are offended at what they consider a vain and foolish presumption of singularity. . . ." He was right. Having been elected by Federalist votes at home, Federalists thought it ungracious and hypocritical to cut loose from the party so soon after being chosen. "Like a Kite without a Tail," one of them described Adams, "he will be violent in his attempts to rise . . . and will pitch on one side and the other, as the popular Currents may happen to strike." In fact, on the question of the Louisiana a number of Federalists outside of Congress agreed with him, including Alexander Hamilton, Chief Justice John Marshall, and of course, his own father. "I do not disapprove of your conduct in the business of Louisiana," wrote the ex-President from Quincy.

"I think you have been right, though I know it will become a very unpopular subject in the Northern states. . . ."

Actually, with the exception of Louisiana, Adams' voting record during his first two years was very close to the Federalist party line. He voted with them on the judicial impeachment cases and on the British boundary treaty. In foreign affairs, with the Anglo-French war temporarily halted, he accused the Republicans of "conjuring up . . . every possible occasion or pretence to quarrel with England." During the presidential election of 1804, as "Publius Valerius," he wrote pro-Federalist essays for the Massachusetts newspapers, accusing the New England Republicans of kowtowing to the Virginian aristocrats. He supported the Federalist attempt to repeal the "three-fifths clause" in the Constitution that gave additional electoral weight to slave states, and without which the Jeffersonians would have lost the presidential election of 1800. He even submitted anonymous verses to the *Port Folio*, repeating the Federalist gossip concerning Jefferson's alleged liaisons with Sally Hemings, one of his slaves. He was still more at ease socially with Federalists, possibly because most of them were northerners like himself. The Republican leaders in Congress, on the other hand, tended to be southern slaveholders, who looked with disdain at the money-grubbing Yankees to the North.

He fancied himself slighted by his colleagues, both Federalist and Republican. He was sure that resolutions and motions made by him were voted against simply because he introduced them, and once he thought he was made chairman of a committee purely as a means for keeping him off the floor. Much if not all of this was in his imagination. He developed a heroic self-image, always maintaining "inflexible principle" against "the spirit of party." It must be said in defense of the other Senators, that John Quincy Adams could find moral issues, as in the crepe-wearing controversy, where others could not. In his first years in the Senate, he was respected but not particularly liked. "He is a man of much information, a bookworm, very industrious," wrote William Plumer, a Federalist Senator from New Hampshire who did like Adams. "A man of handsome natural and acquired abilities far exceeding his age. He is a very correct and animated speaker. A man of strong passions and of course subject to strong prejudices, but a man of strict undeviating integrity. He is free and independent. On some subjects he appears eccentric."

Adams took his job seriously. He spent the summer of 1804 studying the entire United States Code—every law passed since the First Congress in 1789. Then he compiled and analyzed all the Supreme Court decisions. But he was still not satisfied with himself, admitting that the successful legislator required "firmness, perseverance, patience, coolness, and forbearance," qualities that had thus far eluded him. "The intensity with which my mind seizes hold of the public business is greater than suits my comfort or can answer any sort of public utility," he confessed. He did not think himself an effective extemporaneous speaker. The intensity with which he engaged the issues prevented the bantering style and geniality of spirit that characterized the effective lawmaker. Occasionally he would become so excited that he found himself groping for words and bordering on incoherence. "I must, therefore, never flatter myself with the hope of oratorical distinction." He resolved to watch the good orators so as to improve his style, and when the Senate was not in session he wandered over to the House chamber in order to watch the debates there.

From Quincy came all sorts of advice, from his father, who told him to be wary of the southerners, who, along with the Germans, Irish, and Dutch, "have been actuated by an absolute hatred of New England," and from his mother, who thought he needed help on everything from his diet to his wardrobe. "You eat too little and study too much," Abigail Adams lectured the Senator. He needed to pay attention to his appearance, and so should Louisa. "The neatest man, observed a Lady the other day, wants his wife to pull up his coller and mind that his coat is brush'd." His brother told him to relax. "I think it is manifest from the strain of your letters," he said, "that you take the publicke cause too seriously to heart. . . ."

If the presidential election of 1800 was a setback for the Federalist party, that of 1804 was a disaster. Thomas Jefferson was reelected easily, as a Republican tidal wave swept over the nation, even over New England, leaving only Connecticut untouched. Senator Adams, after summering in Quincy, returned undaunted and ready to do battle with the Republicans over the impending trial of Justice Chase.

Chase's "high crime or misdemeanour" was little more than being a bigoted, intemperate, and generally obnoxious Federalist. If the Republicans were successful in removing him on purely political grounds, the next target, so it was said, might well be Chief Justice Marshall himself. Adams, and the handful of Federalist Senators remaining, had hopes of convincing enough moderate Republicans of the dangers in making the judicial system subject to the winds of partisan politics.

The Chase trial was presided over by the lame-duck Vice President Aaron Burr, who had shot and killed former Treasury Secretary Alexander Hamilton in a duel the previous summer. Adams had little use for either man, but had grudging admiration for the fair and fastidious way in which Burr handled the trial, which resulted in a defeat for the Administration. Enough Republicans joined with Adams and the Federalists to prevent the necessary two-thirds vote needed for Chase's removal. He carefully recorded the vote of each Senator on each of the charges against Chase, in what he obviously regarded as one of the key events of his senatorial term. The Republican assault on the judiciary did not raise Jefferson in Adams' estimation.

Three days later he was present as Thomas Jefferson took his second oath of office and delivered his second inaugural address "in so low a voice that not half of it was heard by any part of the crowded auditory." In spite of his father's defeat, and his own removal as Bankruptcy Commissioner, the personal relationship between the two remained polite, even friendly. Adams often found himself an invited guest at Jefferson's dinner table. This was an invitation few refused, regardless of politics. Not only did the President serve the best food in town, but it was backed up by a wide variety of the choicest wines and champagne. "I wish his French politics were as good as his French wines," grumbled one Federalist after leaving Jefferson's house.

When Adams went, there was usually a mix of Republican and

Federalist guests; politics was usually avoided in favor of conversation on historical or scientific matters. The President, a notoriously poor public speaker, was an excellent conversationalist in small groups. His anecdotes often stretched credulity. "Mr. Jefferson tells large stories," Adams recorded one evening after the President declared that he had learned Spanish in nineteen days and that he knew a man in Paris who could make artificial wine. Jefferson seemed to be cured of his early Francophilia, speculating that it might be a good idea for the French people to replace Napoleon with the old royal family. Senator Adams reported these and other conversations to his father in Quincy, who was still licking the wounds of 1800.

Like many who interacted with Jefferson over the years, Adams came to believe that however brilliant, the Virginian could not always be trusted. Jefferson was intensely partisan, but concealed it under a veneer of genial hospitality, such he practiced upon Adams. For his part Adams remained a critic of Jefferson's domestic politics, not only for his attack on the judiciary, but for his cheese-paring budgets. Adams believed that Jefferson's thirst for popularity led him to weaken dangerously the government's authority and its ability to defend the nation in case of a threat from abroad. It was partly for this reason that in 1807 Adams sponsored a resolution calling upon Treasury Secretary Gallatin to report a plan for the purpose "of opening roads, of removing obstructions to rivers; and of making canals . . . which, as objects of public improvement may require and deserve the aid of the government." Already, Adams had a more ambitious view than most of his colleagues of federal responsibility for what later would be called "internal improvements."

THE POLITICAL SEASON IN WASHINGTON usually ran from late November through March in odd-numbered years, and through late spring or early summer in even-numbered ones. Accordingly, Adams made plans for a return home with his family in April, 1805. Still struggling with the results of the collapse of Bird, Savage, and Bird, he bought from his father the farmhouse in which he had been born and had lived until his departure for Europe in 1779. He intended to fix it up as a summer residence. He embarked upon a valiant attempt to become a gentleman farmer, planting dozens of fruit trees and inspecting their progress daily. In the end he concluded it was not worth the effort, given the climate and the time it subtracted from his books, to which, he later admitted, he was addicted "beyond the bounds of moderation."

In Massachusetts, the Jeffersonian tide continued to rise. Should the Republicans capture the legislature, Adams would be a one-term senator, and he made preparations for that possibility. At the time it was permissible for a senator to hold more than one job, and so he continued his legal practice, albeit on a curtailed basis. More to his liking, however, was the opportunity to join the faculty of Harvard, which came his way when he was offered the prestigious Boylston Professorship of Rhetoric and Oratory, named after one of his relatives. Not only would this mean additional income, but it provided the opportunity to immerse himself in an area about which he long believed himself to be in need of instruction. Although his duties would not start for another year, he plunged into the study of the classical Greek and Roman rhetoriticians, from Aristotle and Demosthenes to Cicero and Caesar. He negotiated an arrangement whereby he could teach in the summers, when Congress was not in session, doubling the number of lectures per week so as to complete the normal course over a two-year period. Should he be voted out of office, he would have something to fall back upon. It was a form of unemployment insurance. "My political prospects continue declining," he wrote at the end of the year.

IN FACT, HIS "POLITICAL PROSPECTS" were soon to be dramatically affected by events abroad. The Anglo-French war had resumed in 1803, and with it the renewed possibility of friction between the United States and the belligerent powers. Once again the British were claiming the right of impressment and the right to confiscate neutral shipping headed towards the French enemy. Once again the

French, lacking a powerful navy, were demanding resistance on the part of the Americans, threatening confiscation in French ports if they did not. The conditions of the 1790's were repeating themselves; only this time it was Jefferson and the Republicans who would be faced with the task of negotiation and response.

As before, the most immediate crisis was in Anglo-American relations. For many years the Royal Navy had operated under what it called the "rule of 1756," which declared that neutral trade between the colonies of its enemies—in this case France—and the mother country would not be allowed in wartime if such trade had been closed in peacetime. In the past, ingenious American ship captains had circumvented the rule by taking French colonial goods first to the United States, then to France, thus "breaking" the voyage into two allegedly separate parts. In the summer of 1805, a British admiralty judge ruled, in what became known as the *Essex* decision, that such practices would no longer be allowed. Henceforth, all American merchantmen carrying goods between France and its colonies would be subject to confiscation. In the following weeks, thousands of dollars worth of American property were lost.

When Adams returned to Washington in the fall he found confusion as to how best to meet the new British challenge. Armed resistance was impossible, since Jeffersonian budget-cutting had rendered the navy virtually non-existent. What little remained of the American navy was off fighting pirates in the Mediterranean or rotting at anchor in the Potomac. The Republicans themselves were divided between plantation-minded southerners who had little interest in commercial or naval affairs, and northerners who now favored rebuilding the navy even if it meant raising taxes and spending money in a most un-Jeffersonian manner. Federalists too were torn between their concern for the losses felt by the mercantile community whom they represented, and their long-standing sympathies for Britain in its struggle against Bonaparte and the French.

For Adams there was no dilemma, even though the issue had the potential for driving a wedge permanently between him and the Federalist party. Mindful of his earlier debacles, he had avoided what he called "taking the lead" on issues, usually waiting until others had spoken before entering the debates. Beginning in 1806, however, his strategy changed. He was appointed to a committee charged with the responsibility for responding to that part of the President's Annual Message dealing with foreign affairs. His latent Anglophobia, dormant since the mid-1790's, now re-asserted itself. He was more hawkish than most of the Jeffersonians. "We have come to a situation, with Great Britain," he explained to his colleagues, "in which the more we can raise her jealousies and excite her fears, the better for us." He was one of a minority of senators who favored appropriating money for the purchase of Nova Scotia or other parts of the British maritime provinces. He thought he detected an increase in his influence over his colleagues. "The situation calls for every exertion of my faculties to serve the public," he wrote excitedly in his diary, "and I can never cease to regret that those faculties are so feeble to meet such an emergency. I have set aside all party spirit."

When the committee reported, the first two resolutions submitted to the Senate were from the pen of John Quincy Adams. The first attacked the *Essex* decision and the confiscations that followed as an "unprovoked aggression upon the property of the citizens of these United States, a wanton violation of their neutral rights and a direct encroachment upon their national independence." This passed unanimously; even Timothy Pickering could not avoid voting for it. The second resolution requested that the President "demand and insist upon" reparations for the lost property. After the words "insist upon" were struck out, the resolution passed, although this time Pickering and six other Federalists voted against it. Then, toward the end of the session, Congress enacted a partial boycott of certain British manufactured goods. Adams was the only Federalist in either house to vote in its favor.

That spring, Adams again returned to Massachusetts alone to prepare for his Harvard lectures. Louisa, who was expecting another child, stayed behind with her sister's family. The two boys had been boarded out: George with grandmother Abigail's sister Mary Cranch and her husband, while John stayed with his grandparents. Adams himself planned to live in Cambridge at the home of Benjamin Waterhouse, a family friend and fellow faculty member. For her part, Louisa Adams was not happy with "this separation life," as she once called it, and with good reason. In late June she suffered yet another miscarriage, with her preoccupied husband hundreds of miles away. "Mon Amie," she wrote plaintively a few weeks later, "I grant as you have undertaken the business that it is necessary to attend to it, but your family have some call on you as well." Overcome with grief and guilt, Adams sent for his wife to join him as soon as she was well. He would not make that mistake again. He had already purchased a new home for them in Boston, preparing for the seemingly inevitable return to private life.

The new professor began his course of lectures on rhetoric and oratory, still a major subject in the Harvard curriculum. His inaugural lecture was attended by a claque of parents, relatives, and a host of local dignitaries. But Adams did not see himself as a mere ornamental addition to the Harvard faculty. He took his new job as seriously as he did any other, taking time to hear the students declaim on various assigned subjects, much as he himself had done twenty years before. Like many alumni, Adams detected a decline in standards since his own student days, owing, he said, to "the indulgence of the College."

As tension between the United States and Great Britain continued to mount, the Massachusetts legislature fell to the Republicans. Dozens of British vessels now hovered just off the Atlantic coast, pouncing on American merchantmen as soon as they cleared the three-mile limit. Hopes were pinned on the diplomacy of James Monroe, the American Minister to Great Britain, who like John Jay in 1794, had been charged with the task of defusing the situation.

Back in Washington, Senator Adams found his support of Republican foreign policy rewarded with even more invitations to dine with President Jefferson. More than once it had been hinted by third parties that he was in line for a major appointment, but Adams remained wary. He had, he told a mutual friend, no desire for any appointment from Jefferson, and was quite content in his present situation. But he did not reject the overtures, and he continued to enjoy the president's fine wine and rambling conversation. And he had growing respect for James Madison, the somber, diminutive Secretary of State, with whom he occasionally played chess.

The Congressional session of 1806–1807 divided its attention between the crisis in Anglo-American relations, and the mounting evidence that former Vice President Burr had been plotting either treason in the Louisiana Territory, or an invasion of Mexico, or both. Nothing was known for sure until January, when Jefferson laid before a closed meeting of the Senate the evidence that he said connected his former political ally with a plot to detach Louisiana from the United States. Immediately some Jeffersonians brought forth a bill that would have suspended the right of *habeas corpus* while Burr and his accused conspirators were rounded up. John Quincy Adams surprised his colleagues by his "passionately zealous" support of the measure, which in fact went beyond the administration's wishes.

What Adams knew, and most of his colleagues did not, was that for some time a handful of High Federalists in his own state, led by Pickering, had been contemplating secession, a movement triggered by the Louisiana Purchase. Now, some three years later, Aaron Burr was tied to an even greater secessionist plot, possibly in collusion with the British. The combination of "internal faction, and external power" that he had warned against in Adams' *Publicola* letters in 1791, and that he had seen destroy the Dutch Republic in 1795, appeared to threaten the United States in 1804 and again in 1807. Like Abraham Lincoln more than half a century later, Adams argued that the right of *habeas corpus* was a luxury to be given up in a time of national peril. Fortunately for civil liberties, the suspension bill died in the House of Representatives.

As it was, Burr was later acquitted as a result of a ruling by Justice Marshall that narrowly defined the definition of treason. But neither Adams nor the Senate was through with the Burr intrigue. Later in the year the Senate appointed Adams chairman of a special committee to look into the conduct of a colleague, Senator John Smith of Ohio, who had been implicated but not convicted in the Burr conspiracy. The evidence against Smith was essentially the same as the evidence against Burr, but Adams, in a controversial report, argued that the Senate need not be limited to the narrow rules set down by the Chief Justice. Raising the specter of "a war of the most horrible description, . . . a war at once both foreign and domestic," if Burr had succeeded, Adams and his committee recommended Smith's expulsion. The motion failed by one vote, although Smith later resigned voluntarily. Again, while civil libertarians might disagree with Adams, his actions betrayed his impatience with legal technicalities when confronted with the survival of the Union.

As the Burr affair was unfolding, James Monroe finally sent the results of his negotiations with his Majesty's government. The proposed treaty was a disappointment. There was to be no change in the principles behind the *Essex* decision, and no movement on impressment. Jefferson declined to send Monroe's treaty to the Senate. Further complicating matters were Napoleon's Berlin and Milan Decrees, which declared that neutral vessels that had been trading with Britain, or even submitting to British inspection, would be confiscated by the French wherever they were caught, be it on the high seas or in a European port. Bonaparte had reverted to the same policies followed by the Directory in the 1790's. Federalists, reeling after their losses, could now claim with some truth that the French were as insulting as the British. In Massachusetts the Republican tide began to ebb. Congressional resolutions and boycotts were one thing; the prospect of a second war with the former Mother Country at a time when she was fighting for her survival against the French tyrant was something else. Besides, even with the losses through confiscation, trade with the British Empire was so profitable that a disruption was unthinkable to many who otherwise might have taken the appropriately patriotic stand. Federalists began to take hope.

As the senior Senator from the most commercially-minded state in the Union, John Quincy Adams was faced with increased pressure to cease his hobnobbing with the Jeffersons and the Madisons and return to his Federalist base. Friends argued that New England's true interest lay in continued trade with Old England, whatever the risks. Some even defended the British depredations on American shipping as a necessary evil needed on behalf of a greater good: the defeat of Napoleon. Yet whatever Federalist rumblings there had been against Adams for being too "unmanageable" in the past were nothing in comparison to what lay ahead.

ON JUNE 22, 1807, the British warship *Leopard*, seeking to recover British deserters, attacked without warning and at point-blank range the American frigate *Chesapeake*, following her captain's refusal to permit a search. Three Americans were killed. The attack was illegal even by British standards, for at no time had they claimed the right to stop and search the public naval vessels of a nation with whom they were at peace. Adams was in Cambridge beginning the second year of his course of lectures, and Congress was adjourned for the season. Had Congress been in session, an enraged public opinion might well have pushed a reluctant and unprepared Jefferson into war.

As news of the outrage swept up the coast, town after town held meetings of protest. When the tidings reached Boston, Adams was among those urging the Federalist-dominated Board of Selectmen to call a town meeting and join in the condemnation. They refused. The Boston Republicans then called a meeting of their own. Adams was among those present. Recognizing the significance of this, the Jeffersonians promptly placed him on a committee charged with the drafting of the appropriate denunciatory resolutions. They were voted upon and passed unanimously. Realizing their mistake, the Federalist town fathers called an official meeting at which somewhat weaker resolutions were also adopted, but the damage had been done.

Years later, Adams looked back upon the events of the summer of 1807 as the beginning of "the really important period of my life." Hitherto his departures from Federalist thinking had been tolerated as unfortunate eccentricities. Indeed, Adams still considered himself a Federalist. As recently as the previous April, he had chaired a meeting called to endorse Federalist candidates for state office. But from the moment he crossed the threshold and entered the Republican meeting, his days as a Federalist, and for that matter as a Senator, were numbered. He had already had a "somewhat warm" debate with his former landlord John Lowell, and the day after the meeting, which happened to be his fortieth birthday, he was told by another prominent Federalist that "I should *have my head taken off*" for disloyalty to the party. "I have indeed expected to displease them," he reflected that evening, "but could not help it." Again he struck the heroic pose. "My sense of duty shall never yield to the pleasure of a party."

The President called Congress into session six weeks early that fall in order to deal with the crisis. The British eventually disavowed the *Leopard's* attack, but the disavowal was more than offset by new "Orders in Council" that required *all* American merchant vessels carrying goods to Napoleon's Europe to stop first in Britain and pay duties before being allowed to proceed. Submitting to these new rules would have been, in Adams' mind, the same as giving up independence and rejoining the British Empire. But given American naval weakness, there appeared to be little that could be done.

For years Thomas Jefferson had nurtured the belief that the Old World could be coerced into respecting the New, not by armed might, which America lacked, but by a combination of appeals to abstract justice and the withdrawal of American goods from the international market. His faith in these "weapons" partly explains his unwillingness to spend great sums of money on conventional armed forces. Now, in late 1807, he put his theory into practice. On December 18, he sent to Congress a bill for a total embargo on all American exports. If the Great Powers would not respect American rights, they would no longer enjoy American goods. Nor could impressment continue if American ships were gone from the seas.

Senator Adams did not think much of the idea. Time would prove that the belligerents were not as dependent upon American trade as Jefferson thought. Moreover, the Embargo was unenforceable in many parts of the country, especially in Adams' own New England, whose hundreds of unpatrolled harbors had offered refuge for many a smuggler since the days of Bad King George. Nonetheless, he voted for the Embargo, and to no one's surprise, again was the only Federalist to do so. It was better than nothing, he explained to those who would listen, and it might strengthen the hand of the administration in dealing with the French and British.

But his vote was in effect his resignation from the party. Now the Federalist press turned against him. What Adams thought to be integrity, they called opportunism; what he believed to be patriotism, they called treason. He was, said a western Massachusetts newspaper, "one of those amphibious politicians, who lives on both land and water, and occasionally resorts to each, but who finally settles down into the mud." "I wish to God," fulminated a New York Federalist, "the noble house of Braintree had been put in 'a hole', and a deep one at that, twenty years ago." In January Adams attended and participated in the Republican Congressional caucus that nominated James Madison as that party's candidate to succeed Jefferson as President in the coming election. Even his mother remonstrated with him for that. But his father cheered him on. "You have too honest a heart," he wrote, "too independent a mind, and too brilliant talents, to be sincerely and confidentially trusted by any man who is under the dominion of party maxim or party feelings." He had no choice, his father continued, but to serve out his term and go back to his professorship and his law books. As for the Federalists, "I have long since renounced, abdicated, and disclaimed the Name and Character and Attributes of that Sect, as it now appears."

By the spring of 1808 New England was in full revolt. The same towns that had denounced the *Leopard's* attack on the *Chesapeake* in July were denouncing the Embargo in April, as a violation of the rights of property, the rights of the states, and the rights of the people. Theophilus Parsons, now Chief Justice of the Massachusetts Supreme Court, pronounced it unconstitutional. Timothy Pickering appeared in the Boston press, defending British policies and calling for the "interposition" of the commercial states against the Embargo. Seventy thousand copies of Pickering's letter were distributed throughout the region. For once, the Federalists were on the popular side of an issue. They hoped to use the Embargo to recapture control of the legislature in the spring elections.

Pickering's letter disturbed Adams for many reasons. He knew that his colleague had been involved in the secessionist plot of 1804; now his call for the "interposition" of the commercial states hinted at a replay of the same theme. He knew too, that British agents were communicating with unnamed Federalist leaders, claiming that in the event of a war with Britain, President Jefferson would try to ally America with France. While Adams knew this to be false, Francophobia always lay beneath the surface in New England, so much so that, combined with the anti-Embargo tide, it could play into the hands of whatever secessionist sentiment existed. After reading Pickering's letter, Adams knew that after eight years the time had come for another confrontation between the Adams family and the High Federalists.

It took the form of an open letter to Harrison Gray Otis, his former friend who was now the president of the Massachusetts state senate and an ally of Pickering. Adams wasted little time in defending the Embargo, describing it only as a "temporary expedient" to buy time until something better could be devised. He saved most of his ammunition for Pickering's rationalization of British attacks on American independence and his call for "interposition." Pickering had said little about the real cause for the Embargo—the requirements that American merchantmen stop in England and pay duties before continuing to the continent—and concentrated instead upon the menace of France and Napoleon. Adams refocused attention on the edicts, "thus fatal to the liberties for which the sages and heroes of our revolution fought and bled."

> They strike at the root of our independence. They assume the principle that we shall have no commerce in time of war, but with her dominions, and as tributaries to her. The exclusive confinement of commerce to the mother country, is the great principle of the modern colonial system; and should we by a dereliction of our rights at this momentous stride of encroachment surrender our commercial freedom without a struggle, Britain has but a single step more to take, and she brings us back to the stamp act and the tea tax.

Citing State Department figures, Adams demonstrated that the number of Americans illegally dragooned into the Royal Navy was far greater than Pickering had implied. He pounced on his colleague's unfortunate statement that Britain was only exercising her "right" to regulate neutral commerce in wartime. The whole tendency of the pamphlet, said Adams, "is to reconcile the nation, or at least its commercial states, to the servitude of British protection, and war with the rest of Europe." For this, he continued, Pickering and his allies were calling for the "interposition" of the states. "For this, not only are all the outrages of Britain to be forgotten, but the very assertion of our rights is to be branded with odium."

Adams concluded with an appeal for unity against the attempt to separate the interest of the "commercial states" from the others. Any "interposition," he said, should be "to promote Union and not a division—to urge mutual confidence, and not universal distrust—to strengthen the arm and not relax the sinews of the nation." It may well be true, he said, that the grievances were not evenly shared, but if they were to be dispelled, it would be only through unity. "While the spirit of *independence* shall continue to beat in unison with the pulses of the nation, no danger will be truly formidable."

Although a masterful performance, Adams' letter did not receive the circulation of Pickering's, and it came too late in the spring campaign. Riding the crest of anti-Embargo sentiment, the Massachusetts Federalists swept back into office.

There was a good deal of irony here, and for Adams' enemies, sweet comeuppance. Had he behaved himself and stayed within the Federalist fold, he probably would have been re-elected for a second term. Or if the Republicans had held on, he might have been chosen by them out of gratitude for his defense of their unpopular policy. As it was, he lost everything, and the triumphant Federalists lost no time in twisting the knife. Although the normal time for choosing a national Senator would have been in the fall, the new legislature chose Adams' successor in June. He took the hint and resigned immediately. Timothy Pickering at last had his revenge on the Adams family.

In Massachusetts, to be cast out of the Federalist hierarchy meant more than political ostracism. Given their social and economic power, it meant personal banishment as well. Friends who had travelled out to Cambridge to hear his Harvard lectures came no more. When he walked down Boston's State Street, so it was said, no one spoke to him. He had been prepared for defeat; in fact he welcomed it as a respite from an uncomfortable situation, but he had not been prepared for the cutoff of personal contacts and social relations. Outwardly he maintained his usual stoicism, but inside he bristled with a resentment that would last for the rest of his life.

One consolation was that he now had no shortage of Republican correspondents from Washington. Former adversaries now sought his advice and urged him to run for office as a Republican, again hinting at rewards to come in the future. He answered every letter, declined to run for office, and was non-committal about future appointments. He urged his new friends to revise the Embargo in favor of a ban on trade with the two belligerents until one of them relaxed its violations of American sovereignty. This "non-intercourse" would allow trade with other nations and would ease the pressure on New England commerce; otherwise, he thought, secession might become more than just a topic for discussion in the back rooms of Federalist law offices. Toward the end of the year, Congress enacted legislation similar to what Adams had proposed, but Thomas Jefferson left office without any offer of appointment, diplomatic or other-wise.

And so, for the present at least, Adams' attempt to serve the public outside of the constraints of "the spirit of party" had failed. It was back to the law and his duties as a Harvard Professor. He would now have more time for his family, to which a third son had been added in the momentous summer of 1807. He was named Charles Francis Adams, after his late uncle Charles, and Francis Dana, his father's mentor in St. Petersburg in the 1780's. John Quincy Adams endeavored to bring up his children as he himself had been raised. George, John, and now Charles were inculcated in succession with the same lessons of duty and sacrifice that John and Abigail Adams had tried to instill in their children thirty years before. John Quincy took young George on tours of the Adams farmlands, noting the boundaries and landmarks, impressing him, so he thought, with the heritage for which he would one day be responsible. He tutored him in French and read to him from the classics. But both his mother and his wife thought Adams, unlike his own father, was overly strict and too harsh a disciplinarian. Indeed, disputes over the rearing of their children became a persistent source of discord between Louisa and John Quincy Adams. Although he had a streak of mirth and playfulness that occasionally burst forth, as it did when he wrote racy verses to his wife, or when he played with his nieces and nephews at home in Washington, more typical was his self-admonition after dining with Chief Justice Marshall and other members of the Supreme Court: "This company was very agreeable, and the dinner remarkably pleasant, which made me too sociable, and I talked too much."

In March, 1809, James Madison took the presidential oath of office. Among the witnesses to the inaugural was John Quincy Adams, who was in Washington in his capacity as a private attorney. Two days later he received a note from the new President, asking to see him. Adams complied, and was confronted with an offer of appointment as American Minister to Russia. Madison had to know his response immediately, as the papers were to be sent to the Senate the next day. Adams was thus unable to consult with his family in Massachusetts, although he knew what their answer would be. "I do not wish to see you under existing circumstances any other than the private citizen you now are," his mother had warned before he left for Washington. Louisa too could be counted upon to resist. Their three boys, the oldest of whom of whom was not yet eight years old, would either have to be taken to St. Petersburg, where the winters were eight months long, or placed in the care of relatives. Acceptance would provide grist for the mills of his enemies, who all along had been saying that Adams' support for the Embargo was in return for reward at the hands of the opposition. He would have to give up his cherished teaching at Harvard. The sacrifices involved were more than enough. He had not sought the post; it had come to him. Adams accepted on the spot.

"To serve my country at its call is not merely an ambition, but a duty," he had told his future wife in 1796. Now Louisa Adams would know the full import of those words. A glimmer of hope appeared for her when a combination of Federalists and parsimonious Republicans temporarily blocked the nomination, but President Madison insisted, and it was finally approved. Senator Pickering was heard to say that on the whole, the best thing was to get John Quincy Adams out of the country.

The new Minister received the news of his confirmation and his instructions in Boston while attending a Fourth of July celebration at the Old South Church. There was not much time to prepare for his departure, since they needed to sail immediately if the vessel wished to return before ice closed the Baltic Sea. He had less than a month to wind up his Harvard lectures, pack his things, make the necessary legal and domestic arrangements, and put up with farewell visits from friends and relatives. In a decision he later came to regret, Adams chose to leave his two eldest sons behind. They were placed in the home of his Aunt Elizabeth, widowed in the 1790's, and since remarried. Charles Francis Adams, barely two years old, would accompany his parents.

To friends and family, Adams was outwardly serene, confident in his course of action. But in his farewell lecture to the students at Harvard (the majority of whom, he told his brother, "were made to believe that I was some sort of devil incarnate in politics") he revealed the turmoil that lay within. The love of literature, he said, would never betray them.

> In social converse with the mighty dead of ancient days, you will never smart under the galling sensation of dependence upon the mighty living of the present age; and in your struggles with the world, should a crisis ever occur, when even friendship may deem it prudent to desert you; when even your country may seem ready to abandon herself and you. . . ; seek refuge, my *unfailing friends*, and be assured you will find it, in the friendship of Laelius and Scipio, in the patriotism of Cicero, Demosthenes, and Burke, as well as in the precepts and example of him whose whole law is love, and who taught us to remember injuries only to forgive them.

According to Ralph Waldo Emerson, that passage "long resounded in Cambridge."

Eight days later, John Quincy Adams, his wife and child, his wife's sister Catherine, his nephew William Steuben Smith, and two servants, crossed over the Charles River bridge to Charlestown, where they boarded the private vessel *Horace* for the voyage to Russia.

Chapter Four

"A Bulldog Among Spaniels"

BEFORE LEAVING BOSTON, John Quincy Adams and his wife had their profiles taken by a local silhouettist. They gave no reason for this, nor was it necessary. Everyone knew the hazards of ocean travel, particularly in the North Atlantic and the Baltic, and the new American Minister to Russia wished to have some memento left behind should they not return. His profile reveals that, at age forty-two, Adams in his Senate years had lost most of his hair, disclosing the protruberant forehead that was the trait of several generations of male Adamses. The two profiles show nothing of the tensions that were building between husband and wife following Adams' decision to accept his appointment to St. Petersburg. As a dutiful wife of the early nineteenth century, Louisa Adams never considered rebellion, but as events unfolded, her resentment against her husband for taking her away from her two eldest children increased.

The *Horace* was owned by William Gray, one of the few Republican merchants in Boston. At their own expense, Gray's son Francis, along with the young Alexander Hill Everett, accompanied the Adams party for educational purposes. The first few weeks of the eighty-day voyage were uneventful. Adams fished for cod off the

John Quincy Adams dated these two silhouettes of himself and his wife, taken on August 1, 1809, just before their departure for Russia. The artist was Henry Williams of Boston. *Courtesy of The National Portrait Gallery, Smithsonian Institution.*

Grand Banks of Newfoundland, wrote letters to family and friends—given to passing westbound vessels—and read Plutarch and the Bible. "Our weather is so mild and the sea so smooth that I can employ more time in reading and writing than I ever could at sea before," he happily scribbled in his diary after ten days.

Knowing the resistance of wife and family to his "exile" made it all the more imperative that he justify the decision. He insisted that his motives were of the highest. The appointment, he wrote, "neither suits my own inclination nor my private judgement," but the call of his country, "expressed by the constitutional authority" left him no choice, although, as he told one of his new Republican friends, he thought he could have served the Madison administration better at home. But the alacrity with which he had accepted Madison's offer speaks for itself. Once again, as in 1794 when George Washington sent him to the Hague, the mission was rescuing him from an uncomfortable situation at home. If it meant living in a distant city that was virtually cut off from the rest of the world from October through April, so much the better. No one could accuse him of engineering an appointment like that.

And yet, the indefinite separation from his two eldest sons weighed heavily on his mind. He took the opportunity provided by the calm seas to write an extended letter outlining his hopes for their future and his own understanding of the role of the citizen in a republic. It would be useful, he told his sons—resurrecting an old family theme—"that you should each of you consider yourself as placed here *to act a part*—that is, to have some single great end or object to accomplish, toward which all the views and all the labors of your existence should steadily be directed." In the beginning, everyone has an obligation to provide for oneself and his family, for without that, nothing else was possible. But to one's family, "there is another duty not less sacred than that of giving them bread—the duty of *education*—of training them up in the way they should go; of preparing them for the conflicts *they* may have in their turn to sustain with the world."

Moreover, he who is blessed with a surplus "beyond that which is necessary for himself and his family" has an obligation to do what he can to correct "the inequities of fortune. . . . of becoming the benefactor of his fellow-mortals beyond the circle of his own family." This included the responsibilities of serving society, which under most governments was limited to inherited aristocracies or other privileged minorities. "But under the republican principle," Adams reminded his sons, "every individual has a stake, an interest, and a voice in the common stock of society, and consequently lies under the obligation of attending to and promoting that common interest to the utmost in his power, compatible with the discharge of his more immediate duties of self-preservation and preservation of his kind."

Very often, the privileged do not recognize this obligation, and therefore "pass their lives in idleness, or in dishonorable occupations—mere burdens of human society, mere cumberers of the ground." He hoped this would not be the case for any of his children. But, as Adams had reason to know, there were pitfalls even for those willing to serve the public. In a nation like the United States, most important positions were elective, and for relatively short terms. Never, he warned, become dependent upon them. "For if you choose that which depends upon the will of others, you not only prepare yourself for probable disappointment, but you diminish your means of usefulness by making them precarious. You weaken your power of doing good, by placing the capacity of doing it at the disposal of others." Therefore, he advised, "keep your retreat open," and always be prepared to retire into "the humbler and safer pursuits of private life."

In this most revealing letter, it is not difficult to detect both the republican culture of civic virtue into which Adams was born, and the course of his own life, especially his determination to maintain both personal and political "independence." Through frugal living and wise investments, he had reached a measure of financial security at age forty-two that he hoped would not be threatened by high living in St. Petersburg. Nor did his new affiliation with the Jeffersonians mean that he had abandoned any of his earlier political convictions. His "fundamental principles," he told a correspondent before leaving America, "were *Union and Independence*."

FIVE YEARS BEFORE ADAMS boarded the *Horace*, President Jefferson had opened a correspondence with Russia's Emperor, or Tsar, Alexander I. Jefferson was impressed both by the young monarch's professions of liberalism, and by the more practical need to cultivate the friendship of a major European power whose settlements were beginning to crop up along the Pacific coast of North America. The exchange of full-scale missions between Russia and the United States was the first fruit of this correspondence. Prospects for Russo-American friendship were good, for Alexander had already pledged his support for the principle of "free ships, free goods"—the cornerstone of American commercial policy since independence. "It will be your duty therefore," Adams' instructions read, "to cultivate the good dispositions of the Emperor on every point interesting to the United States." The two nations, Adams was told shortly after his arrival, "could never in any manner be dangerous to each other."

In 1809, the seas upon which Adams sailed were still ruled by Britannia's Royal Navy, but most of the continent of Europe lay in the grasp of Napoleon's *Grand Armée*. Bonaparte had humiliated his most formidable rivals, Prussia and Austria, created puppet states in Italy and the Netherlands, and outflanked the British through alliances with Denmark and Russia. His power and influence ran from the Urals to the Atlantic, from the Baltic to the Mediterranean, although some thought the great Corsican might have reached his limits. "He has stretched the bowstring till it cracks," observed Adams before leaving for St. Petersburg.

Adams got a taste of the problems facing American merchants in Europe when the *Horace* entered the straits between Sweden and Denmark on its way to the Baltic. They were stopped—twice—by British vessels hovering off the Danish coast. Although the *Horace* was not a public ship, she was carrying an accredited diplomat and was allowed to pass. A few hours later, the Danes, who were at war with Britain, mistook them for being English and commanded the *Horace* to put into a Danish port. When the captain refused, the Danes at first ordered an attack but then thought better of it. Then Adams learned of some thirty American merchantmen who had been captured by Danish privateers and whose captains and crew were sitting on land pending decisions by the Danish courts. There was little Adams could do to help. He made a special overland journey to Copenhagen, where, owing to Jeffersonian parsimony, there was no American diplomatic representative. Not having any authority himself, Adams had to be content with sending a long and argumentative letter to the local American consul, a Danish citizen. He was not optimistic about the outcome.

It was now early October, and the delays in Denmark made a timely arrival in Russia doubtful. The American captain favored stopping in Germany and making the remainder of the trip by land in the spring, but Adams persuaded him to push on. Favorable winds brought them to the port city of Cronstadt on October 21st, and a Russian vessel carried them up the River Neva to St. Petersburg the following day.

When he first visited St. Petersburg as a teenager in 1782, Russia was on the periphery of European affairs, and the city was little more than a provincial capital. Now, owing to the efforts of Catherine the Great, Russia had become a major European power and St.

Petersburg the showcase of the continent, "the most magnificent city of Europe, or of the world," as Adams described it to Catherine's grandson the Tsar, without too much exaggeration. This was the city later immortalized in Tolstoy's *War and Peace*, with its endless masked balls, holiday festivals, glittering *soirees*, sleigh rides, *Te Deums*, and intrigue. It was Old World corruption at its finest, a far cry from the forlorn swamps and wooden buildings of Washington. "How much I am delighted with all this is unnecessary for me to say," wrote Adams to his mother a few months after their arrival, "nor how congenial it is to my temper to find extravagance and dissipation a public *duty*." It was in these surroundings that a hostile British observer characterized John Quincy Adams in St. Petersburg as "a bulldog among spaniels." In time he became used to the city, even fascinated by the ceremonial aspects of the Russian Court, recording in detail the rituals and spectacles laid out before him.

Yet the cost of living was so high in St. Petersburg that he considered taking the first boat home in the spring. His annual salary was $9000 (second only to president Madison's) plus another $9000 for an "outfit," or starting-up expenses. But what was thought extravagance by penurious Americans was little more than a week's pocket-money for many of the experienced European diplomats with whom Adams was to mix. Furniture alone ate up his entire expense money, leaving nothing for the $2000 house rent. The French Ambassador, Adams was told, spent $350,000 each year on entertainment alone, featuring banquets of fish and meats, wines and champagnes, fruits and desserts, that dwarfed Thomas Jefferson's little dinners in Washington. Adams feared that he and his wife would not even be able to appear at such functions, let alone imitate them. "Not a particle of clothing I brought with me have I been able to present myself in," he complained, "and the cost of a lady's dress is far more expensive, and must be more diversified than that of a man." If he were to stay, he would have to borrow money—and there were many who were willing to "loan" it to him—or dip into his own savings. Fearing loss of "independence," he resolved upon the latter.

For the reluctant Louisa Adams, the St. Petersburg years were the least happy of her overseas sojourns. "I do not like the place or the people," she reported to her mother-in-law. Things did not improve much, with their Spartan existence complicated by another pregnancy in 1810, followed by a miscarriage. But upon recovering, she and her sister Catherine were able to appear in society, even occasionally to enjoy it. The two sisters became great favorites with the Tsar, who more than once commandeered them as dancing partners. As in Berlin, Louisa's fluency in French made it easy for her to hold her own among the diplomatic corps (only the Bavarian Minister brought his wife with him). Yet late in life, perhaps influenced by intervening events, Louisa Adams would refer to St. Petersburg as "a horrid place."

When Abigail Adams read of her son's financial woes, she sat down and wrote a letter to the President, urging that her son be called home before he went broke. Madison sent Adams an undated letter of recall, to be used when and if necessary. For his part, said the President, he would prefer Adams to stay, but the letter from "your highly respectable mother" impelled him to make the choice available. A few months later, he nominated Adams to the Supreme Court, a choice that was unanimously approved by the Senate. Notwithstanding his principles about never rejecting the call of his country, John Quincy Adams had no desire to serve on its Supreme Court. Taking advantage of Louisa's second pregnancy in Russia, Adams politely turned down the appointment. In a frank letter to the President, Adams admitted that legal studies were "never among those most congenial to my temper," and that he had "long entertained a deep and serious mistrust of my qualifications for a seat on the bench." Whatever regret his parents felt at their son's refusal to return home in 1811 was more than offset by news of the birth of a daughter to the Minister and his wife in August of that year. She was named Louisa Catherine Adams, after her mother, and was probably the first American citizen to be born in Russia.

While in St. Petersburg Adams developed two interests that would remain with him for the rest of his life. The first was in astronomy, cultivated originally as a student in the 1780's and furthered by his little club of amateur scientists in Boston. Because of its latitude, the sun set before 3 pm in December, and in June one could read at midnight without a candle, or so Adams claimed. On the summer solstice in 1811 he stayed up to watch the sun setting at nearly midnight, while the early glow of morning could already be seen in the east.

From astronomy Adams went on to further investigations of measurement, including the historical origins of the English units of measurement as opposed to the Russian equivalents, and the relationship of both systems to the new metric system developed in the days of the French Revolution, and which Napoleon was now imposing on most of Europe. These matters were of more than casual importance, for if American trade with Russia was to increase, Russian equivalents of pounds, ounces, bushels, and tons would have to be calculated with precision. Adams experimented with a small set of scales from his medicine chest, before concluding that they and all the other equipment he could locate were hopelessly inaccurate.

His second emerging interest was in the Bible and religion generally. Despite his background and the number of friends and relatives who had entered the ministry, the young John Quincy Adams had remained a perfunctory churchgoer, seldom mentioning religious or theological matters in his diary or correspondence. His rental of a pew in William Emerson's church in Boston had been as much a social and political gesture as anything else. But in his senatorial years he began attending religious services more regularly, commenting on the quality of the sermon preached that day in his diary. Since there were no Protestant churches in Tsarist Russia, Adams had to be content with attending either Catholic or Orthodox services, which he did more as an observer than a participant.

He compensated for this by a systematic plan wherein he read four or five chapters of the Bible each day, often comparing different translations and commentaries. He approached the Scriptures, not as the Word of God, but as divinely-inspired literature. He was never a fundamentalist, and had rejected Calvinism since the days of his youthful disputations with the long-dead Uncle John Shaw. But his Protestant faith grew with his studies, and in time Adams became one of the leading Biblical scholars of early nineteenth-century America. He accepted most Christian teachings, including that of Original Sin, the divinity of Jesus of Nazareth, and a future state of rewards and punishments—without which, he said, there could be no moral order to the universe. In 1811 he began a series of letters to his son George on the study of the Bible—written, one suspects, as much for the benefit of the author as for the edification of the ten-year-old recipient.

It was well that Adams had the support and consolations of religion, for in September of 1812 the infant Louisa Catherine Adams died. Her father, who had always wanted a daughter, plunged himself into guilt, reading and re-reading those passages in the Bible that implied that the early deaths of children were punishment for the sins of the parents. The Bible taught that "Heaven has given power to every human being the *power* of controuling his passions," he told his son, "and if he neglects or loses it, the fault is his own and he must be answerable for it." Had Adams given in to his "passion" for public office by dragging his reluctant family five thousand miles from home? Was he now being punished for it?

For his grief-stricken wife, the answer was clear enough. Already she had learned of the deaths of her older sister Nancy in 1810, and that of her mother in 1812. She began her own diary, kept intermittently during her St. Petersburg years, in which she now documented her anger at her isolation from her family and her husband's responsibility for it. On the occasion of their fourteenth wedding anniversary, Adams summed up his view of the situation:

> Our union has not been without its trials, nor invariably without dissensions between us. There are many differences of sentiment, of tastes, and of opinions in regard to domestic economy, and to the education of children, between us. There are natural frailties of temper in both of us; both being quick and irascible, and mine being sometimes harsh. But she has always been a faithful and affectionate wife, and a careful, tender, indulgent, and watchful mother to our children, all of whom she nursed herself.

Although the death of their daughter drew them closer together temporarily, her husband's deepening involvement in his work increased Louisa's sense of isolation. She became concerned for the welfare of their sons at home, and her husband agreed to send for them as soon as was practicable. This would turn out to be later than either of them expected.

Adams' responsibilities as American Minister fell into three categories. First, he represented the interests of American merchants and ship captains who, like those he had encountered in Denmark, wished to trade with Russia and other European nations without interference. Napoleon was pressing Alexander to enforce the Continental System against both the British and the Americans, convinced as he was that the latter were only the tools of the former. For his part, the Tsar was willing to cooperate against the British enemy, but not against his American friends. Because Russians and most Europeans had difficulty distinguishing one from the other, and because there were more than a few cases of attempted deception by the British, it became Adams' task to examine papers and interview crew members in order to separate British imposters from genuine Americans.

Second, he outlined and defended American desires for neutrality to the Tsar, Foreign Minister Romantzoff, and any other members of the diplomatic community who would listen. He sparred politely with the Duke de Vicence, the French Ambassador, over the Continental System, which Adams insisted hurt France's allies more than it did Great Britain. He correctly suspected French influence as being responsible for the delay of American vessels seeking entry into Russian ports. On more than one occasion, he patiently explained to Count Romantzoff that unless Americans could sell their cotton, sugar, and tobacco to the Russians, they had no means with which to purchase Russian hemp, naval stores, and other exports. Obstacles to trade did neither nation any good. After a year or so, Adams believed he was making progress, as restrictions loosened perceptibly. "It seems you are great favorites here," ruefully remarked the French Ambassador. Nothing illustrated better the vagaries of international politics than the friendship between the new American republic and the semi-medieval despotism that was Tsarist Russia. Not even the potential for conflict over Russian settlements on the American Pacific coast affected the Tsar's attitude. "Our attachment to the United States is *obstinate, more obstinate than you are aware of*," Romantzoff told Adams.

His third function was to transmit intelligence concerning Eu-

ropean politics and diplomacy, much as he had done before from the
Hague and Berlin. Every ten days or so he wrote a lengthy dispatch
to Robert Smith, the Secretary of State, and later to Smith's successor, James Monroe. Adams was one of the first to report that the
alliance between the two Emperors, Alexander and Napoleon, might
not last, and that one reason for this was their differences over
commercial policy and particularly trade with the United States. In
late 1810 Adams warned the Secretary of State—in code—that a
break between France and Russia was possible. "I think the relations between the two countries are approaching to a crisis on a
point highly interesting to us." By the following spring, Adams was
even more certain. He reported troop movements to Russia's western border, and France's recall of her Ambassador to Paris. "War is
considered as inevitable," he reported in April, 1811—again in code—
"and every arrangement for it is making as speedily as possible by
both governments." In October he wrote "If the war should not
commence soon there is, I believe, nobody who thinks it possible it
should be postponed longer than until the next summer."

As the representative of a second-rank power, Adams was obli-
gated to transact business through Foreign Minister Romantzoff,
with whom he had a pleasant enough relationship. But this did not
prevent frequent unofficial encounters with the Tsar himself, both
at social functions and in their occasional meetings while walking
about the city. Indeed, few episodes in the life of John Quincy
Adams are as captivating as the accounts of his chats with the
Emperor of All the Russias while the two were engaged in their
morning constitutionals. They conversed—in French, still the universal language of diplomacy and of the Russian court—of many
things, including Adams' financial situation (about which the Tsar
seemed to know a great deal), the virtues of flannel underwear in the
Russian winters, the American occupation of West Florida, and the
nature and number of ethnic groups in the United States.

The Emperor confirmed Adams' suspicions about an approaching clash with France. "War is coming," he admitted as the two of
them stood bundled up along the River Neva in March, 1812. "*IL
avance toujours.*" — "HE keeps advancing." Napoleon was massing
his troops along the Polish border. Three weeks later, Adams saw

Alexander I for the last time in Russia, shortly before he left to join his troops. His manner, the American noted, "was graver and less cheerful than I usually have seen him." That spring Bonaparte began his spectacular invasion of Russia, while Adams and the rest of the world watched. By December Adams could write of Bonaparte: "Of the immense host with which . . . he invaded Russia, nine-tenths at least are prisoners of war or food for worms." Napoleon's bowstring had cracked at last in the ice and snows of a Russian winter.

THAT WAR BROKE OUT BETWEEN Russia and France in 1812 surprised no one; that Great Britain and the United States went to war in the same year has puzzled many ever since. Although the United States was poorly prepared for war with Britain or any other nation, and although the most obnoxious of the British "Orders in Council" had been removed, Congress in 1812 bowed at last to the so-called "War Hawks"—led by young Henry Clay of Kentucky and John C. Calhoun of South Carolina—and chose war over what they saw as continued British humiliation. After twenty years of remonstrances, threats, embargoes, nonintercourse, and other strategies, the United States was at last sucked into the vortex of the Anglo-French world war. In vain did Federalists and peace-minded Republicans argue that the French were equally contemptuous of American rights: no Americans were being impressed into the minuscule French navy. Others pointed to the tempting prize of British North America as the real motivation behind the declaration of war. In Russia, the French Ambassador told John Quincy Adams that an army of 5,000 men could take Canada easily.

Adams was not a War Hawk. "I hope that Congress will take special care not to break into a war with England," he had told his brother the previous year. The only reason for fighting was to protect commerce, he said, and once war began, commerce would be annihilated. When the American navy could match the British, then would come the time for a challenge. He knew too well the fate that usually awaits small nations who involve themselves in big wars. "Should we join in the conflict, we could scarcely hope for a better fate than to be sacrificed as one of the victims at its close." Since Britain could never control the whole ocean, nor France all of Europe, the best policy was patience and perseverance.

Adams did not learn of the war until nearly two months after it had been declared, and when he did, he was not pleased. But as a representative of the United States and its President, and out of genuine if belated conviction, Adams became a vigorous defender of the War of 1812, calling it a second war for independence and comparing British impressment to slavery. From Quincy came news of the opposition to the war, led of course by Timothy Pickering, joined by Harrison Gray Otis, and cousin Josiah Quincy. When news of the declaration arrived in Massachusetts, church bells tolled in mourning, ship's flags were lowered to half-mast, shops closed in protest. Federalist banks refused to loan money to the government. After Captain James Lawrence of Salem died in command of the hard-luck *Chesapeake*, murmuring "Don't give up the ship," church authorities, the local militia, and the Federalist establishment boycotted his funeral.

In 1798, John Quincy Adams had denounced the French and their Republican sympathizers. Now, in 1812, he sent forth a stream of letters attacking the British and their Federalist apologists. "No nation," he told former Senator William Plumer, who like himself had broken with the Federalists, "can be independent which suffers its citizens to be stolen from her at the discretion of the naval and military officers of another nation." Once again at home in Massachusetts there was talk of New England secession or possible "neutrality." Once again whole towns and counties in New England were in open opposition to the war and brazenly trading with the enemy. Section was placed ahead of nation; party against country. Wasn't the lesson of a quarrelling and bleeding Europe plain enough? asked Adams of his mother. Unless the Anglophilic Federalists were crushed once and for all, he said, the union established by George Washington and John Adams was done for. European influence in the New World had to be confronted and overthrown so that the American republican experiment might continue without interference. Otherwise, "Instead of a nation coextensive with the North American continent, destined by God and nature to be the most populous and most powerful people ever combined under one social compact, we shall have an endless multitude of little insignificant clans and tribes at eternal war with one another for a rock, or a fish pond, the sport and fable of European masters and oppressors."

The year before, Adams had occasion to study the results of the third United States census, that of 1810. A little calculation revealed that the growth between the first and second census, and that between the second and third, had been almost exactly the same: about thirty-seven per cent. "It is a phenomenon which the world never witnessed before, and which probably will never be seen again." Nearly halfway around the world, John Quincy Adams glowed with enthusiasm for the future of the Republic. "When I reflect upon the capabilities of that people and that territory, I have no curb to enthusiastic hope, but in the recollection of the follies and vices which have proved so fatal to mankind in all former ages, and which threaten to destroy all the glorious prospects of my own country."

This view of the American future was what separated Adams from so many of his New England friends and enemies. It was why he supported the Louisiana Purchase in 1803. It was why he broke with the Federalists in 1808. He half apologized to his father for his repetitive insistence upon the need for a strong union among the American states. He was reminded of the difficulties into which John Adams had fallen twenty years before, when he argued against simple majoritarian democracy and for "balanced government." "*Union* is to me what the *balance* is to you," he explained. He continued to rail against those New Englanders who feared the growth of the United States, and who contemplated its breakup with equanimity. His cousin Josiah Quincy, for whom he had the greatest respect, apparently wanted to limit the United States to Yankees and their descendants. For his part, Adams proclaimed, "I could take by the hand as a fellow-citizen a man born on the banks of the Red River or the Missouri with just the same cordiality, that I could at least half a million natives of Massachusetts. . . ." As he explained to his father, "The whole continent of North America appears to be destined by Divine Providence to be peopled by one *nation*, speaking one language, professing one general system of religious and political principles, and accustomed to one general tenor of social usages and customs. For the common happiness of them all, for their peace and prosperity, I believe it indispensable that they should be associated in one federal Union."

A later generation would call this idea "Manifest Destiny."

SUCH A DESTINY SEEMED ANYTHING but manifest in 1812. As Adams feared, the war went badly from the start. Far from conquering Canada with 5,000 men, the Americans suffered losses all along the northern border, from Maine to Michigan. Only on the ocean, where a few spectacular but strategically unimportant victories over the Royal Navy surprised everyone, did the Americans have cause to rejoice. But the goal was not control of the Atlantic, which was beyond the Americans' grasp, but control of the Great Lakes and Lake Champlain. If these were lost, the way would be open to an invasion of New York and the isolation of New England from the rest of the United States. In Europe, Napoleon's impending downfall promised to free British resources for North America. Time was not on the side of the Americans.

A series of coincidences put Adams at the head of efforts to negotiate a settlement to the War of 1812. When it broke out, the United States had full diplomatic representation at only the three major European capitals: London, Paris, and St. Petersburg. But soon afterwards the American Minister to Britain went home and the Minister in Paris died, leaving Adams the only senior American diplomat in Europe. When Tsar Alexander offered to act as a mediator between his new allies, the British, and his old friends, the Americans, attention was focussed on the Russian capital. Without waiting for a British response, and seeking to extract himself from the war, President Madison appointed a bipartisan delegation to go to Russia, consisting of former Treasury Secretary Albert Gallatin, a Republican, and Senator James Bayard, a Federalist. They were to join Adams in St. Petersburg and be available to meet with the Tsar and the British.

Gallatin and Bayard arrived in the summer of 1813, only to learn after nearly six months that Great Britain had rejected the Tsar's offer. But the British had a counter-proposal: face-to-face negotiations in London, or at a mutually agreeable site other than Russia, where the Tsar's reputation as a defender of the principle of "free ships, free goods," rendered it unacceptable. President Madison named two additional members to the American team: Henry Clay, the hawkish Speaker of the House of Representatives, and Jonathan Russell, former *charge d'affaires* in London. Adams would chair the delegation. The "exile" he accepted in 1809 had resulted in the leadership of the most crucial American diplomatic mission since that of his father, Franklin, and Jay in the 1780's.

So it was that in the spring of 1814, John Quincy Adams left wife and child behind and rushed off to Gothenburg, Sweden, the agreed-upon site of the meeting with the British, only to learn that the location had been changed to the medieval city of Ghent, in what is now Belgium. Thence he travelled as fast as he could, arriving there on June 24th. "You are sufficiently acquainted with my disposition," he told Louisa, "to know that it was some, and not inconsiderable gratification to my feelings to find myself the first here."

THE STORY OF THE NEGOTIATIONS at Ghent that ended the War of 1812 has been told many times, and rightly so, for it was one of the high points of early American diplomacy. With the possible exception of Henry Clay, a Kentuckian who liked to gamble against long odds, no one in either delegation believed a peace treaty would emerge from their efforts. "Scarcely an hour passes," Adams told his wife, "without accumulating evidence to my mind that our antagonists are fully resolved not to make peace this time." His four colleagues disagreed only over whether their stay would be long or short. To save money, they decided to rent a house together, but only for a month at a time.

The British delegation was led by Admiral Lord Gambier, a minor aristocrat distinguished for his role in the British bombardment of the defenseless city of Copenhagen in 1807. Henry Goulburn was a member of Parliament, and the third delegate, Dr. William Adams (no relation, John Quincy learned with relief), was an expert on maritime law. None of them was a major player in British affairs, and they constantly referred back to London for instructions. The cream of British talent was not at Ghent, but at the Congress of Vienna, where the major powers were attempting to settle affairs and redraw the map of post-Napoleonic Europe.

As head of the American delegation, Adams was expected to speak first on its behalf, to deliver notes to his counterpart, Lord Gambier, and to keep the records of the mission. In him, the delegation was thus led by a man who had studied thoroughly not only the short history of his own country, but that of Britain and Europe as well. The long hours spent in study, from Leyden to Newburyport to Harvard College, the hundreds of books digested in half a dozen countries, the years of diplomatic experience in the Netherlands, Prussia, and Russia, would now pay off. Adams was seldom at a loss for a precedent or an analogy, a long-forgotten treaty or obscure law, if it could support the American position. His major handicap was his temperament, especially his fierce disposition whenever he believed American rights to be challenged. When it came to drafting diplomatic notes, he generally preferred a full scale frontal assault, leaving no stone unthrown, hurling his entire arsenal of history, law, custom, and logic. His hard-line approach was balanced by the more mature, soft-spoken, Swiss-born Albert Gallatin, whose suave manner usually took the rough edges off his Yankee colleague's style. The other three, Bayard, Clay, and Russell, played lesser roles.

The summer and early fall of 1814 brought nothing but bad news. The British occupied half of Maine and were sending another detachment of troops toward the Chesapeake Bay, menacing the cities of Washington and Baltimore. Rumors told of a another force headed toward New Orleans, and that the Duke of Wellington himself was ready to go to America and finish the job. Adams hoped he would meet the fate of General Cornwallis. How different the situation was from thirty years before, when Adams' father, Benjamin Franklin, and John Jay confronted the British! There was, he wrote, "little prospect of a like successful issue."

Not until late August were both delegations ready to begin discussion. The British opened by inviting the Americans to meet with them at their quarters for the first session. Adams would have none of this. He referred his colleagues to one of his authorities on diplomacy, which suggested that this procedure was one used by ambassadors when meeting with ministers "of an inferior order." The Americans responded by sending word that they would be happy to meet anywhere *except* at the British lodgings. Eventually the two delegations met at a local hotel.

After this initial sparring, the British then stunned the Americans by presenting, as the price for continuing the negotiations, a demand that the United States agree to the creation of an independent and neutral Indian territory in what is now the upper Middle West. This, they explained, would act as a buffer state between the rambunctious Americans and British Canada. It was intended to put an end to the westward expansion Adams had already described as being "destined by Divine Providence." For good measure, the British also demanded unilateral American disarmament on the Great Lakes. Adams, Gallatin, and the others, primed to discuss "free ships, free goods," impressment, and similar issues, could make no reply. They had no instructions from Washington on Indians, the western border, or the Great Lakes. They had no doubt as to the nature of President Madison's reply to such obvious attempts to block American expansion, but it would take two or three months before it arrived. Adams was certain negotiations would break off. "It is not possible that we should be detained beyond the last of this month," he told his wife in late August. Yet, he noted in his diary, "Mr. Clay has an inconceivable idea, that they will finish by receding from the ground they have taken."

The Indian proposal in particular was troubling, because it was couched in terms that seemed to carry a sense of justice to the natives. Adams had already grappled with this issue in his oration at Plymouth in 1802. Then he had taken a hard line against those whom he sardonically called "generous philanthropists," who had claimed an equality between the rights of Europeans and those of the aboriginal inhabitants of North America. Taking his cue from the writings of John Locke and others, he had defended the superiority of European agriculture over the alleged hunting and nomadic civilization of the natives. He had not changed his mind in 1814, and spent many hours composing a reply to the British proposal that justified white European expropriation of Indian lands. It was they, not the natives, he said, who would make the desert bloom, who would convert the land to the support of thousands, perhaps millions, instead of "a few scattered hordes of savages, whose numbers to the end of ages would not amount to the population of one considerable city." In private conversation, he told Henry Goulburn that if Great Britain wished to stop American expansion, "she must not think of doing it by a treaty. She must formally undertake, and accomplish, their utter extermination." Goulburn was not impressed. "Mr. Adams is a very bad arguer," he told his superiors in London. His colleagues thought Adams spent too much time on the subject.

For their part, the Americans had instructions to insist upon a British renunciation of impressment, but nothing was more popular across the Channel than this manifestation of Britannia ruling the waves. Any ministry that agreed to its abandonment would be hurled from office. Thus each side began by advocating positions that were impossible for their opponents to accept.

Fortunately, the governments of each nation proved to be more flexible than their initial demands suggested. Within hours of their first meeting, the Americans received new instructions from Secretary Monroe permitting them to retreat from the demands regarding impressment. Later the British were told to back off from their insistence upon a separate Indian state in the heart of North America. Henry Clay, the Kentucky poker player, had been right: the British were bluffing. The door to a settlement was now open, but it would still be several weeks before the delegations could be induced by events to walk through it. The Americans renewed the lease on their house for another month.

Living together in bachelor quarters was not easy for five men so disparate in background as Adams, Gallatin, Clay, Bayard, and Russell. There were differences in age, temperament, politics, and regional loyalties. At first, when they were all living in a hotel, Adams took his meals alone, preferring to dine in solitude than to join his colleagues. "They sit after dinner and drink bad wine and smoke cigars," he complained, "which neither suits my habits nor my health, and absorbs time which I cannot spare." But after a friendly remonstrance from Clay, Adams was induced to join the others, with no apparent ill-effects. In the evenings he was generally alone, for no one would join him in his walks about the city, or his attendance at the theaters. "They frequent the coffee houses, the Reading Rooms, and the billiard tables," he reported to Louisa.

In observing his colleagues at close quarters, his respect grew most for Gallatin, a staunch Republican who in the 1790's had been one of his father's severest critics, later Jefferson's Treasury Secretary, and who probably would have been Madison's Secretary of State had it not been for his foreign birth and accent. Perhaps because of his background, Gallatin was better attuned to the European mind, and his re-writing of Adams' confrontational prose usually carried the day with the others, so much so that Adams eventually relinquished his drafting responsibilities to Gallatin. Adams took Bayard and Russell less seriously. The former tended to nit-pick to no real purpose and the latter was erratic and short-tempered, missing several meetings and finally moving out of their joint lodgings altogether.

But it was Henry Clay who intrigued him most, probably because his western frontier background was so different from Adams' own. Clay was a whiskey-drinking, horse-racing, card-playing, ambitious politician. Twice, as Adams rose at sunup to begin his day, he heard the scraping of chairs in the next room, as Clay's poker sessions were breaking up. Yet he felt Clay was in some respects similar to himself. "There is," he told his wife, who certainly knew what he meant, "that same dogmatical, overbearing manner, the same harshness of look and expression, and the same forgetfulness of the courtesies of society in both." Adams and Clay were to have more than one opportunity to size one another up in the next thirty years.

September was spent mostly in delay by the British and in frustration by the Americans. Lord Gambier insisted upon referring everything to London, no matter how small, and Adams suspected they were stalling. "While they are sporting with us here, they are continually sending reinforcements and new expeditions to America," he observed. He was right. On October 1st the American learned that five weeks earlier a British army had landed in Maryland, marched to Washington with little opposition, sacked and burned several public buildings including the Capitol and the President's mansion, and driven James and Dolley Madison into the Virginia countryside. Adams was furious, both at the British and at apparent American weakness and unpreparedness. Now, he was sure, Lord Gambier and his friends could be expected to press their advantage.

But what he did not yet know was that, humiliating as the burning of Washington was, it had been followed by a British defeat at Baltimore, and an even more spectacular loss at Plattsburgh on Lake Champlain. As the news of Baltimore and Plattsburgh filtered back to London, word also came from Vienna of friction between Britain and Russia over the postwar settlement. The Duke of Wellington, who some had expected to go to America, now declared in a private letter that there was little point in continuing the war, given the loss of the Great Lakes and the uneasy situation at Vienna. On the very day Wellington wrote, the Americans at Ghent were putting the finishing touches on a note to the British, which included, at Adams' insistence, an offer to return to the *status quo ante bellum*, with all remaining differences to be subject to negotiation. This the British accepted. By the end of November, Adams was telling his wife that "for the first time I now entertain hope that the British government is inclined to conclude the peace."

And yet, as Adams knew, the negotiations were entering their most difficult phase. So long as the British proposals were unacceptable, the Americans could easily remain united. But the closer the two sides came to agreement, the greater the danger that the details would expose the personal, regional, and political differences among them. This was particularly true of Adams and Clay. One of the unresolved issues was whether the valuable American fishing and curing rights off the Grand Banks of Newfoundland, successfully negotiated by John Adams in 1783, would be continued. Another was the continuation of the British right to navigate the Mississippi from its source (then erroneously thought to be in Canada), also guaranteed by the same treaty. The British took the position that the Treaty of 1783 had been abrogated by the war, and that all matters covered by it were re-negotiable. Clay, the westerner, with the Mississippi now known to be entirely within the United States, was only too happy to agree. As for fishing and curing rights, the War Hawk found

Although painted a century afterward, this painting by Sir Amédée Forestier recreates the scene on Christmas Eve, 1814, as Adams (center) exchanged copies of the Treaty of Ghent with his British counterpart, Admiral Lord Gambier. *Courtesy of National Museum of American Art, Smithsonian Institution.*

no reason to press the matter, given New England's lukewarm attitude toward the war. The others agreed, all except John Quincy Adams.

Although he could not say it, Adams could hardly put his name to a document that gave up rights that his own father had won thirty years before. There were several uncomfortable scenes between him and the others, Clay at one point shouting that he saw little importance in "the mere liberty of drying fish upon a desert." Adams finally said that the others could do as they pleased, but that he would not sign a document that did away with that liberty. At last they agreed to argue for silence on these and other issues, leaving them to be settled by separate negotiation later. To Adams' relief, the British agreed. Had they pressed their position, they would have driven a wedge between him and the others, and the Treaty of Ghent would have lacked the signature of John Quincy Adams.

That treaty, Adams later told his colleagues, would long be remembered for the skill with which it avoided the issues that had brought about the war in the first place. With Napoleon's downfall in Russia and the cessation of the twenty-year Anglo-French world war, the issues of impressment, "free ships, free goods," and neutral rights became merely theoretical. Nothing in the Treaty said anything of consequence about Indians or armaments on the Great Lakes. Territory captured during the war was to be returned. Boundary disputes were to be settled by commissions or by arbitration through a friendly third power. The final document was signed on Christmas Eve, 1814, while a messenger waited in the courtyard, ready to dash for the Channel where a special boat would carry him to England. John Quincy Adams gravely exchanged copies of the Treaty with Lord Gambier. "I told him," Adams later recorded, "I hoped it would be the last treaty of peace between Great Britain and the United States."

"THUS ENDS," HE WROTE a week later, "the most memorable year of my life." He could not be sure of the Treaty's reception in America, whether its signing would be considered "as a day of joy or of sorrow," but he did know that no better settlement could have been made. "We have obtained nothing but peace, and have made great sacrifices to obtain it," he told his wife. "But our honor remains unsullied; our territory remains entire." In mid-March, Adams learned that not only had the Treaty been approved by the Senate, but by a unanimous vote. It had arrived in Washington at virtually the same time as the news of General Andrew Jackson's repulse of the British attack on New Orleans. Americans had a new hero in Jackson, and his victory made it possible for them to retire from the war more gracefully than anyone had thought possible.

Weeks before the conclusion of the negotiations, when the outcome was still in doubt, Adams told his wife to prepare to leave St. Petersburg. Five years in the Russian capital was long enough, and he had requested his recall by President Madison. In the event the negotiations failed, Adams intended to return to America and join the rest of his family. In the event they succeeded, he was prepared to "receive the President's orders." By this he meant an anticipated appointment as American Minister to Great Britain. Adams now sent instructions for Louisa to break up their household, sell what furniture and effects she could, say the appropriate goodbyes, and with the young Charles Francis Adams, join him in Paris.

While awaiting his wife's arrival, Adams took what (for him) amounted to a vacation. He walked about the streets of the city he had first visited as a child with his father more than thirty years before. He attended dozens of plays, and spent hours in the new Louvre Museum, admiring the great paintings that Napoleon's armies had looted from all over Europe and the Near East. He ate well and grew fat. Through the agency of William H. Crawford, the American Minister to France, Adams met the newly-restored Bourbon King Louis XVIII, brother of the unfortunate victim of the French Revolution in 1793. And he met once again the aging but indestructible La Fayette, whom he had first met as a young man in 1785.

It was in Paris that Adams learned of the success of the Treaty of Ghent and of Andrew Jackson, but these faraway events were dwarfed by the news of Napoleon's escape from his exile on the Mediterranean island of Elba, and his dramatic march toward Paris with an ever-increasing army. As Napoleon moved toward Paris from the south, Louisa Adams and her seven-year-old son were approaching from the east, in a hair-raising dash across war-torn Europe that would long be remembered in the Adams family. As she neared the French border Louisa was at some risk, for she was an English-speaking lady travelling in a carriage with Russian markings, and both England and Russia were the enemies of France. At one point she and Charles were threatened with arrest, but her fluency in French once again came to her assistance. After explaining her American nationality, and shouting "Vive la France" whenever appropriate, she successfully made the final leg of her journey, rolling into Paris on March 23, more than five weeks after her departure from St. Petersburg.

The Adamses were thus in Paris during the first of the so-called "Hundred Days," Napoleon's bid to regain power that was to end at

Waterloo. Adams became fascinated by the man who had alternately befriended and despised America for so many years. He developed a sneaking admiration for Napoleon and his audacious return, and contempt for the fleeing French aristocrats who depended upon foreigners like the British and the Russians for their status. He went to the Tuileries more than once in order to get a glimpse of the Emperor, hoisting Charles up on his shoulders so that he too might see the Man of Destiny. When word went round that Napoleon was to attend the theater, Adams procured tickets. "Never at any public theatre," he later told his mother, "did I witness such marks of public veneration, and such bursts of enthusiasm for any crowned head, as that evening exhibited for Napoleon."

His commission as Minister to Great Britain arrived in early April. Although it was a high honor from a grateful James Madison (he also appointed Gallatin Minister to France, Bayard Minister to Russia, and Russell Minister to Sweden), Adams did not look forward to his new assignment. At St. Petersburg he had been accredited to a friendly power and had enjoyed the personal confidence of most of the rest of the diplomatic corps. Now he would have to deal with the supercilious arrogance of the British. There was still the matter of the fisheries to be resolved, boundaries to be drawn, and a commercial treaty to be negotiated. "I have never been charged with a public trust from which there was so little prospect of any satisfactory result," he told his father. Still, few could overlook the fact that this was the highest overseas diplomatic assignment that could be conferred on an American, or that for the second time an Adams was going to London after an Anglo-American war. The family crossed the Channel to England in late May, passing on the road to London a regiment of soldiers headed for the Continent to grapple with Napoleon for the last time. After a brief period of settling-in, Adams rented a house in the London suburb of Ealing—already conveniently named "Boston House"—where they were to stay for most of their two-year residence.

Unforeseen problems soon arose in addition to those already anticipated. There had been a riot at Dartmoor prison in which several American prisoners of war had been killed. The British were already suspected of cheating on the Treaty of Ghent by not evacuating Mackinac Island in the Great Lakes and by not returning slaves they had allegedly lured or kidnapped, much as they were accused of doing during the Revolutionary War. After the news from Waterloo and Wellington's victory over Napoleon, the Royal Navy demobilized so quickly that hundreds of impoverished American sailors illegally impressed into His Majesty's service now crowded the streets of London seeking passage home. Adams had to dip into his personal funds to assist them. To top it off, a minor postal official not only continually opened his mail, but insisted on referring to Adams as a mere "consul." The British still did not take Americans seriously.

John Quincy and Louisa Adams were more than impatient for the reunion with their two eldest boys. George and John had originally been placed with their great-aunt Elizabeth, but without notice had been transferred to the care of his brother Thomas and his wife. Neither George nor John was an enthusiastic letter-writer, and sometimes several months would go by without any word from either Adams' brother or his sons. In fact, all was not well with Thomas Boylston Adams, who, after a period of promise as a young man, was slipping into a prolonged decline not unlike that of his dead brother Charles. It was with more than the usual sense of relief that the Adamses greeted their two long-lost boys in England.

The reuniting of the family gave Adams the opportunity to supervise personally the education of all three sons at once. He focussed his attention on George, the eldest, for whom he tried to re-create the atmosphere he thought his own father had provided years before. He roused George up early in the morning for Bible study (in both French and Latin), followed by tutoring in Greek, Italian, and penmanship. He spent long hours in walks and conversation with the boy, who was experiencing the usual trials of adolescence. Eventually George and John Adams II were sent to an English boarding school where, if they did not sparkle, they at least survived. Their father was uneasy. The welfare and education of his sons was among the deepest concerns of his heart, Adams told his diary, but he was prepared for the possibility that "none of my children will probably ever answer my hopes." He would be content if "none of them ever realizes my fears."

For Louisa Adams the years in London were easily the happiest of the three tours of duty she experienced with her husband. She had her whole family with her in the city where she had been born, and in which she still had many friends. The months she had spent alone in St. Petersburg, raising Charles Francis Adams for nearly a year as a single parent, and her wild ride across Europe gave her a sense of confidence she had not felt before. She and her husband grew closer together, and she took a new interest in his work.

ANTI-AMERICAN FEELINGS in Britain were "keener, more jealous, more envious, more angry than ever," Adams wrote after six months. He based this on his reading of the London newspapers and quarterly journals of opinion like the *Edinburgh Review*, a notoriously anti-American production. A postwar recession was stimulating many Englishmen and Englishwomen to consider emigrating to America, and there seemed to Adams to be a concerted effort on the part of the press to portray the United States as a primitive, uncouth, lawless, violent, and unstable society, full of promise but little performance; in the words of one critic, "a people eternally on stilts." But in spite of what one might read in the newspapers or the quarterlies, such feelings were considerably less evident in the upper echelons of the conservative government of Lord Liverpool, the Prime Minister. As in America, a new generation of political leadership was emerging. Liverpool, Foreign Secretary Castlereagh, and the Duke of Wellington, were all of Adams' generation. They had replaced the Pitts, Foxes, and Grenvilles, whose very names suggested an earlier period. Old King George III, now a blind derelict wandering about Windsor Castle, had been replaced by his son, the Prince Regent. These men had few memories of the American Revolution and consequently fewer resentments. Two wars had shown not only that American independence was an incontrovertible fact, but so was American expansion. As Great Britain moved forward in its Industrial Revolution, as the income from its mines and factories surpassed that from its ships and colonies, the United States loomed more as a potential market for British goods and less a rival for British trade.

Lord Castlereagh belonged to that school of diplomacy which believed that if difficult issues could be avoided as long as possible, they might go away or become irrelevant, a stance not always congenial to that of John Quincy Adams. It meant, however, that the delicate issues Adams feared most were put off until another day. Thus the matter of the Grand Banks fisheries, for which Adams was prepared to do diplomatic battle to the utmost, was transferred to Washington for negotiation, while temporary licenses were granted to the Yankees on a year-to-year basis. The question of armament on the Great Lakes was likewise transferred to Washington. Outstanding boundary disputes involving islands in the Passamaquoddy Bay and the Maine border were eventually settled amicably by joint commissions. The northern forts were evacuated, if not on time, at least without provoking ill-will. On only two issues, impressment and the return of slave "property," did Liverpool and Castlereagh dig in their heels.

Already, Adams had taken steps to defuse the first issue. At his first meeting with Castlereagh, he reported that President Madison was recommending legislation to Congress that would prohibit foreign seamen from enlisting in the navy or the merchant service of the United States. And while he knew the British would never abandon the principle of the right to search vessels for their escaped citizens, this law, plus the end of the Anglo-French world war, meant that the principle was just that, an abstraction. "It was not the disposition of the American Government," he told the Foreign Secretary, "to apply the force of arms to the maintenance of any abstract principle." Since British citizens could not serve, there could be no reason for the British to search American vessels. And if there were no searches, there could be no problem. "When the evil ceased to be felt, we should readily deem it to have ceased to exist."

The matter of the slaves proved to be more delicate. The Treaty of Ghent called for the return of all private property taken by either side, but the wording of the Treaty was such that the British were able to claim that in the case of slaves, it applied only to those held within British forts, not those who had somehow wound up in the hands of British officers. In a tense discussion with Lord Liverpool, Adams insisted that slaves were private property and should be returned as such. Liverpool agreed they were property, but maintained that there was a difference nonetheless. "A table or a chair, for instance, might be taken and restored without changing its condition; but a living and a human being was entitled to other considerations." While agreeing that there might be such a distinction, Adams maintained that the Treaty did not make it, and therefore slaves who had escaped or who had been lured to the British armed forces should be returned or their owners indemnified.

Like most New Englanders, Adams disapproved of slavery in the abstract, but was ambivalent about it in the concrete. At this stage of his life his militant nationalism still overrode any other concerns, and commitment to a strong union made him sensitive to the demands of those outside his own section. Besides, as an American official charged with the responsibility for defending the rights of American citizens, including slaveholders, Adams felt he had no choice, and stuck to his guns. So did the British. Slaves who had been kidnapped or abducted under false pretenses would be restored, he was told, but those who had voluntarily fled from their masters would not, nor could there be indemnification. There was little use, Adams told Secretary Monroe, in pursuing it further. Eventually this matter too was referred to a commission for arbitration.

The only concrete product of Adams' sojourn in London was the adoption of a relatively low-level commercial agreement pledging nondiscrimination in tariffs and permitting direct American trade with certain British East Indian colonies. But even here Adams managed to score a small victory. Until 1815 Great Britain, along with most nations, had treated the United States as a power of the second rank, which meant that in treaties and agreements Britain was always mentioned first in the text, and the signatures of her negotiators came ahead of those of the United States on the final page. Acting on a strong hint from the Secretary of State, Adams insisted on what was known as an *alternat*, a second copy in which the United States was named first and his signature, along with those of his colleagues Clay and Gallatin, came ahead of the others. This was the procedure followed when dealing with powers of equal rank like Spain, France, or Russia, but had not been followed by Great Britain regarding the United States. It seemed purely symbolic, and neither Clay nor Gallatin thought it of much importance. Adams insisted, however, to the point of threatening not to sign unless the *alternat* was included. As much to humor him as anything else, the others agreed. The fact that the British made no objection was further evidence of their changed attitude toward the United States.

WITH THE MOST DELICATE issues transferred to Washington, and the others proving to be irresolvable, Adams found time to turn to more personal matters. He took advantage of his spare time to attend the theater once again at Covent Garden and Drury Lane, and read the novels of Sir Walter Scott aloud to his wife and children. He prowled among London's many bookstores, searching for obscure editions that his octogenarian father was seeking for his library at home in Quincy. He renewed his interest in astronomy, studying the heavens along with his son George and "an amiable young lady of eighteen who is here on a visit to my wife." In London he became a great favorite with the Whig opposition party, who fancied themselves friendlier to America than their Tory opponents. He was a frequent guest of the Lord Mayor at civic banquets at which eloquent toasts were offered to Anglo-American friendship, and to which Adams was always expected to deliver a spontaneous reply. This was something that required a little practice, but in time he adapted to it.

Although he had begun his political career as a moderate conservative, critical of Thomas Paine and the French Revolution, in postwar London he was regarded as a staunch republican. This suited Adams' temperament. In letters written to friends at home, he contrasted the Old World with the New in language that was little different from that of Paine or Jefferson decades before. "Emperors, kings, princes, priests, all the privileged orders, all the establishments, all the votaries of legitimacy, eye us with the most rancorous hatred," he told his father. Europe, he declared to another friend, had returned to "monkery and popery" in the aftermath of the French Revolution. "She has cast up the code of Napoleon, and returned to her own vomit of Jesuits, inquisitions, and legitimacy or Divine Right."

He also stepped up his nationalist attacks on the "spirit of party," by which he usually meant the critics of the late war. In late 1814, a group of New England Federalists had met at Hartford, Connecticut, to discuss revisions in the Constitution to protect that region's interests (including the abolition of the three-fifths clause, something that John Quincy Adams had favored when he was a Federalist) and ways to oppose more effectively the ongoing war. A minority of the Hartford Convention, as it came to be known, favored outright secession if the war were not brought to an end. The convention had just appointed representatives to "negotiate" with the federal government when news of Andrew Jackson's victory at New Orleans arrived, followed by word of the Treaty of Ghent. From that time forward, the very phrase "Hartford Convention" became a synonym for Federalist sectionalism and disloyalty. "They have erected their old political system on the perverted axiom that a part is greater than the whole," Adams wrote of his former Federalist allies. "They see nothing in the American Union but New England." Adams found it embarrassing. "As to our beloved native New England, I blush to think of the part she has performed, for her shame is still the disgrace of the nation. . . . I feel the infection of their shame, while I abhor the acts by which they have brought it upon us."

I will give to you one word," Adams told his his young admirer Alexander Hill Everett, "which you may lay down as the foundation of the whole political system to which you may boldly and safely devote from this moment all the energies of your character, all your talents, and all your genius—that word is *Union*." Just as a society must be a successful union of individuals, he told his diary, America must be a successful union of states, with a strong government based on a strong army and navy, backed by a stronger financial system than anything heretofore developed.

While Adams was writing his letters denouncing partisanship and sectionalism, the United States was moving toward another presidential election. Following the precedent established by Washington and Jefferson, President Madison declined a third term, leaving the way open for James Monroe, who narrowly defeated William H. Crawford for the Republican party's nomination. Once Madison's rival, Monroe had served him faithfully as a competent if not brilliant Secretary of State. The Federalists, still reeling from the effects of the Hartford Convention, offered no real opposition. Monroe was elected president with 183 out of 217 electoral votes. It was the last presidential election in which the Federalist party provided opposition.

The postwar period in America signalled the beginning of what was somewhat inaccurately called the "era of good feelings." The political animosities engendered by the Anglo-French world war dissipated rapidly, and many wondered how it was possible for the nation to have been so divided twenty years before. John Adams and Thomas Jefferson had resumed writing letters to one another in 1812. In Philadelphia, a Republican printer named Mathew Carey wrote a best-selling pamphlet entitled *The Olive Branch, or Faults on Both Sides*. In London, John Quincy Adams had already anticipated the spirit of the "era of good feelings." The time had come, he wrote in 1815, for "the wise and honest men of both [parties] to discard their prejudices and turn the experience of the war to the benefit of their common country."

Adams had a stake in the outcome of the election, for Monroe's elevation left open the post of Secretary of State. Even before the outcome was clear, his parents and others were urging him to come home, to be on the scene, to be more visible. Adams resisted such transparent "electioneering," repeating his notion that public office should be neither solicited nor avoided. "I have made it the general principle of my life to take the situation assigned to me by the regular authority of my country," he explained to his father in early 1817. He would wait upon events and not try to influence them. Civic office in a republic was neither a prize to be awarded, nor a goal to be sought, but a verdict to be rendered.

The verdict came the following April, and after the usual expressions of reluctance and self-doubt, Adams wrote his letter of acceptance. It took two months for him to wind up his affairs, attend the usual farewell dinners, make the ceremonial rounds of leave-taking, and pack his now formidable collection of books. Although he had been in London barely two years, less than any of his previous diplomatic assignments, he could leave with the assurance that Anglo-American relations were in better shape than at any time since independence. He spent his last weeks there often in the company of the eccentric philosopher-reformer Jeremy Bentham, who pelted him with questions about America and suggestions for its improvement. He also found time for visits from Robert Owen, the Scottish socialist, and William Wilberforce, the English aboli-tionist. But time was running out. In the early afternoon of June 10, 1817, Adams and his family crossed over Westminster Bridge and bade a final farewell to London and Europe. (Final, that is, for all but young Charles Francis Adams, who would return forty-four years later, in the midst of the American Civil War, as Abraham Lincoln's Minister to Great Britain.) Five days later, they embarked upon the American ship *Washington,* and were on their way home.

Chapter Five

---○---

"Leave the Rest of the Continent to Us"

WHEN JOHN QUINCY ADAMS left Boston in 1809, few were there to see him off other than his brother and a few friends. Eight years later his arrival in New York city was followed by a huge banquet, attended by Governor De Witt Clinton, Mayor John Jacob Astor, and most of the important men of the state. Not to be outdone, the Boston town fathers gave him one twice as large. His past sins in supporting the Republican Embargo were, at least for the present, forgotten. Once again, there were faces that were missing (including those of his sister Nabby and her husband, both of whom had died in his absence), and there were new, younger ones that he did not recognize. But both his parents were there, his father full of the usual questions and opinions about national and international affairs. He dipped his portly frame for a swim in the waters off of Black's Wharf in Quincy, and marvelled again at the new buildings in Boston (though frowning at the levelling of once-prominent Beacon Hill in order to fill in part of the harbor for yet more homes).

After leaving their sons in the care of relatives, Adams and his wife journeyed from Boston to Washington, taking advantage of the new steamboats that shortened the journey considerably. The nation's

capital was still a far cry from St. Petersburg or London. At one end of
Pennsylvania Avenue stood the President's house, in an open field
without trees. Sheds and stables emanated from its sides. Four
buildings flanked it, containing the four Departments: State, Treasury, War, and Navy. The city still showed the effects of the British
attack three years before. The President's house had been given
several coats of white paint to conceal its scorched walls, from which
it would eventually derive its name, "the White House." Adams had
barely enough time to meet the President before Monroe fled to his
Virginia estate in order to escape the smell of paint and plaster.
Congress not being in session, and the cabinet not scheduled to meet
for another month, there was ample time for the new Secretary of
State to study the political landscape of "the Era of Good Feelings."

JAMES MONROE WAS THE fourth and last of the "Virginia Dynasty" of
presidents. In the 1790's he had been the sort of pro-French Republican that John Quincy Adams had disliked the most. A fierce partisan
of the French Revolution, his conduct as Minister to France had led
to his recall and virtual humiliation by George Washington. He fared
little better under the presidency of his friend Thomas Jefferson, who
had sent him back to France, where he played a minor role in
negotiating the Louisiana Purchase, and then to Great Britain, where
as Minister he negotiated a treaty so inadequate that Jefferson refused
to submit it to the Senate. Again, Monroe returned home under a
cloud. In 1808, after briefly challenging James Madison as Jefferson's
successor, he retired to Virginia. But three years later, Madison coaxed
him out of retirement and appointed him Secretary of State, where his
conduct of that office led to the Republican party's nomination in
1816. Mellowed in his partisanship, Monroe was the last president to
have fought in the American Revolution. On formal occasions, such
as his inauguration, he wore the cocked hat, knee-breeches, and
shoe-buckles of an earlier day.

John Quincy Adams had mellowed too, especially toward James
Monroe. "Our sentiments upon subjects of great public interest
have at particular periods of our public life been much at variance,"

he admitted. But he had been impressed by Monroe's handling of his office, and besides, he was sure that the new President did not want a sycophant as Secretary of State. Should a matter of principle arise over which he could not compromise, then "it will be my duty seasonably to withdraw from the public service." The occasion never arose.

Having served as American Minister to two major powers and nearly five years as Secretary of State, Monroe was no stranger to foreign affairs. He had firm ideas about the direction of American diplomacy, which coincided for the most part with those of Adams. Given the jealousies raised by the domination of Virginians in the presidency, Monroe explained to Jefferson, "I have thought it advisable to select a person from the eastern states, in consequence of which my attention has been turned to Mr. Adams, who by his age, long experience in our foreign affairs, and adoption into the republican party, seems to have superior pretensions to any there." He might have added that no American in 1817 was more knowledgeable in diplomacy, history, and geography, or who had more experience with the Old World's leaders.

To Henry Clay, whose star had continued to rise since his return from Ghent, Monroe offered virtually any post except the one Clay wanted: that of Secretary of State. Clay chose to remain Speaker of the House of Representatives. For his Treasury Secretary, Monroe appointed William H. Crawford of Georgia, who had opposed him for the Republican nomination the year before. Adams had met Crawford briefly in Paris, where he had been Minister to France during the Hundred Days. For his Attorney General, Monroe chose the pleasant but dull William Wirt, and the secretaryship of the Navy, never an important office under Republicans, was bestowed upon a succession of three northern nonentities.

The cabinet member for whom the hypercritical Adams had the most respect was the young Secretary of War, John C. Calhoun. From South Carolina, Calhoun was only thirty-five years old in 1817, and had yet to emerge as the gaunt, spectral figure who in later years would formulate and articulate so much of the political and social ideology of the Old South. He was easily the most effective Secretary of War the nation had yet seen. "Calhoun thinks for himself, independently of all the rest, with sound judgement, quick discrimination, and keen observation," Adams wrote in early 1818. His seriousness of purpose and commitment to duty as he saw it, and his orderly and intellectual approach to decision-making, were proof that Puritanism was not a monopoly of New Englanders.

Monroe's cabinet was drawn from a new generation of American political leaders, men who, like John Quincy Adams, had been born in the eighteenth century but who had been too young to have played a role in the heady days of the Revolution or its aftermath. Others included Andrew Jackson of Tennessee, born in the same year as Adams, Martin Van Buren of New York, busily crafting one of the first state-wide political machines, and Congressman Daniel Webster of New Hampshire and Massachusetts, a Federalist critic of the recent war, but who nonetheless commanded growing respect for his oratorical style and his legal talent.

Although by birth Adams belonged to this second generation, he was never at home with them. He had matured early, had overlapped, as it were, the generation of the American Revolution, of which he was quite literally a son. Although his ideas on foreign policy had driven him to the Republicans, Adams remained the product of the older eighteenth century deferential society. Unlike other conservatives, he endorsed the principles of majority rule and the Declaration of Independence, but he balked at the notion that the majority was always right, or that elected and appointed officials were always bound to follow its wishes. No product of Puritan culture could accept the idea that right and wrong were determined by the power of numbers. And when the American naval hero Stephen Decatur made his famous toast: "Our country, right or wrong!" Adams dissented. "I can never ask of heaven success, even for my country, in a cause where she should be in the wrong," he told his father. He hoped America would always be successful, "but whether successful or otherwise, always right."

Although able men like Jefferson, Madison, and Monroe had preceded him as Secretary of State, Adams nonetheless found the Department in considerable disorder when he arrived. Whereas the great foreign ministries of the Old World had rank upon rank of under-secretaries, assistants, messengers, couriers, and servants, the penurious Republicans had provided for a State Department consisting of just twelve employees, plus a laborer and a watchman. Housed in a wooden building four blocks from the White House, the Secretary of State struggled with correspondence from over a dozen ministers and over a hundred consuls abroad, and from the ten to fourteen foreign ministers residing in Washington. He was also responsible for issuing passports, recording the names of all arriving passengers from abroad, preserving the public papers and documents of the United States, supervising the Patent Office and the decennial census, and keeping the Great Seal of the United States. It was an impossible task, and no Secretary of State, not even John Quincy Adams, ever mastered the position until it was reorganized and some of the responsibilities redistributed.

He was shocked to learn that no records were kept of incoming correspondence. There was no index for quick access to letters once they were filed. "A lover of order in all things," Adams set about reorganizing the Department. He taught one of the clerks the mysteries of proper accounting, clamped down on irregularities and slipshod procedures, and instituted recording and filing practices that were still in use in the twentieth century. He reorganized the Department's library, neglected for many years. He paid close attention to the recording of all public laws and in 1820, the issuing of instructions to the federal census marshals. Both of these were statutory duties but had often been ignored by his predecessors. He spent a large part of the summer of 1820 researching and writing a monumental *Report on Weights and Measures* that plumbed the depths of the existing scientific and historical knowledge on that subject. Yet he found time to receive personally each and every visitor of whatever rank and for whatever purpose. When he wasn't doing these things, he was busy laying what one authority has called "the foundations of American foreign policy."

ADAMS' CONCEPTION OF AMERICAN interests and the diplomacy that should support them had not changed since his "Publicola" letters, written as a young man in the 1790's. If anything, his experiences

abroad in four different countries had only strengthened them. He
believed more than ever in the uniqueness of America and its
republican social and political system, that it would be folly for
Americans to identify themselves with any Old World power, and
that foreign policy should not be the basis for partisan differences at
home. To these however he had added his militant expansionism,
developed in the letters written from Russia and Ghent to his
parents and others. North America was destined to be "one *nation*."
In short, the foreign policy of Secretary Adams consisted of
non-involvement in Old-World matters that did not involve the
New, non-partisanship in foreign policy, and the expansion of the
United States across the North American continent.

Before that could happen, however, the claims of two major
European powers, Britain and Spain, would have to be confronted.
Britain was the more powerful of the two, but since 1815 she had
shown signs of accepting the inevitability of American growth.
Spain, on the other hand, was a declining power that still claimed
Florida and the territory south and west of the Louisiana Purchase.
Indeed, it still questioned the legality of the Purchase itself.

Adams' two years in London had prepared the way for an
adjustment of most Anglo-American differences except the dormant
issue of impressment. Even before Adams arrived in Washington,
acting Secretary of State Richard Rush had signed an agreement
pledging each nation to virtual disarmament on the Great Lakes.
That left the matters of the North Atlantic fisheries, the slaves
allegedly still in the hands of the British, and the Canadian-Ameri-
can border, from Maine to the North West Coast. Adjustment of
these was to be among his first assignments as Secretary of State.

Under instructions from Monroe and Adams, Rush, who became Minister to Great Britain, negotiated a multifaceted "Convention" in 1818, whose terms further signalled Britain's willingness to
accept the pre-eminence of the United States in North America,
provided its own interests were not threatened. The Canadian
border was drawn from the Great Lakes to the Rockies along the
49th parallel. This placed the Mississippi entirely within the United
States and put an end to any British claim of navigation rights. The
Americans wanted to extend the boundary straight to the Pacific,

but the British claimed the entire Columbia River basin, or what is now most of Oregon and Washington. This Monroe and Adams rejected. Both countries agreed instead that the territory west of the mountains—Oregon Country—should be left open for settlement by citizens of either nation for a period of at least ten years, with the agreement to be renewed for ten-year intervals thereafter if both parties consented. The matter of the slaves was left to a third party to arbitrate. The British accepted Adams's casual suggestion of Tsar Alexander of Russia as a suitable arbiter, and to Adams's delight, his old friend decided in favor of the Americans.

As for the fisheries, Adams' persistent defense of the "right" of Americans to fish off the Grand Banks and to use the islands there to dry and cure their catch paid off as well. Castlereagh, having no desire to spark a conflict with the Americans, proposed a compromise. If the Yankees would agree to give up their claim to fish anywhere off the Banks, the British would agree to guarantee American use of the very best grounds "for ever." Thus, while giving up the general principle, the Americans were given the substance. These agreements were victories for the United States, placing land and resources eventually worth billions of dollars within its domain. The resolution of the fisheries was a personal victory for Adams as well. Thanks to him and his father before, American fishermen continued to use some of the richest fishing grounds in the world.

But Adams was still not satisfied. An enemy of colonialism everywhere, he merely tolerated the remaining British presence in North America because he could do no more. In the year following the Convention of 1818, he laid his beliefs before Monroe's cabinet. The world, he said, should "be familiarized with the idea of considering our proper dominion to be the continent of North America. From the time when we be came an independent people," he told his colleagues, "it was as much a Law of nature that this should become our pretension as that the Mississippi should flow to the sea." While Spain had possessions to the south and Britain controlled Canada, "it was impossible that centuries should elapse without finding them annexed to the United States." This would not come through conquest, he confidently predicted, but because it was "a physical, moral, and political absurdity" that such pieces of territory, of little or no value to the European powers, should lie next to "a great, powerful, enterprising, and rapidly-growing nation."

In 1819 few Americans had any conception of what lay beyond the Rockies, and many regarded them as a "natural" boundary. Not Adams. As Secretary of State, his views extended even beyond the continent. In 1823 he told the new American Minister to Spain that in the case of Spanish Cuba, "there are laws of political as well as physical gravitation," and that once severed from its "unnatural connection" with Spain, Cuba "can gravitate only towards the North American Union." He had a spectacular argument with Stratford Canning, the British Minister, over American settlements on the Columbia River. He proclaimed that the British had no rights in any part of North America that was claimed by the United States. Britain, shouted Adams, claimed territory all over the world. "You claim India; you claim Africa; you claim—" "Perhaps," interrupted Canning, "a piece of the moon." No, continued Adams, he hadn't heard that, but if they did, it made as much sense as claiming the Columbia River. Was Adams challenging the British presence in Canada? asked the incensed Minister. "No," replied Adams. "There the boundary is marked. . . . Keep what is yours, but leave the rest of the continent to us." Canning took eighteen pages to report this extraordinary session to Lord Castlereagh, calling Adams "determined," "acrimonious," "impatient," and "rude." Significantly, however, Castlereagh told Canning to drop the subject. Time would settle the matter, he said.

"LEAVE THE REST of the continent to us." As Adams pointed out to the cabinet, while Britain hemmed the Americans in to the north, Spain blocked their way to the south. But unlike the British Empire, which was still growing, that of Spain was crumbling. Nearly all of its American colonies were in revolt against the corrupt and reactionary government of King Ferdinand in Madrid. Even the Spaniards at home were restless and would soon rebel. Americans watched these revolutions with vague sympathy, but were mainly interested in their impact in North America. An expansionist-minded United

States lay in wait for what was widely regarded as the inevitable result of Spain's collapse: the acquisition of Florida, possibly Texas, and, with the passage of time, Cuba. The real question was when, and by what means.

Most immediately, there was Florida. Originally settled by Spain in the sixteenth century, it was now little more than a haven for assorted European pirates and adventurers, hostile Seminoles, and runaway ex-slaves. During the War of 1812 the British had violated Spanish neutrality by organizing the Seminoles and ex-slaves to harass the American border, and although the British had officially left, there had been continued friction and bloodshed. Spain was pledged to control the situation, but was clearly unable or unwilling to do so. Plantation owners in nearby Georgia maintained that the presence of so many runaways across the border set a poor example to their own "property," and looked to Washington for help. Monroe and Adams pointed out to the Spanish Minister that his country had its hands full contending with revolutions in Latin America and therefore could not hope to control the inhabitants of Florida. They pressed the Madrid government to cede it to the United States while there was still time to do it gracefully. For good measure, they claimed as well the Spanish province of Texas, which, they said, was part of the old Louisiana Territory and therefore rightly belonged to the Americans.

Thus while he was keeping one eye on the negotiations in London, Adams was also engaged in hard bargaining with the Spanish Minister for as much of the Spanish Empire as he could get. He was determined not only to obtain Florida, which the Spanish were willing to give up, but to draw the Spanish border as far south and west as possible. This would give the Americans Texas, and bring them that much closer to the "South Sea," the name often given to the Pacific. For his part, Don Luis de Onís, the Spanish Minister, was equally determined to keep the Americans away from Texas and silver-rich Mexico. He maintained that Napoleon's sale of Louisiana in 1803 had been illegal, and that the proper western border of the United States was not the Rio Grande, but the Mississippi. That left considerable territory to bargain over. Perched, so to speak, on their respective rivers, the two diplomats surveyed the lands in between, looking for the most advantageous compromise.

They were still there in the spring of 1818 when General Andrew Jackson, acting under orders, so he said, from Secretary of War Calhoun, invaded Spanish Florida in a punitive expedition against marauding Indians and slave runaways. In the process, the General captured two Spanish forts, executed several Seminoles without trial, and imprisoned, tried, and executed two British citizens whom he accused of inciting the Indians. He then returned in triumph to Tennessee, having set the diplomatic world ablaze in Washington, London, and Madrid.

At first no one knew what to do. Adams was shocked at the summary execution of the Indians, and told Secretary Crawford that he was "not prepared for such a mode of warfare." The execution of Arbuthnot and Ambrister, the two Britishers, could hardly help Rush's negotiations in London. Faced with the possibility of censure, General Jackson loudly defended his actions as justified by his orders, and privately maintained that he had been given the go-ahead to try and capture Florida by the President himself. The facts are unclear even today. What was clear was that Jackson had shaken the Spanish tree so severely that it might drop not only Florida but a lot more besides. Recognizing this, Adams swallowed his earlier objections to "such a mode of warfare," and rushed to Jackson's defense. Indeed, in Monroe's cabinet, he was the General's only advocate.

Since the careers of John Quincy Adams and Andrew Jackson were eventually to collide and result in one of the bitterest and longest-lasting hatreds in American politics, it is important to note this earlier phase of their relationship. It is difficult to conceive of two more contrasting backgrounds. Whereas Adams was born into secure surroundings in Massachusetts, Jackson first saw the light of day in the primitive frontier setting of the Carolinas. Whereas Adams's parents were a major force in his education and character development, Jackson's father died before he was born and his mother died when he was a teenager. While Adams was writing compositions and declaiming in Latin at Harvard College, Jackson was gambling, fighting, and drinking in the North Carolina and Tennessee backwoods. While Adams was pursuing his diplomatic assignments at the Hague and Berlin, Jackson briefly represented the new State of Tennessee in Congress, and then resigned in frustration. (Thomas Jefferson, who presided over the Senate in his capacity as Vice President, later said that Jackson was ineffective as a speaker because he often was so overcome with rage and emotion as to become inarticulate.) While Adams was in the Senate, Jackson was back in Tennessee achieving notoriety as a hot-tempered dueler, and hoping for war to break out with the British, or Spanish, or both. He got his wish, and fortune eventually brought him to New Orleans in 1814 at the same time Adams was in Ghent. Yet, in spite of their different backgrounds, Adams and Jackson had much in common in 1818. Both were ardent expansionists, both hoped to remove all "foreign" influence from North America, and both, in different ways to be sure, succeeded in doing so. This explains Adams's defense of his future adversary.

All the Presidents since Washington's time had used their cabinets as informal discussion groups, with no clear-cut divisions of authority. Often matters were decided by majority vote. In the case of Andrew Jackson's invasion of Florida, with Henry Clay and many Congressmen demanding punishment, every member of the cabinet except Adams favored some form of disavowal if not censure. This was especially true of Calhoun, who as Secretary of War was Jackson's nominal superior. Calhoun's orders to Jackson gave him permission to cross the Spanish border if he was in hot pursuit of the Seminoles, but he had been told not to attack should they take refuge in a Spanish fort. And he certainly had not been given orders to capture Spanish officials, nor to hang British citizens. But Adams now had his eye on the map of North America, and the possible territorial consequences of Jackson's act.

"I continue to oppose," Adams told his diary, "the unanimous opinions of the President, the Secretary of the Treasury Crawford, the Secretary of War Calhoun, and the Attorney-General Wirt. I have thought that the whole conduct of General Jackson was justifiable under his orders, although he certainly had none to take any Spanish fort. My principle is that everything he did was *defensive*; that as such it was neither war against Spain nor violation of the Constitution." Then, as at Ghent, he proceeded to show his colleagues the relevant texts on international law and usage which supported his point of view. He succeeded in persuading them that Jackson should not be disavowed.

Having thus convinced himself and the cabinet, he set out to persuade the nation and the world. In a masterful series of letters to Onís and George Erving, the American Minister in Spain, Adams demonstrated that in diplomacy, as in other things, the best defense is often a strong offense. Ignoring weaknesses in his case and bristling with sarcasm and indignation, Adams went on the attack. The real fault, he said, lay with Great Britain, for not preventing incendiaries like Arbuthnot and Ambrister from going to Florida, and with Spain, for being unable or unwilling to do anything about it. If Spain could not control people in her own domain, then she should turn it over to a nation who could. As for the executions, Adams defended them on the grounds of "retributive justice." All knew, he said, the nature of frontier warfare, "that savages make no prisoners, but to torture them; that they give no quarter; that they put to death, without discrimination of age or sex." White men who "degrade themselves beneath the savage character by voluntarily descending to its level" could expect nothing but Jackson's methods of dealing with them. "Is this not the dictate of common sense? Is it not the usage of legitimate warfare? Is it not consonant to the soundest authorities of national law?"

Many could, and some did, answer "No", but the note to Erving (which Adams took care to publish even before it reached Madrid) effectively obscured the case against Jackson for the time being. At Monticello, Thomas Jefferson pronounced it one of the best-written diplomatic notes he had ever seen. In Congress, Henry Clay's attempt to censure Jackson collapsed.

Indeed, Adams's defense was weak in law, logic, and fact. The truth was that General Jackson ran into very few Indians in Florida and at no time was his army in danger. That he had other things on his mind than chasing natives was later made clear when his private correspondence with Monroe was published, revealing a letter in which he pointedly suggested that Florida could be captured in sixty days. Jackson's enthusiastic support among frontier land speculators and Georgia slaveholders should have been warning enough to

Adams, if he cared, that the real motives behind the Florida invasion had little to do with defending Americans and more to do with protecting slavery. As for the British, had an American general hanged two subjects of King George at any time prior to 1815, the result would have been certain war. Even in 1818, as Lord Castlereagh told Richard Rush, war could have been had merely "by holding up a finger." But the finger was not held up. Adams had calculated, shrewdly enough, that Britain had no interest in defending the two renegades. Arbuthnot and Ambrister were disavowed, and Spain was served notice that she would receive no help from Britain in resisting American expansion.

Throughout the summer and autumn of 1818, with the debate over Jackson raging in the background, Adams and Onís continued their fencing over Florida, Texas, and the southwestern boundary. Adams knew from letters received from Minister Erving in Madrid that Onís had instructions to cede Florida to the United States even before Jackson's invasion. He now was determined to make a treaty that would satisfy the nation's western interests. Then, President Monroe made a momentous decision: the United States would give up its claim to Texas (dubious, in any event) in exchange for a Spanish boundary to be drawn to the Pacific. Adams reluctantly agreed. Onís said he would have to send to Madrid for instructions. But as Adams retreated from Texas, he pressed for a line as far south as possible. As Onís retreated from the Mississippi, he pressed for a boundary as far north as possible. When Onís's instructions arrived, they reflected the impact of Andrew Jackson's invasion. The Minister was told to settle for whatever he could get, even giving up Texas. In February, 1819, Adams and Onís finally agreed to a line beginning at the Sabine River (the current Louisiana-Texas border), working to the northwest, by way of the Red River, the Arkansas River, and the Continental Divide, to the the forty-second parallel (the present northern border of California). To make sure that the Spanish would never be able to use the river boundaries for trade or transportation, Adams insisted that the border lie on the south and west banks of the rivers, not in the center, as was customary. The Transcontinental Treaty also ceded Florida to the United States for $5,000,000.

One more step had been taken to fulfill Adams' continental

vision, but the price was Texas. At Monroe's suggestion, he consulted with General Jackson before going ahead with the change in strategy. The General was in Washington to defend himself against Clay's censure motion. Adams stopped by at Jackson's residence and the next day Jackson returned the call. The two studied the appropriate maps and agreed the price was worth it. Jackson later made the same point in letters to Monroe and Calhoun. "I am clearly of your opinion," he told the President, "that for the present, we ought to be content with the Floridas." Whether Adams consulted Jackson to protect himself against criticism later on, or whether he was genuinely interested in the General's opinion, is unclear. At any rate, twenty-five years later, Adams and Jackson would have conflicting recollections as to what was said about Texas in the winter of 1819. But John Quincy Adams kept a diary, and Andrew Jackson did not.

The Treaty was signed—with the *alternat*—on February 22, 1819, Washington's Birthday. For Adams this was more than appropriate, for it had been Washington who had launched him on his diplomatic career, who had predicted accurately enough that he would one day be found "at the head of the diplomatic corps, let the government be administered by whomsoever the people may choose." Two days later the Senate approved the treaty by a unanimous vote. "The acknowledgement of a definite line of boundary to the South Sea," declared the triumphant Secretary of State, "forms a great epocha in our history."

Indeed it had. Only in its abandonment of the shaky claims to Texas did the Treaty appear to be vulnerable. In Congress, Speaker Clay, always looking for an issue that might discredit the Administration, complained loudly, but nothing came of it.

THE PREVIOUS SUMMER, in the midst of the Florida crisis and the Spanish negotiations, Adams took a six-week vacation to be with his parents and family at Quincy. It was well that he did, for less than a month after his return to Washington he received word that his mother was seriously ill. Abigail Adams was now seventy-three years old. Adams chose not to return to Quincy but to stay on the job.

Then he received a letter from one of his sons telling him of Abigail's death after a three-week battle with typhus.

From the time when he stood by her side while she melted her pewter spoons into bullets after the battle of Lexington, and when he climbed with her to the top of the hill from which they watched the smoke rise from Bunker Hill, Abigail Adams had been to him what she became for later generations of Americans: a symbol of patriotism, sacrifice, and duty. Now almost without warning, she was gone. He mourned her with more than a touch of guilt, for he had stayed on in Washington when he knew she was seriously ill. "My lot in life," he reflected, "has been almost always cast at a distance from her. I have enjoyed but for short seasons, and at long, distant intervals, the happiness of her society, yet she has been to me more than a mother. She has been a spirit from above watching over me for good, and contributing by my mere consciousness of her existence to the comfort of my life." "She was," Adams later told his brother, "a contradiction of every libel written about her sex."

His Puritan background taught him that life was rarely unmixed success, that goodness and pleasure were quite often followed by failure, evil, or pain. It was not man's lot to bemoan tragedy, whether in private or public life, but to accept it as a test of strength, and to be stronger for it. Such was the case with his mother's death and with the previous deaths of his sister, his brother, and the numerous stillbirths and miscarriages that had afflicted his wife. So too in his public career. The Transcontinental Treaty had been such a re-sounding success that he could not help wondering if the pendulum might swing again. "May no disappointment embitter the hope which this event warrants us in cherishing," he wrote apprehensively after it was signed.

Less than two weeks later he learned that the Treaty was flawed. Depending upon how it was read, it could be construed as giving substantial amounts of Florida real estate to a small number of Spanish noblemen who had established last-minute claims there. More embarrassing was the fact that Minister Erving had warned him from Madrid several months before to be alert for such a possibility, and Adams had uncharacteristically filed and forgotten the letter. And, to twist the knife even more, the news of the Treaty's

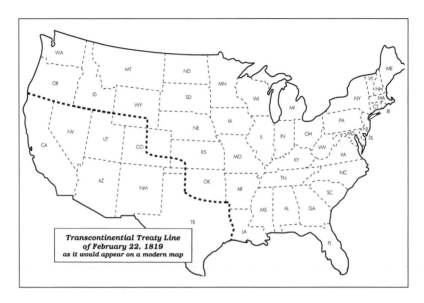

*Transcontinential Treaty Line
of February 22, 1819
as it would appear on a modern map*

The Transcontinental Treaty Line began at the Sabine River (the current Louisiana–Texas border), and worked to the northwest, by way of the Red River, the Arkansas River, and the Continental Divide, to the the forty-second parallel (the present northern border of California).

defects was brought to President Monroe by a no-doubt gleeful Henry Clay. Although nothing was lost in the long run, much of his pride in himself and the Treaty evaporated. "Never will the treaty recur to my memory but associated with the remembrance of my own heedlessness," he remonstrated to himself. "Should it hereafter be, as it probably will, exposed to the world, and incur from my country reproach as bitter as my own, it will be no more than I deserve." It took two more years and a change in government in Spain to straighten things out. The final document was ratified, again on Washington's Birthday, February 22, 1821.

THE TRANSCONTINENTAL TREATY proved to be only half of the equation that described Spanish-American relations, for in the background of the negotiations that led to the Treaty could still be heard the sounds of the Spanish Empire breaking up. Pressure was building, not only for American diplomatic recognition of the insurgents, but for outright support as well. Speaker Clay led the charge. In 1818 he delivered a three-day speech in Congress urging that the United States take the lead in the movement for colonial liberation. In revolting against Spain, he said, the Latin American rebels were merely re-enacting the great struggle of 1776.

Adams, too, saw history repeating itself, but not in the same way. Clay and his followers were repeating the same errors that Jefferson and the early Republican party made in the 1790's. "Now, as at the early stage of the French Revolution, we have ardent spirits who are for rushing into the conflict, without looking to the consequences," he told his father. One of the "consequences" was the possible disruption of the transcontinental negotiations. Any suggestion that the United States was about to aid the Latin American rebels against Spain would lose the Treaty. For the time being, Adams discouraged any talk of support for the revolutionaries to the south.

It was not that Adams opposed Latin American independence. Like most Americans, he abhorred colonialism, especially by Europeans in America. "The contest cannot and ought not to terminate otherwise than by the total independence of South America," he told Richard Rush. But the reality of Latin American independence had yet to be shown. Merely because a nation had the right to independence did not mean it was independent in fact. Americans "may indeed infer the right from the fact," he explained to the President, "but not the fact from the right." Moreover, as with the French Revolution, he saw little hope for true republicanism emerging from the Spanish colonies, given their history and social system, both of which were quite different from that of the United States. He outlined his position in a little lecture to Henry Clay in 1821. He wished the Latin colonials well, he said,

> but I had seen and yet see no prospect that they would establish free or liberal institutions of government. . . . Arbitrary power, military and ecclesiastical, was stamped upon their education,

upon their habits, and upon all their institutions. War and mutual destruction was in every member of their organization, moral, political, and physical. I had little expectation of any beneficial result to this country from any future connection with them, political or commercial. The United States would have little to gain from any connection with them.

But the virus of revolution was spreading nonetheless. In 1820 King Ferdinand of Spain was forced by liberals to accept a constitution. With that, many of the European monarchies trembled, fearing that another revolutionary era was about to begin. Russia, Prussia, and Austria had already formed what they called the Holy Alliance, led by Tsar Alexander, now a prematurely aging reactionary mystic. The Alliance was dedicated to suppressing revolutions everywhere, and there was talk that it might come to Ferdinand's aid. Significantly, Great Britain refused to join the Alliance.

Monroe and Adams cared little what happened in Spain. Of greater concern was the prospect that the Alliance might not stop at restoring Ferdinand in his own country, but would move on to restore his American colonies as well. The chances of such an intervention were remote, but the very idea challenged the role John Quincy Adams was attempting to define for the United States in the New World. As he put it in his instructions to one of his ministers, "to stand firm in cautious independence of all entanglements in the European system" had been a cornerstone of American policy since 1783, but this also meant that "for the repose of Europe as well as of America, the European and American political systems should be kept as separate and distinct from each other as possible." In other words, the United States would stay out of Europe, and it expected the European powers to stay out of the Americas. This was the essence of what later would be called the Monroe Doctrine.

Until the difficulties over the Transcontinental Treaty were ironed out, however, Monroe and Adams took care to refrain from any statement or action that might alienate Spain or upset the Holy Alliance. When the Greeks rose up in 1821 against their Turkish rulers, Adams opposed any diplomatic action on their behalf, in spite of the personal sympathy he and most classicly-educated

Americans had for their cause. It was an Old World matter, he said. But Henry Clay, in a speech given in his home town of Lexington, Kentucky, was calling for the United States to join with the Latin Americans in "a sort of counterpoise to the Holy Alliance." And the *Edinburgh Review*, for many years a leading British journal of opinion, was calling upon Americans to stand with Great Britain against despotism and oppression everywhere. Not until after the Transcontinental Treaty had at last been ratified did Adams feel free to speak his mind and to define America's future role on both sides of the Atlantic.

The occasion came on the Fourth of July, 1821. Adams was at the peak of his prestige as Secretary of State, and had been invited by the citizens of Washington to deliver the annual patriotic address. As always, these speeches were exercises in self-congratulation combined with abuse of Great Britain. Adams did not disappoint his audience in that respect. Appearing in the academic regalia of a Professor of Rhetoric and Oratory, he held aloft the original Declaration of Independence (for whose custody, as Secretary of State, he was responsible) and recited bloodcurdling tales of the Revolution. But the kernel of his address lay not in his anti-British hyperbole but in his warning to those Americans who thought that the Revolution of 1776 could be exported to Greece or South America in 1821. Intervention in foreign wars, even on the right side, he argued, would undermine the nation's unique position in the world. She had become a symbol of liberty to all, both friend and foe. To intervene in a cause not her own would alter her meaning "from *liberty* to *force*. . . . She might become the dictatress of the world. She would be no longer the ruler of her own spirit."

Only if the nation's own rights or security were directly threatened would war be justified. "Wherever the standard of freedom and Independence has been or shall be unfurled," declared Adams, "there will her heart, her benedictions and her prayers be."

> But she goes not abroad, in search of monsters to destroy. She is the well-wisher to the freedom and independence of all. She is the champion and vindicator only of her own. She well knows that by once enlisting under other banners than her own, were they

even the banners of foreign independence, she would involve herself beyond the powers of extrication, in all the wars of interest and intrigue, of individual avarice, envy, and ambition, which assume the colors and usurp the standard of freedom.

It was the most important speech John Quincy Adams ever made. In a few sentences he defined the course of American foreign policy for most of the nineteenth century. Other nations fighting for their freedom might earn the sympathy of the United States and its citizens, but they should not expect aid or intervention.

IN THE FOLLOWING YEAR, 1822, the new nations of Chile, Peru, Colombia, Mexico, and Argentina established their independence beyond doubt, and Adams saw to it that the United States was among the first to establish diplomatic relations with them. The Spanish Minister in Washington protested, but to no avail. With the Transcontinental Treaty ratified, Spain was no longer in a position to bargain. That autumn the emperors, kings, dukes, and ambassadors of the Old World assembled in Verona, Italy, to discuss what should be done about Spain and her decaying empire. Six months later French troops invaded Spain with the blessings of the Holy Alliance and restored King Ferdinand to his old powers. Would they stop there or would they turn their attention westward? And if they did, what should be the proper response of the United States?

While Monroe and Adams contemplated these questions, a dispatch arrived from Rush in London. The new foreign Secretary, George Canning, was proposing a joint Anglo-American declaration warning against outside intervention in the struggle between Spain and her colonies. With an eye on the potential trading possibilities with Latin America, Britain was now as determined as the United States to keep the Holy Alliance out of the New World. Moreover, she had the Royal Navy to back her up.

The proposal placed Monroe in a dilemma. If he accepted it, he guaranteed non-intervention, but at the price of an alliance with Great Britain. Was this a special case, justifying abandonment of "no entangling alliances?" As he frequently did on such occasions, Monroe turned for advice, not to his Secretary of State, but to his two predecessors Madison and Jefferson, who, along with Monroe himself, had built their early careers as fierce opponents of Great Britain. But times had changed. He was inclined, he said, "to meet the proposal of the British govt., to make it known, that we would view an interference on the part of the European powers, and especially an attack on the Colonies, by them, as an attack on ourselves. . . ." Overcoming a lifetime of Anglophobia, Jefferson too counselled an alliance. With Britain on our side, he wrote from Monticello, "we need not fear the whole world." Madison agreed. "There ought not to be any backwardness . . . in meeting her the way she has proposed." Without telling anyone of his correspondence, Monroe laid the matter before his cabinet in early November, 1823.

Secretary of War Calhoun, Attorney General Wirt, and the Secretary of the Navy, Samuel Southard, all favored the idea of a joint declaration. The President also inclined to it; Secretary Crawford was absent. Only Adams opposed it. Ever since the 1790's he had argued that whatever Americans might owe to Great Britain in the form of their cultural and political heritage, that nation stood no differently in its strategic relation to the United States than any other European power. This belief had led to his break with the Federalists in 1808, and now, fifteen years later, he had not changed his mind. If there was to be any declaration, he said, it was better to stand alone, "to avow our principle explicitly . . . than to come in as a cock-boat in the wake of the British man-of-war."

As in the Jackson affair, Adams found himself a minority of one within the cabinet, and unknowingly against Jefferson and Madison as well. He doubted very much the possibility of an invasion of South America by the Holy Alliance, especially in the face of British opposition. He was more interested in using the occasion to call a halt to European colonization in the New World. Recently, the Russians had been making noises about their territorial rights in the Pacific Northwest, and Adams had already told the Russian Minister that "we should contest the right of Russia to *any* new European colonial establishments." Perhaps the time had come for a *unilateral* statement by the United States asserting the separateness of the two hemispheres and opposing further colonization or intervention by any European power: Russia, Spain—or Great Britain itself. Since the British had already committed themselves privately against intervention, there was nothing to be lost.

For two weeks Monroe vacillated between the Jefferson-Madison position and that of Adams. The news from Europe was not good: the French were advancing in Spain and the King was back in full control. Monroe showed Adams the letters from the two ex-Presidents, but Adams stuck to his position. There was no chance that Spanish rule could be restored in Latin America by force, he maintained, and therefore no reason to throw in with Great Britain. After more thought, Monroe deferred, not to Jefferson and Madison, but to his Secretary of State. The notion of an Anglo-American alliance was dropped.

Adams intended to confine the non-intervention and non-colonization statements to a series of diplomatic notes to the Russians and the British, but the President had other ideas. He thought them important enough to be included in his Annual Message for 1823. Thus Adams listened with pleasure as Monroe read to the cabinet the draft of the Message, to be delivered at the opening of Congress. He used Adams's own anti-imperialist words when he declared that "the American continents, by the free and independent condition which they have assumed and maintain, are henceforth not to be considered as the subjects for further colonization by any European power." But the Secretary of State was less pleased with what followed, as Monroe proceeded to attack the French for invading Spain and called for early recognition of Greek independence. Having demanded that Europe stay out of the Americas, he then took sides in European affairs. Adams dissented. The nation, having at last severed itself from European affairs, was not prepared for what he called "a summons to arms—to arms against all Europe, and for objects of policy exclusively European—Greece and Spain. It would be as new, too, in our policy as it would be surprising." The next day he pressed his non-interventionist argument privately. "The ground I wish to take," he told the President "is that of earnest remonstrance against the interference of European powers by force with South America, but to disclaim all interference on our part with

Europe; to make an American cause, and adhere inflexibly to that." Americans could not have it both ways: if they wished the Old World to keep out of the affairs of the New, they would have to remain aloof from Europe's quarrels, no matter where their sympathies might lie.

Again Adams prevailed. The paragraphs in question were revised so as merely to take note of the troubled European scene, but not to take sides. In its final form the Monroe Doctrine was thus both a warning and a promise: a warning to Europe not to meddle in the Western Hemisphere, and a promise that the United States would stay out of European quarrels not affecting its rights or security. "In the wars of the European powers in matters relating to themselves," said the President in his Annual Message, "we have never taken any part, nor does it comport with our policy to do so."

> It is only when our rights are invaded or seriously menaced that we resent injuries or make preparation for our defense. With the movements in this hemisphere we are of necessity more immediately connected, and by causes which must be obvious to all enlightened and impartial observers. The political system of the allied powers is essentially different in this respect from that of America. . . . We owe it, therefore, to candor and to the amicable relations existing between the United States and those powers to declare that we should consider any attempt on their part to extend their system to any portion of this hemisphere as dangerous to our peace and safety. . . .

In view of the role that John Quincy Adams played in the shaping of the Monroe Doctrine, some have maintained that the ideas within it should more properly be called the "Adams Doctrine." But the Secretary of State believed—rightly—that he was only following in the tradition of neutrality first laid down in Washington's administration. And in fairness to Monroe, it should be recalled that it was his idea to elevate them to the dignity of a presidential message, rather than issuing private communiques through the State Department.

Realists have since pointed out that the United States in 1823 was in no position to resist an allied invasion of South America without British help; that the Monroe Doctrine meant nothing without the Royal Navy. Adams knew this. His real achievement was in his insistence that the United States use the occasion to assert its leadership in the emerging New World, to sail ahead of, not behind, "the British man-of-war." Accordingly, the President's Message was received with mixed feelings in London, with cold silence in Madrid, and with warm satisfaction in Latin American republics. As Adams suspected, the allied invasion never materialized.

BY THE EARLY 1820's, the long hours spent in reading and writing, often before sunup and in poor light, had taken their toll on John Quincy Adams. His eyes perpetually watered, adding to his grim appearance, and he had developed a slight tremor in his right hand, sometimes requiring a brace to steady it while he wrote. Most evenings he spent by himself in his "writing chamber," bringing his diary up to date, catching up on personal correspondence, or drafting state papers. When lured out of his house to mix with society, he often complained of wasted time. Yet another side to Adams occasionally peeped through his forbidding exterior. For one thing, he was aware that his sedentary life encouraged his tendency to gain weight. As a corrective, he engaged in a strenuous program of running in the winter and swimming in the summer. In cool weather he could be seen determinedly jogging through the streets of Washington. In the summer, there were many stories of the Secretary of State, clad only in cap and swimming goggles, clambering out of the Potomac to collect his clothing, heading for another day's work at the office.

John Quincy and Louisa Catherine Adams entertained guests at their rented home at 4 1/2 and F Streets every Tuesday evening when Congress was in session. Their home ranked with the White House itself as a social center, for Mrs. Monroe was a semi-invalid, rarely seen in public. Louisa Adams filled in the resulting vacuum, and took the lead in planning the dinners and parties at the Adams home. Guests rarely went away thirsty or underfed. Often there was music, singing, and dancing, while the Secretary of State was an anxious spectator.

"Mrs. Adams is, on the whole, a very pleasant and agreeable woman," wrote a Massachusetts friend to his wife in 1820, "but the Secretary has no talent to entertain a mixed company, either by conversation or manners." Once, though, following a successful evening, Adams danced a reel with his wife and sons, much to the amusement of the servants and musicians. Pleased with himself, he attended a party a few weeks later and danced with the wife of a prominent Washington editor. People talked about that for weeks. But these were exceptions. For the most part he could be found in his office, at his desk at home, or trudging from one to the other. Usually he took a month's vacation in late summer to visit family and friends in Massachusetts, but other than this, there was little time for travel or recreation.

After his mother's death in 1818, with his father in his late eighties, Adams became the effective head of the entire clan. He supervised not only the education and welfare of his three sons, but was responsible for that of his brother Thomas's growing family as well. As for his own sons, John Quincy Adams, forgetting his own experiences, planned their lives to include preparation for the law after attendance at Harvard. He continually impressed upon his sons the importance of being an Adams and the responsibilities that went with it. His letters, warning them to buckle down or face his wrath, are in contrast to the demanding but affectionate letters written by John Adams to his children in the 1770's. Indeed, John and Abigail warned their son that he might be pushing his children too hard, but he dismissed their advice as grandparents' indulgence.

When, in the fall of 1821, he learned that both John and Charles Francis Adams were doing poorly at Harvard, he refused to let them come to Washington for the Christmas holidays. "I could take no satisfaction in seeing you" he told John. Whether because of or in spite of these tactics, George Washington Adams graduated in 1821 after winning the coveted Boylston prize (beating out Ralph Waldo Emerson), and Charles graduated in 1825. But John Adams II did not graduate at all, having been expelled from college in 1823 for leading a student riot. His father was crushed. He tried to have the matter reopened, but not even the Secretary of State could blunt the wrath of Harvard College. John eventually became his father's personal secretary, while George studied law with Daniel Webster and then was admitted to the Massachusetts bar. But neither of them seemed interested in a life of public service, and Adams slowly transferred most of his hopes to the youngest son, Charles. Louisa concealed her doubts about her husband's methods, but she never doubted his motives. "A better father could not exist" she told old John Adams.

THE FAMILY TENSIONS WERE interwoven with Adams's work on the Florida cession, the negotiations with Great Britain, the Spanish boundary question, and the formulation of the Monroe Doctrine. Of his non-diplomatic duties, that which consumed most of his time in his earliest years as Secretary of State was the research and writing connected with his *Report on Weights and Measures*, submitted to Congress on February 22, 1821, simultaneously with the exchange of ratifications of the Transcontinental Treaty.

In the last days of the Madison administration, the House of Representatives had passed a routine resolution calling upon the next Secretary of State to submit a report on the systems of measurement prevailing in the various states and foreign countries, and to make recommendations for an appropriate system to be adopted by the United States. Behind the resolution was the belief that Americans might want to abandon the English system of pounds, ounces, feet, and inches, and adopt the new metric system devised by the French. When Adams arrived in Washington seven months later, the resolution was sitting on his desk.

The project appealed to him. Even before its completion, Adams' reputation for scientific inquiry and research had resulted in his election as President of the American Academy of Arts and Sciences. He investigated the subject with his customary thoroughness, which meant gathering information from all over the nation and adding to it what he could learn about the historical origins of the English and French systems, with commentary on the strengths and weaknesses of each. He consulted with no one, for there was no one in Washington whose knowledge of the subject approached his.

Frustrated by lack of resources and materials, at one point he was reduced to carrying out his research with a rusty set of scales that once belonged to the Bank of the United States. When he finished, the result was a remarkable piece of work; nothing better illustrates the depth of Adams's mind and the sweep of his imagination. Subsequent experts have pronounced the *Report* to be the most complete survey of its kind up to that time. It still may be read today with profit by anyone interested in the historical origins of measurement and its evolution from ancient and biblical times through the early nineteenth century.

Adams thought highly of his *Report*. He managed to convince himself that differing monetary and measuring systems were a contributing factor to war. The establishment of a world-wide uniform system of weights and measures might therefore advance the cause of peace.

It was a unique, if somewhat mystical, idea. How curious it was, Adams told Congress, that while there was near uniformity in the weapons of war, there was continual disagreement on the instruments of peace, "that they should use the same artillery and musketry, and bayonets and swords and lances, for the wholesale trade of human slaughter, and that they should refuse to weigh by the same pound, to measure by the same rule, to drink from the same cup, to use in fine the same materials for ministering to the wants and contributing to the enjoyments of one another." To establish a uniform system throughout the world, he concluded, "would be a blessing of such transcendent magnitude that . . . the being who should exercise it would be among the greatest of benefactors of the human race." But, he said, the time had not yet arrived for such a momentous step forward. The French system had logic and precision on its side, and obviously was a step in the direction of a universal system, but custom and usage remained on the side of the English system, at least for Americans. He therefore refrained from making any recommendation. Much to his disappointment few of his countrymen read the *Report*, not even his own father. For himself, he believed he would never write anything that was "more important to the best ends of human exertion, public utility, or upon which the remembrance of my children may dwell with more satisfaction."

THE END OF THE ANGLO-FRENCH world war had released the energies of the nation toward the westward expansion that Adams had
confidently believed was its destiny. Americans swarmed over the
Appalachian Mountains, down the Ohio River, and across the
Mississippi. Six new states, all but one of them from beyond the
Appalachians, entered the Union during Monroe's first term. The
rise of the "New West" altered the political scenery, for now people
thought in terms of three great sections instead of two.

Expansion brought with it a changed economic atmosphere.
The attraction of the West, as always, lay in the opportunity offered
by cheap land. But the land, however cheap, was never free, and to
take advantage of it usually meant borrowing money. Thus, the
postwar years saw an increase in the number of banks chartered in
the states, most for the purpose of providing easy credit to those
wishing to buy or speculate in western lands. Partly out of a fear of
an uncontrolled expansion of credit, Congress in 1816 re-chartered a
second Bank of the United States, hoping that it would act as a
brake upon "wild-cat" speculation. The possibility of a dangerous
land boom and the inevitable bust to follow was only one potential
threat to the economic stability of postwar America. The nation's
farmers, who for the most part had prospered in the war years by
feeding Europe's armies, now faced the loss of their market. Manufacturers, who also had not done badly during the war, now looked
on with dismay as ship after ship—mostly from Great Britain—
landed in American ports and disgorged clothing, furniture, shoes,
books, and ironware priced below their own products. Again in 1816,
Congress raised the import duties on most items with the idea of
raising revenue for the federal government and protecting domestic
industry at the same time.

These and other measures raised important questions as to the
powers and responsibilities of the federal government, questions
that had been largely dormant since the 1790's. Nowhere in the
Constitution was Congress given specific powers to create banks or
protect industry. Those who thought Congress had that authority
were thrown back on the "loose" construction of the Constitution
first put forward by Hamilton and the Federalists a generation
before, but resisted then by Jefferson and Madison. In the postwar

period many "Old Republicans" complained that by chartering banks, enacting protective tariffs, and sponsoring "internal improvements," Congress was reverting to the "monarchical" federalism of the 1790's.

Then, in 1819, while John Quincy Adams was fretting over the defects in his Transcontinental Treaty, the national economy collapsed. Food and grain prices fell in the face of reduced demand from abroad, and with them, the value of land. Those who had bought land on credit with the expectation that it would continue to rise in value had no way to meet their debt payments. Pioneers, investors, and speculators alike went bankrupt, in time pulling banks down with them, along with thousands of depositors. Farms were abandoned and factories closed their doors. The nation was experiencing its first full-scale depression. The "Era of Good Feeling"—if there ever was one—was over.

From his office in the brick State Department building on Pennsylvania Avenue, Adams read about the unravelling economy. True, domestic affairs were not his direct responsibility, but as a member of the cabinet, and possibly Monroe's heir, he could not escape involvement. The "Old Republicans" blamed the Bank and the Tariff for the depression, and called for a return to strict construction and limited government.

Adams rejected this point of view. He favored a national bank as the only means to hold the local banks in check, he had no objection to protecting the infant industries of America from foreign competiton, and he had no sympathy for land speculators who had hoped to get rich quick by buying low and selling high. Above all, he believed that the federal government not only had the power, but the duty, to stimulate the internal improvement of the nation. As a Senator in 1807, he had sponsored a resolution calling upon the Secretary of the Treasury to devise just such a comprehensive plan for the future. But as Secretary of State, Adams kept most of these thoughts to himself.

He was equally reticent about the other major domestic crisis of the Monroe Administration: the controversy over slavery and its future in America, sparked by the proposed entry of Missouri as a slaveholding state. The new state was the first to be made up of territory entirely west of the Mississippi. If it entered with slavery merely because the white inhabitants wished it, did this mean that slavery was destined for the entire West? Many northern Congressman were determined to prevent this, and moved in 1819 to block the admission of Missouri unless it eliminated slavery from its proposed constitution. They demanded that slavery be limited to the existing southern states, and not expand further. Adams tried to follow the Missouri debates, regretting that "my time is so much absorbed by other more immediate and indispensable duties that I scarcely have any left for investigating this." He added "we are approaching a crisis that will shake the Union to its centre."

Up to then, Adams' reservations about slavery had always taken second place to his militant nationalism, as in the case of the slaves allegedly abducted by the British during the recent war. As Secretary of State he had resisted any treaty with Britain for suppressing the international slave trade, because that would lead to British inspection of American vessels on the high seas. To grant the Royal Navy this right, he pontificated to Stratford Canning, would be worse than the slave trade itself. He was still a better nationalist than abolitionist.

The Missouri debates unleashed an unexpected flood of emotional and acrimonious oratory. Men and women alike flocked to the Capitol to hear northern and southern Congressmen denounce each other in terms never before used. As he joined the throngs in the Congressional galleries, the attitude of John Quincy Adams toward the "peculiar institution" began to harden. It may have indeed been included in the guarantees in the Constitution, he reflected, but it nonetheless was "the great and foul stain upon the North American Union." He had not supported the Louisiana Purchase in 1803 and negotiated the Transcontinental Treaty in 1819 only to see the West populated with slaves and denied to free white labor. He told a northern Senator that if he were in Congress he would insist that the Treaty be amended to prevent slavery from entering any new American territory.

He had several searching conversations with John C. Calhoun, the Secretary of War. Although a South Carolinian, Calhoun had been educated at Yale and was in Adams's view the only cabinet colleague with whom he had anything intellectually in common. But he was shocked and depressed to learn that Calhoun was a defender of slavery. It was the means, Calhoun told Adams, of maintaining equality among whites in the South. By relegating manual labor to blacks, white people in that section were able to preserve their status and their democratic values. Calhoun's logic alarmed Adams. Here was an institution that could take a mind as brilliant as Calhoun's and twist it into the defense of things clearly false and ugly. After talking with the South Carolinian he poured his thoughts about slavery into his diary:

> What can be more false and heartless than this doctrine which makes the first and holiest rights of humanity to depend upon the color of the skin? It perverts human reason, and reduces a man endowed with logical powers to maintain that slavery is sanctioned by the Christian religion, that slaves are happy and contented in their condition, that between master and slave there are ties of mutual attachment and affection, that the virtues of the master are refined and exalted by the degradation of the slave; while at the same time they ... burn at the stake negroes convicted of crimes for the terror of the example, and writhe in agonies of fear at the very mention of human rights as applicable to men of color.

The Missouri question, wrote the aging Jefferson, was "like a fire-bell in the night." To Secretary Adams, it was the "title-page to a great tragic volume." But again, for the most part, he kept these thoughts to himself.

Eventually the arrangement known as the Missouri Compromise emerged. In exchange for northern acceptance of Missouri as a slave state, the south would accept a federal restriction on slavery north of a line extending west from Missouri's southern border. Not sure of the constitutional right of Congress to limit slavery's growth, Monroe submitted the matter to his cabinet before signing the measures. The entire cabinet, including Calhoun, approved the federal limitation. Adams reluctantly agreed to admitting another slave state (Maine would shortly be added to retain the balance in the Senate) but had second thoughts when he came home. "Perhaps," he mused, "it would have been a wiser as well as a bolder course to have persisted in the restriction upon Missouri, till it should have terminated in a convention to revise and amend the Constitution." If this resulted in a new and smaller Union, "unpolluted with slavery," what of it? "If the Union were to be dissolved, slavery is precisely the question upon which it ought to break." His anti-slavery feelings were now competing with his nationalism.

And the crisis was not over. Missouri proposed to exclude all free blacks from its borders, even if they happened to be citizens of other states. Here, Adams was less cautious, at least among those he thought to be his friends. If Missouri persisted in this, he said, Massachusetts and the other free states should retaliate by excluding Missouri whites, regardless of the consequences. This might lead to a breakup of the Union, but that, said Adams, would be followed by a slave insurrection. The end of slavery would soon follow after much bloodshed, but "so glorious would be its final issue, that, as God shall judge me, I dare not say that it is not to be desired." Henry Clay resolved the matter in a "second Missouri Compromise" that merely stated that nothing in the Missouri Constitution should be interpreted as restricting the rights of citizens of other states. There the matter of black citizenship remained for the next thirty-five years.

In 1823 Adams was presented with a subtle political challenge by the House of Representatives. By an overwhelming margin it passed a resolution calling upon the Monroe administration to negotiate the "abolition of the African slave trade, and its ultimate denunciation, as piracy, under the law of nations, by the consent of the civilized world." Adams had always resisted such agreements before, but now he was ready to reconsider. He studied the resolution carefully, particularly the word "piracy." Pirates were international outlaws, at war with all nations, not possessing any rights at all. If America and Britain were to agree in advance that international slave traders were pirates, searching their vessels would not be a breach of national rights. After convincing himself of this, he went to the President and cabinet. Secretaries Crawford and Calhoun, both slaveholders, were dubious, but eventually the entire cabinet voted to support an agreement with Britain, provided Parliament first declared the slave trade to be piracy.

It took nearly a year for the agreement to be negotiated by Rush and sent back to Washington, and by that time the 1824 presidential election was well under way. Not wishing to add yet another credit to Adams's growing list of accomplishments, his opponents in the Senate lined up with nervous southerners to amend the treaty to death. Secretary Crawford, who had approved the proposal the year before, now denied attending the meeting at which it was discussed. It was Adams' only major defeat on a treaty as Secretary of State and was the closest the United States would come to an international agreement on the slave trade until the Civil War.

The difficulties Adams encountered in 1824 with the treaty against the slave trade were only to be expected. From the day of his arrival in Washington he was well aware that he was being watched as a leading candidate for the presidency itself. At times he was convinced that one or another of his fellow cabinet members were undermining his work, to say nothing of the opposition coming from Henry Clay. At first, he refused to "electioneer" for any advancement, but events soon made him an active participant in one of the most fateful presidential elections in American history.

Chapter Six

◯

"Liberty is Power"

"OF THE PUBLIC HISTORY of Mr. Monroe's administration," John Quincy Adams wrote immodestly to his wife in 1822, "all that will be worth telling to posterity hitherto has been transacted through the Department of State." James Monroe had been reelected in 1820 without significant opposition, receiving every electoral vote but one. Former Senator William Plumer of New Hampshire, his colleague from the old Embargo days, cast his vote for Adams, much to the latter's embarrassment.

Monroe and his two predecessors, Jefferson and Madison, had each served as Secretary of State at some point prior to becoming President, and all were aware that Adams might stand to benefit from this tradition. Notwithstanding the confusion over the Transcontinental Treaty, he had made no major errors, had not been involved in any political scandal, had supervised the improvement of relations with Great Britain, had acquired Florida, extended the American boundary to the Pacific, developed a moderately progressive policy toward Latin America, and had gained the confidence of the President more than any other member of the cabinet.

Yet when Adams had been appointed in 1817, his mixed political background, his regional affiliation, and his own personality were assumed to be serious handicaps, if not disqualifications, in any presidential effort. "It is thought here that J. Q. Adams will not be a successful candidate," wrote Supreme Court Justice Joseph Story, who admired him. "It seems that the great objection to him is, that he is retiring and unobtrusive, studious, cool, and reflecting; that he does nothing to excite attention, or to gain friendships." Stratford Canning, who as Minister from Great Britain crossed verbal swords with Adams more than once, remembered him as "more commanding than attractive in personal appearance, much above par in general ability, but having the air of a scholar rather than a statesman." Adams' own diary and letters are scattered with self-descriptions like "dogmatical," "peremptory," "cold," "overbearing" and "harsh." Yet he also wrote that "with a knowledge of the actual defect in my character, I have not the pliability to reform it." The world would have to take him as he was. "I well know that I never was and never shall be what is commonly termed a popular man," he told his wife.

THE MANEUVERING TO SUCCEED Monroe began as soon as he took office. Henry Clay hoped to succeed him by leading the opposition in Congress, particularly against the foreign policies of John Quincy Adams. Treasury Secretary Crawford was biding his time, quietly using the enormous patronage of the Treasury Department to build his own following in Congress and the federal bureaucracy, such as it was. And if it was true that the last three presidents had served as Secretary of State, it was also true that they also had been native Virginians. So too were Clay and Crawford. Secretary of War Calhoun was also a candidate, with a surprisingly strong following in the North. Andrew Jackson was occasionally mentioned, but the General professed no great interest in the presidency.

For his part, Adams was well aware of the situation. "This Government is, indeed," he wrote after a little more than a year in Washington, "assuming daily more and more a character of cabal, and preparation, not for the next Presidential election, but for the one after. . . ." He had not been in Washington six months before he

was approached by Alexander Everett, the ambitious Harvard graduate whom he had taken with him to St. Petersburg, and who had
become something of an adopted son. Was Adams going to do
anything to promote his chances of succeeding Monroe? "I should
do absolutely nothing," Adams told Everett. Others would not be so
scrupulous, Everett replied. "I told him that was not my fault—my
business was to serve the public to the best of my abilities in the
station assigned to me, and not to intrigue for further advancement.
I never, by the most distant hint to any one, expressed a wish for
public office, and I should not now begin to ask for that which of all
others ought to be most freely and spontaneously bestowed." One of
his friends, Judge Joseph Hopkinson of Philadelphia, jokingly called
Adams's approach to office the "MacBeth policy", citing MacBeth's
declaration that "If chance would have me king, why chance may
crown me, without my stir." Adams, the Shakespeare expert, agreed,
reminding Hopkinson of Macbeth's ultimate destruction after he
began to conspire for the office. His friends in Philadelphia, Adams
told his wife, "send me kind messages to inform me that unless I
mend my manners, I shall never be President. Well, and what then?
There will be candidates enough for the Presidency without me."
Regardless of what the future held, Adams professed to be ready for
retirement from public life.

Yet Adams never said that he did not want the presidency, or that
he was unqualified for it. That he was destined for greatness had
been in the minds of his parents since he was old enough to read.
The hope continued to burn brightly in the mind of his father, still
turning out letter after letter from Quincy, although he was approaching his ninetieth year. In fact, John Quincy Adams wanted
very much to be President, but he wanted the office on his own
terms. "If my country wishes for my services," he told a friend, "she
must ask for them."

His behavior was consistent with the norms of the deferential
society into which he had been born. His models were George
Washington and his own father, neither of whom had publicly
maneuvered or conspired for the presidency. The people should
recognize and reward their leaders for their achievements without
encouragement or manipulation by the leaders themselves. For the

candidate to try to affect the result by intrigue or "electioneering," he wrote to a well-wisher, was like moving the hands on a defective watch. "If your watch has no main-spring, you will not keep time by turning round the minute-hand." If the office was to be "the prize of cabal and intrigue, of purchasing newspapers, bribing by appointments, or bargaining with foreign missions," he declared unctuously "I had no ticket in that lottery." Andrew Jackson, born in the same year as Adams, felt the same way. "I have no desire, nor do I expect ever to be called to fill the Presidential chair," he said, "but should this be the case, contrary to my wishes or expectations, I am determined that it shall be without any exertion on my part."

In the absence of organized political parties, Adams expected that a deserving candidate would emerge through an almost mystical form of political spontaneous generation, as Washington had years before. Although he could not admit it, he hoped to be that candidate. Any other result amounted to a vote of "no confidence" in his service as Secretary of State, indeed his entire career. Thus, while he remained aloof, he had more at stake emotionally in the outcome of the election of 1824 than any other candidate.

As the election approached, Adams began to distinguish between the active conniving for the office practiced by most of his potential rivals, which he condemned, and seeing to it that the public had a clear understanding of his own record, which was not only justified but necessary if the public were to make an informed decision. He refused to encourage his friends, but he would not allow his enemies to distort or undermine his achievements.

He twice fired warning shots at those considering an attack on his reputation or his record. In 1822 his former colleague at the Ghent negotiations, Jonathan Russell, thought he might advance the prospects of his friend Henry Clay by authoring an election tract claiming that Adams in 1814 had truckled to the British on the questions of the fisheries and the control of the Mississippi. Adams was furious. He swooped down on the unfortunate Russell, and spent the entire summer writing a book-length document demonstrating that Russell's evidence was not only inaccurate, but forged. Some of his friends, including his wife, thought that in the case of Russell he engaged in overkill, but Adams persisted. Nothing was

Although better known for his invention of the telegraph, Samuel F. B. Morse was also an accomplished painter. This depiction of the old House of Representatives was made in 1822, when Adams was Secretary of State. Adams would later serve there as a Congressman from 1833 to his death in 1848. *In the Collection of The Corcoran Gallery of Art, Museum Purchase, Gallery Fund.*

ever heard again of Russell or his charges. In the following year a Virginia Congressman attacked Adams for the "Publicola" letters, his vote against crepe-wearing in 1803, his alleged opposition to the Louisiana Purchase, and a host of other errors. Adams was happy to set the record straight, which he did in a lengthy letter to the *National Intelligencer*, later published as a pamphlet.

Then there was the matter of the Monroe Doctrine. Adams knew that the Republican party had always appealed to American Anglophobia, and that no one claiming to be a Republican could afford to be accused of being "soft" on Great Britain. Hence the denunciation of the Mother Country in his address of July 4, 1821. It was perhaps no accident that Adams was the only member of Monroe's Cabinet to argue against the alliance with Britain in December, 1823. Had he gone along with the majority and supported the alliance with

Britain, Adams, the ex-Federalist from Massachusetts, would have been vulnerable to critics seeking soft spots in his record.

Finally, he did not overlook any opportunity to remove his rivals from the scene. At various times he suggested to President Monroe that Clay, Calhoun, or Jackson be appointed to a ministerial post abroad, either in Europe or Latin America. Nothing came of these gambits. So while Adams had the greatest personal and psychological stake in the outcome of the election in 1824, he pursued his goals in a way different from the others, but no less effective.

THE ELECTION OF 1824 produced the only occasion in which the House of Representatives chose the president from among the three leading candidates as provided for in the Constitution of 1787 as revised by the Twelfth Amendment. It remains also the only contested election in which there were no national political parties. Absence of parties meant absence of issues. Further complicating matters was the fact that in 1824 there was no agreed-upon way of determining nominees. In the past, when there had been discrete political parties, Congressmen and Senators from each had gathered in separate caucuses and chosen the nominees. But with all potential candidates calling themselves Republicans, this method could no longer work, for without Federalist opposition, the Republican nominee would automatically become President.

Instead, the "friends" of candidates Adams, Clay, Calhoun, Crawford, and Jackson organized on the state level and attempted to influence legislatures or voters through unofficial "conventions" of supporters. Specially created (and very temporary) newspapers cropped up in 1824, trumpeting the virtues of their man. There was no standard time or method for choosing the presidential electors in the various states. Some were elected at-large on a statewide slate, others were chosen by district, still others were appointed by the state legislature. All of these activities were carried on at different times. The decline of parties, far from restoring national unity, had resulted in political chaos.

With five candidates in the field, it was recognized from the start that in all probability the House of Representatives would choose the President. This in turn meant that no one of the five would be chosen without help from at least one of the other four. Supporters of the candidates therefore had to be circumspect in what they said about the opposition, since today's enemy might be tomorrow's ally. The least likely alliances, however, would be among men from the same region. Hence the competition between westerners Clay and Jackson, and southerners Calhoun and Crawford, was particularly fierce. Adams, the only northern candidate, was in a strong position, since only he, if he chose, could ally himself with any of the other four.

The candidate for whom Adams had the greatest respect was Andrew Jackson. Adams not only supported the General in 1818 but backed him again in 1821 when Jackson got himself in trouble as Governor of the Florida Territory. Jackson and the Spanish ex-Governor had managed to insult each other over a minor legal matter, resulting in the latter's arrest by Jackson. Once again Adams was Jackson's only advocate in Monroe's cabinet. After reading Adams's defense of his conduct, Jackson praised his "bold, manly and dignified refutation of falsehood." Unless Secretary Calhoun (of whose condemnation of the Florida invasion Jackson was still un-aware) were to be a candidate, the Secretary of State was his own choice as Monroe's successor. "You know my opinion of Mr. Adams Talents, virtues, and integrity. . . ," the General told a friend in 1821, "I think him a man of the first rate mind of any in America as a civilian and scholar, and I have never doubted of his attachment to our republican Government." For his part, Adams was critical of those whom he thought were seeking "to put down poor old Hickory," and told his diary that "General Jackson has rendered such services to this Nation, that it is impossible for me to contemplate his character or conduct without veneration."

Adams associated with Jackson privately as well. In the midst of Jackson's difficulties with Congress over the Florida invasion he invited the Tennessean to dinner with a small number of friends. "Our hero looked depressed and dejected," Louisa wrote to old John Adams. According to William Plumer, Jr., Adams preferred Jackson to any of the other candidates. In January, 1824, a few weeks after the General arrived in Washington as Tennessee's new Senator,

John Quincy and Louisa Adams honored him with a magnificent ball at their home on the anniversary of the battle of New Orleans. Adams then let it be known he would not be opposed to Jackson's serving with him as Vice President. Were Jackson to accept the vice presidency, Adams wrote condescendingly, it would "afford an easy and dignified retirement to his old age."

Adams was one of the first to sense Jackson's political strength, but Jackson did not rise to the bait. If he had, and the Adams-Jackson coalition prevailed, the political history of the United States in the second quarter of the nineteenth century would have been quite different. But Jackson and his advisors were well aware of his appeal to the voters at large, aware that he represented a new type of candidate whose appeal transcended sectional lines and who there- fore could still win the presidency on his own. Jackson was different from the other four. His political experience was minimal, but that did not seem to matter. His achievements lay elsewhere.

Another who realized Jackson's strength was Calhoun. Badly defeated by the General in a Pennsylvania convention in 1823, he suddenly withdrew, and announced that he would gladly serve as Vice President under either Adams or Jackson. The forty-one-year- old Calhoun could afford to wait. Almost at the same time it became evident that the candidacy of Crawford was in trouble. The Treasury Secretary had suffered a partial cerebral stroke, which had been complicated by an overdose of medication. Slow to recover, he was unable to generate the strength expected of him by his numerous friends in Congress.

By the summer of 1824, the continued uncertainty of Crawford's health and Calhoun's withdrawal effectively reduced the field to three: Adams, Clay, and Jackson. But when the returns were finally in, Crawford's supporters were strong enough to prevent the Speaker from placing among the top three candidates. The Twelfth Amend- ment—which John Quincy Adams had opposed in 1804—reduced the number of finalists from five to three, thus eliminating Clay. Had he been a candidate, the probability of his selection by his Congres- sional colleagues would have been great indeed. As expected, no one received a majority of the electoral votes, with Jackson receiving

99, Adams 84, and Crawford 41. The state of Crawford's health now effectively reduced the choice to two: Adams or Jackson.

Partisans of Jackson, then and since, have pointed to the fact that their candidate received 153,000 popular votes as opposed to Adams' 114,000, and thus was the popular choice and should have been elected by the House in 1825. In response, partisans of Adams have pointed to the fact that their candidate's support came from many states where electors were not chosen by the voters, and had there been direct elections in all the states, the popular vote margin would have been much smaller. Moreover, the additional electoral votes generated by the non-voting slave population in the South inflated Jackson's electoral count, just as it had Jefferson's in 1800.

Nevertheless, those who wrote the Constitution did not believe the people should choose the president by popular vote. That was why they created the Electoral College in the first place, and why they provided for the selection by the House of Representatives in the event that no candidate received a majority of the electoral votes. Under the procedure, the House votes by states, not by members, with each state having one vote as determined by the majority of each delegation. There were twenty-four states, making thirteen necessary to elect. If no candidate could gain that number by March 4, then the new Vice President, John C. Calhoun, would become President.

As Congress assembled that winter, the leanings of each member were scrutinized, analyzed, and recorded over and over again. Daniel Webster later recalled that there were those who claimed to be able to predict a man's vote simply by the way he put on his hat. As he scanned the list of states and votes, Adams knew he could count on the six New England states. He had narrowly carried Maryland against Jackson, but this was no guarantee that its Congressmen would vote for him. New York, thanks to some crafty maneuvering by his supporters of which Adams was blissfully ignorant, had given him most of its electoral votes, but there were many New York Congressmen who favored Jackson or Crawford. New England, New York, and Maryland made up eight states: he was still five short. But then so too were Jackson and Crawford. Adams told his friends to stand pat and await developments.

Then, in the early weeks of 1825, as the day for the selection of the President approached, Washington saw a new John Quincy Adams. Throwing off his objections to socializing, he suddenly turned up at banquets, called on key Congressmen, and answered all sorts of questions on a variety of issues. No, he told the handful of Federalists still left in Congress, he did not bear a grudge against them for ending his Senate career in 1808. Yes, he told Republicans, he still regarded himself as one of them, although he wanted at the same time to rise above parties. "Conciliation, not collision," he said, was his principal aim.

In the meantime, all eyes were on Henry Clay, the man who could not be President, but whose personal influence as Speaker of the House controlled the outcome. Enjoying his role, the Kentuckian listened courteously to the cases put to him by the friends of his former rivals. Actually, he had already made up his mind. Crawford was out of the question because of his physical condition. As for Jackson, against whom he had led the unsuccessful censure movement in 1818, relations between the two were such that they could never trust one another. Besides, Clay had genuine doubts about military men in high office, especially when they came from his own part of the country. That left Adams, with whom he had quarrelled at Ghent, whose subsequent diplomacy he had criticized, and who had been libelled by his feckless friend Jonathan Russell.

But by 1825 foreign policy had faded as a national issue. The Anglo-French war had been over for a decade, all important issues had been resolved with Spain and Great Britain, and the Latin American republics had been recognized, although not as quickly as Clay would have liked. On domestic matters, Clay and Adams had similar views on the need for an active, rather than a passive, federal government, one that assumed responsibility for economic development by means of a protective tariff, a national bank, and internal improvements. Anticipated by Adams in his resolution back in 1807, Clay had dubbed this ambitious approach "The American System." It was markedly different from the states-rights and limited-government principles of the "Old Republicans" that were flourishing in Virginia and South Carolina. Thus, both temperamentally and philosophically, Clay was pushed away from Jackson and Crawford, and drawn toward Adams. There was one other factor. If the next President were to come from the East, that might increase the chances of his successor coming from the West, and vice versa. To temperament and philosophy, Clay could add self-interest.

On New Year's Day, 1825, Clay casually asked if he might see Adams soon, privately. Eight days later they came together in Adams's study in a meeting that would not only determine each of their political futures, but which would also influence the nature of American politics for the next thirty years. Clay pledged his support to Adams and said he would advise his friends to support him. This meant his own state of Kentucky, plus Ohio and Missouri, maybe more. Adams listened but made no commitments. He left a blank space in his diary, intended for an account of the conversation, but never filled it in. "*Incedo super ignes*" he had written in his diary: "I walk over fires." A week before the House vote, Adams told President Monroe that Jackson's election was "more probable" than his own.

The House met on February 9, 1825, with Clay in the Speaker's chair. It was high political drama matched only once or twice in the nation's history. The Speaker first announced that no candidate had received the necessary majority of electoral votes, and then directed the House to proceed immediately to its vote. The roll was called, as was the custom in those days, from North to South. There were no surprises when the New England states lined up with Adams, when Georgia and Virginia stuck with Crawford, and when Tennessee, Pennsylvania, and New Jersey supported Jackson. But the strength of Henry Clay was felt when Kentucky, Ohio, Louisiana, and Missouri voted for Adams, to which were added the votes of New York, Maryland, and Illinois. Adams had his thirteen states on the first ballot, and was President-elect of the United States.

Upon learning of the result, Adams quickly penned a note to his father in Quincy. The expectations of his parents had been fulfilled. "I can only offer you my congratulations and ask your blessings," he wrote. The years of preparation and education, of financial, social, and marital sacrifice, had been recognized and rewarded. But at what price? In his recent actions, Adams had violated his own rules, which for him was a far greater consideration. Public office was like death, he had once said, never to be sought, never to be avoided. Had he lived up to that maxim? He conceded that perhaps two-thirds of the country was opposed to the result. Had Adams really changed from the aloof and unbending statesman to the clever and unscrupulous politician? Many believed they had their answer when he announced that Henry Clay was his choice for Secretary of State.

In the opinion of most historians and biographers, the so-called "corrupt bargain" between Adams and Clay, which "stole" the presidency from Andrew Jackson, blighted Adams's presidency from the start. It was not Clay's support of Adams—he had to support someone, and few could have expected him to go for Crawford or Jackson—but his acceptance of the "reward" that was the major blunder of Clay's career, tied to him, as one historian has written, like a tin can to a dog's tail, for the rest of his life. For Adams, it created a situation in which he forever had to dodge the charge that he bought the presidency with the appointment of his long-time rival and critic.

Yet, as Adams prepared to become sixth President of the United States, the forces had not yet gathered that would limit his administration, like that of his father, to one term. His presidency was by no means doomed. How he conducted himself as President, the proposals and measures he advocated, and how he responded to the evolution of American politics away from the era in which he grew up, would also play roles in his fate.

From a legal or constitutional standpoint there was nothing improper in House election: if the Constitution required the leading popular vote-getter to be chosen, it would have said so. But he was about to become President partly as a result of his own good luck in being the only northern candidate, but also because of his "electioneering," his courtship of key people in Washington, including Henry Clay. This was hardly the "MacBeth Policy." The people had not come to him and asked him to be President in recognition of a life of service. He knew that Andrew Jackson and his friends felt cheated by the result. He was also aware that many regarded him as an elitist who had never really shed the Federalism of his earlier days. Nor was he helped by his status as the son of a President. Already there were complaints about the monarchist "House of Braintree," and the dangers of making the presidency an hereditary office. Adams hoped to use his inauguration to pacify these critics, and heal whatever wounds had been created.

On March 4, Adams left his home, accompanied by companies of militiamen, and proceeded to the Capitol. There, in the presence of Congress, President Monroe, Vice President Calhoun, Andrew Jackson, Henry Clay, and other friends and rivals, he delivered his Inaugural Address. To those who doubted his commitment to popular government he affirmed his political creed, "that the will of the people is the source, and the happiness of the people the end of all legitimate government. . . ." Thomas Jefferson himself could not have put it better. But Adams went even further than Jefferson, describing the United States as a "representative democracy." No President before him had ever used the word "democracy" in a public address. Once it had been a term of opprobrium; now he helped it gain respectability, at the same time hoping to strengthen his standing as a believer in the popular will.

He then turned to the recent election. There was danger, he said, when partisanship was mixed with sectionalism. He hoped that Congress would lay aside these considerations in favor of "the sentiments of mutual respect, the habits of social intercourse, and the ties of personal friendship." And then, while Andrew Jackson stared stonily ahead, Adams plunged on. "Less possessed of your confidence in advance than any of my predecessors," he conceded, "I am deeply conscious of the prospect that I shall stand more and oftener in need of your indulgence." After the speech, he took the oath of office from Chief Justice Marshall. Jackson stepped forward and shook his hand, for the last time.

Congress stayed in session long enough to approve of Adams' cabinet nominations. He tried to retain as much of Monroe's cabinet as he could. Treasury Secretary Crawford declined to continue, and so was replaced by Richard Rush, the American Minister to Great Britain, in whom Adams had great confidence. John C. Calhoun having advanced to the vice presidency, Adams first thought of Andrew Jackson as Secretary of War, but decided against it. The prospect of Clay and Jackson in the same room, let alone the same cabinet, was enough to discourage that. He offered it instead to James Barbour, a Crawfordite and former Governor of Virginia.

Barbour accepted. Monroe's Navy Secretary, Samuel Southard, and Attorney General William Wirt agreed to stay on. With Clay replacing Adams as Secretary of State, his official family was complete. The only Senate opposition came against Clay, with fifteen Senators, including Jackson, opposed. After approving the cabinet, Congress adjourned and its members scattered to their respective states and districts. A new Congress would take office in December. Adams had nine months in which to set an agenda for his Administration and to build on the conciliatory approach of his Inaugural Address.

IN 1825 THE EXECUTIVE OFFICE of the President consisted of exactly two people: the President and his secretary. Its powers were extremely limited in comparison with later years. Indeed, for most Americans not only the presidency, but the federal government was, to use Alexander Hamilton's words, "at a distance and out of sight." Most of the functions performed by the federal government in the twentieth century were performed by the states or localities, or not at all. The Washington establishment, including Congress, numbered approximately 600 people, not counting the military. With some exceptions, most Americans were content with this. The heritage of the American Revolution had taught them to be suspicious of remote, centralized power.

As for the President, there were no national media to confront or manipulate. There were comparatively few appointive offices to dangle before potential supporters, nor were there, at this time, nationally-organized political parties to rally in his support. There were few ceremonial trappings to the office, and no concern whatever for personal security. When Adams travelled between Washington and Quincy, he usually went by private coach or bought stagecoach tickets like anyone else. He continued his early morning "races" around the Capitol square (the fifty-nine-year-old Adams claimed he could make it from the White House to the Capitol and back in an hour flat), and his summertime swims in the Potomac. He had a favorite rock on which he would leave his clothes before diving in.

As an administrator, Adams differed little from Monroe. The cabinet met sometimes as a group; more often Adams met with each secretary individually. When they did meet in common, each member was invited to discuss all matters before them, whether or not they lay in his particular area of responsibility. When not meeting with officials, Adams was available to virtually any citizen who stopped by. The rest of Adams's regimen remained as it had been for several years: early risings, study of the Bible, exercise in the morning, letter-writing and catching up with his diary in the late evenings. Actually, he found that he often had more free time as President than he had as Secretary of State. Naturally, this bothered him. He accused himself of spending too much time "wasted in idleness or at the billiard table."

Much of the summer of 1825 was taken up by what turned out to be an interminable Farewell Visit by America's favorite Frenchman, the Marquis de La Fayette. There were not many of his old revolutionary comrades left, but the Marquis managed to visit the aged John Adams at Quincy and the aged Thomas Jefferson at Monticello, and ex-Presidents Madison and Monroe in Virginia. He also travelled to New Orleans, and visited Andrew Jackson at the Hermitage near Nashville. There were many ceremonies and pageants, but after reluctantly crossing the Potomac with La Fayette on his visit to Monroe, Adams recorded that he took "no pleasure in such scenes." Large gatherings of people disturbed him, even when they were friendly. After taking leave of La Fayette with a moving farewell speech in September, Adams departed to Quincy for his annual vacation. He spent two months visiting with his father, now ninety and almost blind, but mentally as sharp as ever. He returned to Washington in late October.

By then it was clear that Jackson and his followers had not been mollified by Adams' attempt at conciliation. Old Hickory, originally confining his anger to Henry Clay, had returned to Tennessee in high dudgeon, and his feelings became stronger the closer he came to his home in Nashville. In due course, and with the active encouragement of his Tennessee friends, his ire expanded to include Adams, his former benefactor. He had resisted the idea that Adams had bargained with Clay, he told a correspondent, but when

Clay was actually appointed, he could no longer doubt that Adams was "a participant in the disgraceful traffic of Congressional votes for executive office. From that moment I withdrew all intercourse with him." In that same month the Tennessee legislature, with only three dissenting votes, nominated Jackson for President in the next election—three years in advance.

Adams' major task upon his return to Washington that fall was the composing of his first Annual Message—what in a later age would be called the "State of the Union" address. In it, he hoped to persuade Congress and the nation of two things: first, that the time had come for the United States to play a leading role in inter-American affairs, and second, of the need for the federal government to undertake an ambitious program of economic, educational, technological, and social improvement.

The Old World powers—Spain, France, Britain, and Russia—had already been given notice by the Monroe Doctrine not to make plans for further colonization in the New World. The United States was expanding from sea to sea to control the North American continent in the name of "representative democracy." Now it was time to follow up on these successes, and Adams knew, or thought he knew, just how to do it. Several Latin American republics had called for an inter-American conference in Panama, to discuss, among other things, the questions of neutral rights in time of war (a long-held goal of American diplomacy) and the suppression of the international slave trade (which Congress was on record as favoring). To make its interest and influence clear, Adams believed the United States should be represented.

Although a child of the American Revolution, Adams had never imbibed its hostility toward power that for many had been its basic heritage. As "Publicola" in 1791, Adams dismissed the "imaginary apprehension" that an elected government would over-extend itself. Ever since his 1807 resolution as a Senator, Adams was committed to the idea of federally-supported internal improvements. He elaborated his position as Secretary of State, and presidential candidate: "The question of the power of Congress to authorize the making of internal improvements," he said, was simply one of whether the American people, in setting up their government, had been "so ineffably stupid as to deny themselves the means for bettering their own condition. I have too much respect for the intellect of my own country to believe it." Freedom did not mean weak government. Unfortunately, however, the "prevailing doctrine" prevented the federal government from "discharging the first *duty* of a nation, that of bettering its own condition by internal improvement." Adams believed not only in the responsibility of the federal government for economic improvement but of intellectual and moral improvement as well. He recognized that this too was against the "prevailing doctrine," but intended to use his first Annual Message to make his plea nonetheless. He acknowledged that it was a "perilous experiment."

His cabinet agreed, and counselled against it. They either doubted the constitutionality of some of his proposals, or, given Adams's precarious political position, objected to the timing of them. He listened to their comments, but he went ahead with his original plan. In his Annual Message Adams re-asserted his belief that "the great object of the institution of civil government is the improvement of the condition of those who are parties to the social compact." To this end he proposed a package of measures that included an accelerated program of road and canal construction, the establishment of a new Department of the Interior, the creation of a national university, the building of a national astronomical observatory, the financing of scientific expeditions of exploration and research, the creation of a new Naval Academy, the passage of a national bankruptcy law, and the establishment of a uniform system of weights and measures. "The spirit of improvement is upon the earth," he told Congress. There was no need to be obsessed by the old eighteenth-century conflict between liberty and power:

> Let us not be unmindful that liberty is power; that the nation blessed with the largest portion of liberty must in proportion to its numbers be the most powerful nation upon earth, and that the tenure of power by man is, in the moral purposes of his Creator, upon condition that it shall be exercised to the ends of beneficence, to improve the condition of himself and his fellow-man.

How ironic it would be, he concluded, if while the Old World monarchies were moving ahead in improving themselves, Americans "were to slumber in indolence or fold up our arms and proclaim to the world that we are palsied by the will of our constituents."

The twentieth-century reader of Adams's Annual Message will note that nearly everything he advocated eventually came to pass. But his cabinet had been right in suggesting caution in 1825. Already there was increased hostility to further extension of Congressional power in the slaveholding South in the wake of the Missouri debates. His suggestion that Congress not be "palsied by the will of their constituents" was especially unfortunate, since there were many who thought their will had already been "palsied" by the outcome of the recent presidential election. It made it possible to portray Adams as one who cared little for popular government or public opinion. His suggestion that America imitate Europe in scientific and intellectual improvement enabled his critics to accuse him of a sneaking admiration for the effete and corrupt societies of the Old World in which he had spent much of his life. His injection of literary metaphors into the message—as when he called his astronomical observatories "lighthouses of the skies"—brought only laughter.

THE ANNUAL MESSAGE was the first element in the undermining of Adams' presidency. The second contributing factor was his evolving attitude toward Native Americans and their relationship to the federal government. This touched not only upon race relations, but upon economic development in the South and West, and contributed to Andrew Jackson's already formidable political strength in those regions.

Soon after he assumed office, Adams learned that one of the treaties negotiated by the federal government with the Creek Indians in the state of Georgia was fraudulent. The Creek agents, led by a man named McIntosh, had been bribed by state and federal officials into ceding all of their territorial rights. Adams, not knowing the situation, had ratified the treaty as one of the first acts of his presidency. When the main body of Creeks found out about the treaty, they promptly killed McIntosh and refused to abide by it. But the Georgia whites, led by their Governor, were already preparing to survey the Creek lands prior to the expected departure of their original inhabitants.

The Creeks were one of the so-called five "civilized" tribes of the old Southwest, a name given them by whites to indicate that they had abandoned their alleged hunting and nomadic past and had adopted agricultural habits. But the Creeks, along with the Cherokees, Choctaws, Chickasaws, and Seminoles, lived on land that was rich in potential for cotton and other cash crops in the South, and which white pioneers and speculators meant to have for themselves as soon as possible. This consideration lay behind all discussion of white-native relations in this era.

Up to then, Adams had not been a particular friend of the American Indian, whether in 1802, when he had ridiculed "moralists" and "philanthropists" who had defended their rights to the land, or at Ghent in 1814, when he led the charge against the British proposal for an independent Indian nation in the Old Northwest, or in 1818, when he had come to the defense of Andrew Jackson's savage treatment of the Florida Seminoles.

But in 1825 the English were gone from the Old Northwest, the Spanish were gone from Florida, and the Creeks now seemed to be farmers no different from the whites who wanted their land. When Secretary of War Barbour, under whose jurisdiction the matter lay, proposed to halt implementation of the Creek Treaty until it could be re-negotiated, Adams and the rest of the cabinet agreed. Ignoring a series of insulting and threatening letters from Georgia's Governor Troup, Barbour moved to stop the white surveying of Creek lands. Troup breathed defiance at the slightest hint of any alteration of the original pact, however dishonest, and threatened force against federal officials who might intervene on behalf of the Native Americans. The Georgia-Creek controversy threatened to provoke the most serious federal-state confrontation since the Whiskey Rebellion of the 1790's.

Adams spent many late-night hours studying the old treaties and legislation pertaining to them, and found himself more and more in sympathy with the Creeks. But he could find no solution, given the determination of the Georgians to resist, and the support they expected and received from the old Indian-fighter, Andrew

Jackson. The former hunters of the forest were now themselves hunted, Adams told a visitor, "like a partridge on the mountains." But there was little hope that Jackson's partisans in Congress would support the administration in its search for a more equitable treaty. A collision with Georgia was avoided at the last minute by a revised treaty, which ceded all the Creek lands to the state. The Creeks themselves were given the option of submitting to the white man's rule in Georgia, or leaving for the trans-Mississippi West. Although in the end the Georgia whites prevailed, they and other southerners resented the delay caused by Adams' interference.

THE THIRD FACTOR CONTRIBUTING to the Administration's downfall was President Adams' refusal to promote his own ideas, to protect himself from his enemies, and to reward through his appointive power those who believed in him. Although Adams himself lost his job as bankruptcy commissioner in 1802 at the hands of the Jeffersonians, as yet no clear precedents existed for the removal of unsympathetic officeholders by a President. Adams was not interested in creating one. He not only refused to fire those known to be hostile to him, he persisted in renominating anyone whose term of appointment expired, so long as there was no complaint of dishonesty or incompetence. To do otherwise, he said the day after he was sworn in, "would make Government a perpetual and unremitting scramble for office. A more pernicious expedient could scarcely be devised." It was not long before the message became clear: nothing would be lost by opposing the Adams administration, and little could be gained by supporting it.

Adams seemed impervious to the claims of his own supporters in key states like New York, Pennsylvania, New Jersey, and Kentucky. Early in his term, Joseph Blunt, a correspondent in New York, urged that "public testimony of your confidence in men, whose principles and qualifications are unquestionable, should not be withheld." Two years later Blunt warned that the Jacksonians were making it clear that when the General won, "party services shall be rewarded." Adams's friends, he continued "only give lukewarm aid to

In Asher Durand's engraving of an earlier painting by Thomas Sully, John Quincy Adams is surrounded by books and papers illustrative of his diplomacy as Secretary of State. Charles Bird King's portrait of Louisa Catherine Adams, done at about the same time, reminds the viewer of Mrs. Adams love of music. *Courtesy of National Museum of American Art, Smithsonian Institution.*

the cause." Another New Yorker lamented that the appointment of "a known Jackson man" to the federal district judgeship only strengthened "the power of men bent on Mr. Adams' overthrow." The President lost the support of a New Jersey newspaper in 1827 over another judicial appointment. "I can not understand this policy," wrote a supporter to Henry Clay. But Adams would not change his position. Honesty and competence were to be his only criteria, he told his critics. He regretted the loss of personal and political friends because of "the faithful and fearless discharge of my duty," but he would not turn the Presidency into an "electioneering machine."

"Electioneering" was a word Adams now applied to anyone who wrote pamphlets, made speeches, organized committees, or solicited support in the presidential cause. Having "electioneered" briefly in 1824-25, he quickly returned to the higher ground of the MacBeth policy—never to descend again. Although the presidency was "at a distance and out of sight" for three years out of four, there still were gestures that could be made and actions taken that would remind the people from time to time who held the office. Adams did little of this, perceiving his duty to be at his desk in Washington or in Quincy. "Seest thou a man diligent *in his* business?" he said, quoting the Bible by way of explaining his refusal of an invitation to attend a cattle-show and agricultural fair outside of Baltimore. "From cattle-shows to other public meetings for purposes of utility or exposures of public sentiment, the transition is natural and easy. . . . This is no part of my duty." He did not wish to be an exhibit. Even an invitation to attend the fiftieth anniversary celebration of the Battle of Bunker Hill in his own state met with a similar refusal. He rejected the suggestion that he attend the opening of a canal in Pennsylvania "so as to show myself among the German farmers and speak to them in their own language." Adams, one of the few American statesmen fluent in German, told his friends that "this mode of electioneering suited neither my taste nor my principles."

Sometimes, when travelling between Washington and Quincy, he attracted crowds of people without any effort. This both puzzled and disturbed him. Several thousand people gathered at the wharf in Philadelphia in 1827 just to see him, many wanting to shake his hand and give three cheers. He responded with a one-line speech: "God bless you all!" There was no disorder, he remarked to his diary, as if there was some danger that the crowd might run amuck. Slightly pleased, he hoped that it came from no "vain or unworthy sentiment of exultation." A year later, on the Fourth of July, Adams ventured out from Washington to participate in the opening of the construction of the Chesapeake and Ohio Canal. He was to turn over the first shovelful of dirt, but in so doing hit a tree root. He promptly shed his coat and attacked the submerged tree until he came up with his shovelful. The crowd loved it, and he went home pleased with himself. "If he would only lend himself a little to the usages and manners of the people," wrote Louisa Adams to one of their sons, "without hiding himself and . . . rejecting their civilities, no man could be more popular because his manners are simple, unostentatious, and unassuming." But the incidents in Philadelphia and at the Canal were exceptions.

IT HAD BEEN EVIDENT for some time that Adams could not count on the loyalty of his own Vice President. Even before his inauguration a mutual friend told him that unless a pro-Calhoun cabinet was appointed, he could expect trouble. "I am at least forewarned" Adams wrote. Once a nationalist with ideas about the vigorous use of federal power similar to those of Adams, Calhoun was moving steadily in the direction of states' rights and limited government, largely in response to the growing insecurity of the white minority in his own slaveholding state of South Carolina. By June of 1826 he was in active correspondence with Jackson, and many of his friends were announcing their support for the General in 1828.

Jacksonians and Calhounites did not wait long to attack the proposed Panama Conference, using constitutional objections combined with racial slurs on Latin Americans generally. While unable to torpedo the proposal to send delegates, they succeeded in tying up the procedures and delaying approval until it was too late for the President's nominees to depart in time. As for Adams' proposals for national "improvement," reaction against them continued to reverberate. Three of Henry Clay's strongest allies, Francis Blair and Amos Kendall, both of Kentucky, and Senator Thomas Hart Benton of Missouri, promptly defected to Jackson. Old Hickory himself declared that Adams' ideas showed that he had only "a hypo-critical veneration for the great principles of republicanism." Perhaps Adams "was not the man of real wisdom, that had before been ascribed to him."

At first the Administration was strong enough in the House of Representatives to control the election of its Speaker and thus the leadership of the key committees, but it could not control the Senate, where Calhoun presided. In early 1826 the opposition reached a peak of sorts with a speech delivered by Virginia's eccentric John Randolph of Roanoke, a lifelong enemy of the Adams family. Not everyone took Randolph seriously, as he occasionally appeared in Congress with hunting dogs, a whip, and a slave carrying a jug of porter. But when he accused Henry Clay of forging the invitation to the Panama Conference, raked over the charges of "corrupt bargain," and referred to the alliance between "the puritan and the black-leg," Clay challenged Randolph to a duel. The two exchanged inaccurate pistol shots before agreeing that honor had been served. It was, said Missouri's Senator Thomas Hart Benton, who was hiding in the bushes at the time, one of the last high-toned duels he had witnessed in Washington. That Vice President Calhoun, as presiding officer of the Senate, failed to control Randolph, was further evidence of his disloyalty.

The stalemate over Panama, the hostility to the Annual Message, the alliance between Jackson and Calhoun, and the comic-opera duel between Clay and Randolph, were the main products of the first session of the Nineteenth Congress, which adjourned in the spring of 1826. Adams was glad to see them leave town. As the summer approached, plans were laid in Washington and elsewhere for the celebration of the fiftieth anniversary of the Declaration of Independence on July 4th. Old John Adams' prediction to Abigail that the event would be celebrated by "Pomp and Parade, with Shows, Games, Sports, Guns, Bells, Bonfires, and Illuminations" had long since come true. Among the signers, only Adams, Jefferson and Charles Carroll of Maryland were still living. All three had been invited to Washington for the celebration, but each declined owing to age and health. Ceremonies were held in the Capitol building with President John Quincy Adams attending. He then returned to the White House where he received visitors until three in the afternoon. Unbeknownst to him, both his father and Thomas Jefferson lay dying on the anniversary of the document with which their names would be forever linked. This was, Adams later wrote, "visible and palpable marks of divine favor," and most Americans agreed.

Adams left Washington as soon as he learned his father was ill, but did not arrive in Quincy until after the funeral. With Congress not due in Washington until December, there was no reason to return immediately, and so Adams remained in Massachusetts for nearly four months. Important documents and information were forwarded to him for action. Meanwhile, the deaths of Adams and Jefferson inspired a second round of observances and memorial services. Adams attended as many as he could, the most spectacular of which was a thundering two-and-one-half-hour declamation by

Daniel Webster. The entire audience sat "mute", according to the President's diary.

By the terms of his father's will, John Quincy Adams inherited the Adams home in Quincy, provided he paid $12,000 into the estate. As the executor of the will, he was also charged with the responsibility for overseeing the payment of regular income from the estate to each of fourteen heirs, including the children of his two brothers and sister. For the moment he concentrated his attention on the problems of his brother Thomas and his own son George. Thomas Boylston Adams had continued to deteriorate, and was on the verge of becoming a public nuisance. Temporarily sobered by his father's death, Thomas agreed to stay on in the Adams mansion (rent-free because he had no employment) until John Quincy cared to claim it. As for George Washington Adams, he too showed signs of future trouble. Aged twenty-five, and by many accounts a most charming person, he had never been able to get his feet on the ground. He too was drinking too much, and although he had been elected to the lower House of the Massachusetts legislature, had shown no real interest in the post, and subsequently lost it. He had been given the responsibility for managing his father's real estate ventures and investments, but was bungling the job. The two had frequent arguments and as many reconciliations. It was with a mixed sense of relief and foreboding that the President returned to Washington in late October.

UPON HIS RETURN, Adams was greeted by a new and unanticipated crisis in an area he least expected—foreign affairs. As Secretary of State, he had brought pressure upon the British to allow American trade with the West Indies (Jamaica, Barbados, and certain of the Leeward Islands) on an equal competitive basis with the rest of the Empire. Prior to independence, the West Indies trade had been an important part of the colonial commercial economy and an equally important source of supplies for the islands' sugar planters. Indeed, the traffic between American ports and the Caribbean, and the attempts by the British to disrupt it, had been a major factor in the coming of the War of 1812. Thus, when the British closed the traffic to outsiders in 1822, Adams persuaded Congress to impose retaliatory duties on certain kinds of British shipping until they changed their minds. That was in 1823. Now, three years later, the British moved further with a law forbidding *all* American trade with their colonies except Canada. Once again, the Jackson-Calhoun forces pounced on him. People who had once claimed that his Federalist background made him "soft" on Great Britain now criticized him for demanding free trade with the West Indies. As Secretary of State, they said, Adams had hoodwinked Congress. The hostile Senate attempted to repeal the earlier law, but was blocked by the pro-Adams House. Congress adjourned without taking any action, which meant that Adams, under the terms of the act of 1823, was required to counter-retaliate by further restrictions on British vessels coming from the Western Hemisphere. The loss of the West Indies trade would be used against him in the coming election.

The attacks on the administration in the Senate were now led by the genial Senator from New York, Martin Van Buren. In 1824 he had been the chief organizer of Crawford's presidential campaign, only to see his efforts frustrated by his candidate's illness and the stronger appeals of both Jackson and Adams. Van Buren was one of a new breed of politicians. Whereas the conventional wisdom inherited from eighteenth-century republicanism held that political parties and partisanship were bad, Van Buren believed they were good. He and his New York followers believed political parties were useful for educating the people about issues, for getting them involved in the political process, and for making it possible for people from undistinguished social backgrounds—Van Buren was the son of a tavernkeeper—to achieve elective office. In New York he had built one of the nation's first statewide political machines—the Albany Regency, it was called—which was noted for its efficiency, organization, and discipline.

When Van Buren came to Washington in the early 1820's, it was with the avowed purpose of re-creating the two-party rivalry that had disappeared during the Era of Good Feelings. He had hoped to use the Crawford candidacy for this purpose, blending it with a states-rights, Jeffersonian philosophy he knew would be attractive to much of the South. The result, he often said, would be a new Jeffersonian-minded coalition of "the planters of the South and the plain republicans of the North." With Crawford out of the way, Van Buren was looking for another candidate with whom to ally. Andrew Jackson seemed the logical choice in spite of the fact that the General appeared to have no fixed political ideology. By the winter of 1826–27 Van Buren had decided that Jackson was his man, and passed the word along to his Regency machine. Thus a third element was added to the Jackson-Calhoun alliance. "You may rest assured that the re-election of Mr. Adams is out of the question," Van Buren told a friend in February, 1827, not long after the West Indies crisis had broken out.

Adams watched Van Buren very closely. In his carefully crafted partisanship the New Yorker was almost the antithesis of everything the President stood for, yet the man retained a certain fascination, for, unlike most partisans, he also prided himself on maintaining friendly social relations with his bitterest opponents whenever possible. Thus it was that after a successful tour through the South in which he cemented his alliance with the Calhounites and Jacksonians, Van Buren had no compunction against stopping by the White House for a chat with the man whom he was planning to defeat. The topics covered were carefully chosen, centering on non-political matters. But Adams knew what the New Yorker had been up to and where he had been. "Van Buren is now the great electioneering manager for General Jackson" he told his diary, and has "every prospect of success."

With the South and West moving toward Jackson, and with New England safe for Adams, the decisive areas in 1828 would be the "middle states" of New York, New Jersey, and Pennsylvania, the Old Northwest states of Ohio, Indiana, and Illinois, and Henry Clay's Kentucky. Some of these states Adams could still win, and enough electoral votes were available from the others to give him an edge over the General, had different attitudes and strategies prevailed in 1827 and 1828.

THE NEW TWENTIETH CONGRESS assembled in late 1827, offering

another opportunity for a test of strength between the Adams administration and the Jacksonian coalition. Two years before, the House of Representatives had elected a friendly Speaker, John W. Taylor of New York. This time, however, under Van Buren's direction, the Jacksonians replaced Taylor with a Virginian, Andrew Stevenson. The vote was 104 to 94, with over half of the thirty-two New York representatives voting against Taylor. Van Buren's ability to turn his fellow New Yorkers against the administration was an ominous sign.

With the election of Stevenson as Speaker, the presidential election campaign began in earnest. Congress gave its printing contract to a South Carolinian, Duff Green, whose *United States Telegraph* had been established in 1826 as an advocate of his friend John C. Calhoun, and who was now in the Jackson camp. The *Telegraph* proceeded to berate Adams, Clay, and the administration throughout 1828. Considerable time was consumed in early 1828 by a resolution introduced by a Jacksonian Congressman to inquire into the expediency of placing a colossal picture of the Battle of New Orleans in the Capitol rotunda. The Adams forces responded with a resolution calling for the publication of a Jackson-led court-martial that had resulted in the execution of several Tennessee militiamen during the War of 1812. With Congressional committees in unfriendly hands, there was little possibility of gaining the initiative against those whom President Adams called "the skunks of party slander."

The Jackson campaign was not run out of Washington, but from Nashville. There a small group of long-time friends and advisors of the General co-ordinated the effort with Van Buren and Calhoun in Washington, and with a number of strategically located newspapers, including the *Telegraph*, the Albany, New York *Argus*, and the Richmond, Virginia *Enquirer*. This three-cornered organization, featuring a central committee, Congressional leaders, and a group of selected newspapers, would set the pattern for future presidential campaigns for many years. In Jackson's case, it was helped by the distance from Washington, which, said many of his followers, was the center of "corruption," going back to the Adams-Clay "bargain," if not before.

The Adams campaign, if it can be called that, was run by Henry Clay and Daniel Webster. There was no central committee of friends and advisors in Quincy or Boston. Many newspapers supported the administration, including the widely-read *National Intelligencer*, whose editors were friends of the president. But there was none of the co-ordination between candidate, committee, and Congress that marked the opposition. Nor did the *Intelligencer*, which saw itself as a semi-official newspaper of record, play as partisan a role as the *Telegraph*. For his part, the President thought the notion of spending money to secure this state or that newspaper, or to print huge quantities of handbills or pamphlets, as "altogether venal." His continued refusal to use patronage as a means of building morale and support for his political allies and potential followers undermined his campaign, especially in the crucial states of New York, Pennsylvania, Ohio, and Kentucky.

The most conspicuous example of Adams' patronage miscues was the Postmaster General, John McLean. Originally a holdover from the Monroe years, when he had been an ally of Calhoun, McLean time and again professed his loyalty to Adams. Yet McLean's own appointments soon acquired a reputation for Jacksonian or Calhounite leanings. When Clay and others complained, Adams responded that he had no hard evidence against McLean, and besides, he was modernizing and improving the Post Office to an unprecedented degree—which was true. Only in the summer of 1828 did Adams become convinced of McLean's disloyalty, but by then it was too late. Soon after he took office in 1829, President Andrew Jackson rewarded McLean by appointing him to the Supreme Court.

Not only did the 1828 election break new ground in campaign organization, but in the defamation of presidential candidates and their families as well. What in earlier days might have been the subject of jokes and smirks in the back rooms of taverns and saloons now appeared in print and in Congressional speeches. One Jacksonian tract accused Adams of providing a young woman for the pleasure of the Tsar of Russia while he was American Minister. It was hinted time and again, without evidence, that the fastidious Adams had padded his expense accounts while in the foreign service. Louisa Adams' English birth was cited as an example of his truckling to Great Britain, and he was again falsely accused of opposing the Louisiana Purchase while in the Senate in 1803. John Adams II, while carrying a message for his father to the capitol building, was roughed up in the rotunda by a young Jacksonian, and the incident became the subject of a predictably inconclusive Congressional investigation. But the anti-Adams campaign hit its most ludicrous point when it was charged that the President had spent public funds on a billiard table and a set of chessmen for the White House, with which he was presumed to have spent many an hour carousing with his friends.

Not to be outdone, the administration supporters rehashed all of the old charges against Jackson that had been raised by Henry Clay years before. His frontier brawls and duels, the harsh justice delivered against the Tennessee militiamen, and his alleged illiteracy were paraded before the public in election handbills and broadsides. Not content with this, however, administration supporters added the far more inflammatory charge that Andrew Jackson had stolen his wife Rachel from another man and had lived with her for many months in the 1790's before marrying her. (The facts suggest that Jackson had actually rescued the unfortunate woman from a tyrannical husband and had married her in the belief that she was divorced. Upon finding this was not the case, he married her again, thus leaving himself open to the charge of adultery and her with the charge of bigamy.) Nothing infuriated the General more than this accusation, and when Rachel Jackson suddenly died following the election, he blamed her death on his political enemies, including, for a while, John Quincy Adams. Although Adams had nothing to do with the charges, he was aware of them and did nothing to stop them. Himself a victim of libel and slander, he was not prepared to come to his opponent's defense. He had already done that, in 1818 and 1821.

JUST BEFORE ADJOURNING in May, Congress sent to the President a curious piece of legislation that in time would be denounced in the

South as the "Tariff of Abominations." Its origins are in dispute, but its effect is not. In the short run the Tariff helped strengthen the Jacksonian forces in the Middle States and thus further weakened Adams' chances for re-election. In the long run it became the occasion for a spectacular confrontation between the state of South Carolina and the federal government in 1832.

The idea of tariff protection for domestic industries had long been a favorite of Clay, and to a lesser extent, Adams. By 1828 a carefully-organized protectionist campaign in the Middle States— especially Pennsylvania—indicated growing support for a new and more comprehensive tariff. In the North, both Jackson's and the administration's supporters were prominent in demanding a bill that raised the price of nearly every imported item, as well as those of many raw materials. On the other hand, most southern Jacksonians, including Vice President Calhoun, had concluded by 1828 that tariff protection of industry was exploitative and even unconstitutional. Southern opposition to the Tariff of 1828 thus posed a problem for men like Martin Van Buren, who was promoting the alliance be- tween "the planters of the South and the plain republicans of the North." Clearly, the issue threatened Jackson's election.

Some contemporaries and later historians have maintained that Van Buren and his friends deliberately concocted a tariff bill so "abominable" to the shipping interests in Adams's own New En- gland that they were sure the Yankees would ally with the Calhounites to defeat it. The plan allegedly was then to blame the administration in the North for its failure to pass, take credit for its non-passage in the South, and thus preserve both wings of the Jacksonian coalition. But others have argued that the bill was meant to pass all along, since everyone knew that Calhoun and the South had nowhere to go in 1828 except for Jackson. In any event, the commerce-minded New Englanders swallowed whatever misgivings they may have had about the bill and lined up, not with the southerners against it, but with the manufacturing states in favor of it. When Adams signed the measure, southerners were furious, and the factory-owners and workers delighted. Had the administration taken credit for the bill in the Middle States, it undoubtedly could have turned that Tariff to its advantage, but Adams' passive view of the political process did not allow for this. As it was, northern Jacksonians took the credit while southern Jacksonians denounced both the tariff and the President. John Randolph was heard to mutter that the Tariff of 1828 referred "to manufactures of no sort, but the manufacture of a President of the United States."

As the net drew tighter in the spring of 1828, members of Adams's cabinet contemplated resignation or sought other positions. Clay talked of quitting because of poor health. Barbour, the Secretary of War, wanted to be appointed Minister to Great Britain, as did Daniel Webster, who felt he had earned it by his work for the administration in Congress. He couldn't blame them, Adams told his diary, for trying to seek "a harbor from the storm." In the end, the cabinet stuck with him, except for Barbour, who did go to London. Treasury Secretary Rush agreed to be his vice presidential candidate, although Clay would have been a better choice.

Although custom still forbade the personal appearance of presidential candidates for the purpose of soliciting support, it did not stop Jackson from making a triumphal return to New Orleans early in 1828 for the purpose of commemorating his famous victory there thirteen years before. The celebration lasted four days and was reported in detail all over the country, especially in the *Telegraph*, the *Argus*, and the *Enquirer*. Adams was disgusted by anyone who could so "exhibit himself in pompous pageantry." Jackson's flowery speeches at New Orleans were obviously ghost-written, his critics cried, for they contrasted starkly with the spelling in the General's hand-written letters, some of which were printed verbatim in order to show his unfitness for high office. Few seemed to care.

Duty, custom, and personal preference kept Adams at his desk until August, 1828, when he left for Quincy—alone. Louisa refused to accompany him as long as his brother Thomas lived in the family home. For her the White House years were the unhappiest of her life, next to the years in St. Petersburg. In contrast to her sparkling enthusiasm while a cabinet wife and hostess, she took no pleasure in her official duties as "First Lady." She disliked the White House, which she found cold and drafty, with the furniture threadbare and worn. A fragment of an autobiography written at the time reveals a depressed woman, resentful of her husband's ambition, guilt-ridden at the long separation from her two oldest boys in their childhood, and suffering from frequent incapacitating nervous ailments. The knowledge of his wife's discontent and depression hung heavily on the President's mind. His son George's situation had not improved. To complicate matters further, his second son John became engaged to Mary Hellen, who was originally brother George's fiancee, but whom George neglected, along with most everything else. Mary was the orphaned daughter of Louisa's sister Nancy, and thus a first cousin to John. The two were married in a private ceremony in March, 1828, with the barest approval from the Adamses. In the waning months of the year, not only was his political career unravelling, but his marriage and family as well. His diary makes frequent references to both "public" and "private" cares in 1827 and 1828.

No ENTOURAGE OR ADVANCE-MEN accompanied John Quincy Adams on his last journey home as President of the United States. In fact he rode on horseback with his son John and a servant from Washington to Baltimore, stopping only to rest the horses. He was sixty-one years old, and, he admitted to his diary, "somewhat sore." That evening there was a Jackson rally in the square next to his hotel, and Adams went to sleep with the speeches ringing in his ears, "like the beating of a mill-clapper." There were pro-Adams meetings in the city as well. "A stranger," the President remarked, "would think that the people of the United States have no other occupation than electioneering."

The next day at Philadelphia, in the crucial pro-tariff state of Pennsylvania, another large crowd turned out to see the President, just as they had the year before. They gave him three cheers, and many followed him as he walked to his hotel. Adams now felt compelled to give a speech. He stepped to the porch and said: "Fellow-citizens, I thank you for this kind and friendly reception, and wish you all a good-night." That was it. To do more would be to "electioneer," to exhibit oneself in Jacksonian "pompous pageantry."

Significantly perhaps, Adams discontinued his daily diary entries from the time of his arrival in Quincy that August until his return to Washington late in September. Thereafter, until the end of the year, there is little comment on political affairs or the election results that began to trickle in during October. At first things looked well, with pro-Adams results in Maryland and Delaware. But devastating news came shortly thereafter from Pennsylvania, where the Jackson ticket won handily over a poorly-organized and divided administration effort. By the end of the month Charles Francis Adams, who by then was twenty-one years old and keeping his own diary, would write that the results were clear enough, at least to him. "Our family are at last to cease being the eternal subjects of contention and abuse." A week later he wrote from New York City "I advise the family to prepare for defeat. . . . The general opinion seems to be that little short of a miracle can save the P[resident]." A few days later, the results were complete. Andrew Jackson had triumphed over John Quincy Adams.

The General did as well as expected in the South and West. (One of the results of Adams' Indian policy was that his name did not appear on the ballot in Georgia at all.) But Jackson also overwhelmed Adams in Pennsylvania, rolled up majorities in New York, Ohio, Indiana, Illinois, and even won in Henry Clay's Kentucky. New England held firm for Adams (one elector in Maine voted for Jackson), and the President carried New Jersey, Delaware, and Maryland—the last by only a handful of votes. He also did well in western New York—heavily populated with transplanted Yankees— picking up some electoral votes there under the state's district system. Jackson won 178 electoral votes, Adams, 83. The popular vote was a little closer: 647,276 to 508,064. John C. Calhoun was re-elected Vice President.

Nearly all political historians agree as to the significance of the presidential election of 1828. It marked a watershed in American politics, in the nature of the presidency, and perhaps in the evolution of American society itself. Ideologically, it signalled the beginning of a thirty-year period in which the concepts of limited government, states' rights, and strict construction of the Constitution were in the ascendancy over their opposites. It marked the beginning of an equally long period of dominance by Martin Van Buren's coalition of southern planters and northern "plain republicans." Socially, it was another step in the disintegration of the deferential society in America, as it saw the accession to power of a frontiersman of obscure background and little formal education to the highest office in the land. Andrew Jackson became forever the symbol of the destruction of class lines and hereditary privilege—this in spite of his great personal wealth, much of it invested in slaves.

For Adams, the very things that he thought had qualified him for high office—experience, education, sacrifice, and commitment to public service—now worked against him and others like him. Jackson, declared one of the General's supporters, "had not the privilege of visiting *the courts of Europe at public expense*" nor was he "dandled into consequence by lying in the cradle of state." Adams came to symbolize an obsolete society, the decadent East against the vibrant West, inherited status as opposed to the self-made man. These things in the end worked against him as much as did the machinations of Martin Van Buren and John C. Calhoun.

Finally, the result was in part determined by the fact that its principal victim entered the contest a reluctant warrior. Although he often complained of the continual press of visitors, many of whom were seeking jobs or merely wished to shake his hand, the President found plenty of time in 1828 for reading his beloved classics, debating fine points of Cicero's orations through the mails with his youngest son Charles, and keeping his diary up to date. While in the White House, he developed a renewed interest in botany, devoured several books on the subject, and filled the nursery with seedlings from all over the country and around the world. Adams reported the progress of his botanical experiments with the same detail that he commented on public or political matters. His actions describe a man handicapped by an awareness that he had "electioneered" to obtain the presidency. To this was joined a conception of the office that limited his abilities to use it to its full advantage. Toward the end, he seemed to be losing interest in his position.

In November Adams went about the business of compiling his Fourth Annual Message. He would leave his successor an economy stronger than when he entered office. Revenues, he told Congress, were greater than expected, leaving the surplus to be applied to the reduction of the national debt. Initiatives had begun in the area of internal improvements, including roads, canals, and harbors, that he hoped would continue for many years. Indian affairs, with the re-negotiation of the Creek Treaty, appeared to be quiet for the moment. In foreign affairs, the nation remained at peace. Henry Clay's stewardship as Secretary of State had resulted in the negotiation of no less than nine commercial treaties (more than in any comparable period prior to the Civil War) and in the settlement of a large number of individual claims against foreign powers. Under Adams' direction, Clay attempted to fulfill the earlier promise of the Trans-continental Treaty by offering to buy all or part of Texas from Mexico—now independent from Spain—but was unsuccessful. Only this, and the continued British exclusion of Americans from the West Indies trade, clouded the scene.

While his personal financial situation no longer required him to face the dreaded practice of law, Adams still had to decide the nature and location of his impending retirement. For various reasons, including his wife's health and his brother's delicate situation, he elected to remain for the time being in Washington. His extended family consisted of servants and his son John and his wife, who added to the total by contributing a daughter of their own in December—the first child born in the White House. He rented a suitable home for all the Adamses about a mile and a half away from the White House.

As Adams and his family were preparing to depart, the Jacksonians were preparing to enter. The newly-bereaved General arrived in mid-February, 1829, and set up headquarters at Gadsby's Hotel, which soon became a focal point for sightseers and would-be political appointees. The President-elect made no attempt to contact Adams because he still held him partly to blame for the attacks upon his late wife. For his part, the President refused to make the first move. All but one of his cabinet advised against his attending Jackson's inauguration. In not doing so, Adams left himself open to the charge that he was a poor loser, following in the footsteps of his father, who likewise could not bring himself to witness the swearing-in of Thomas Jefferson in 1801.

So the President and President-elect communicated through an intermediary, the U. S. Marshal for the city of Washington. Adams told the Marshal to tell Jackson that the White House would be available on March 4th so that he could receive guests. Jackson told the Marshal to thank Adams and to tell him not to hurry, that he and his family could stay as long as they needed to, even as long as a month. Adams told the Marshal that would not be necessary and made plans to leave the day before. He spent part of March 3rd on Capitol Hill, signing last-minute legislation. Then he walked alone back to the White House and departed at about nine o'clock.

THUS ENDED THE presidency of John Quincy Adams. The office was easily the most frustrating of the many that he held. His vision of a federal government capable of guiding and directing the economic and intellectual development of the nation through internal improvements and the subsidization of investigation and learning was at least a generation, perhaps a century, ahead of its time. Yet his hostility to organized politics made him, as he himself was to admit, an anachronism, a throwback to an earlier day. "The sun of my political life sets in the deepest gloom," he wrote after the election results were unmistakable. "But that of my country shines unclouded."

Yet his most spectacular career still lay ahead of him.

Chapter Seven

————————◯————————

"I Was Born for a Controversial World"

ON THE DAY OF ANDREW JACKSON'S inaugural, Adams was out doing errands in the city. "The day was warm and spring-like," he later wrote. "Near the post-office I was overtaken by a man named Dulaney, who first inquired whether I could inform him how he could see John Quincy Adams." Such was the fleeting nature of power in a republic. Adams believed, or professed to believe, that his public life was over. His retirement was, he told a group of well-wishers, as complete as "a nun taking the veil." He repeated this to his diary, to his friends, to his family. "The State of the nation is one of such profound peace and tranquillity that I have none of that deep concern for public interests which followed me into retirement in 1801 and in 1808," he told his youngest son Charles. "These are piping times of Peace compared with them."

Two years later he was back in Washington as a Congressman, his promises to retire tossed aside. His critics always maintained that his return was proof of both his ambition and his thirst for revenge against those who had beaten him in 1828. His admirers believed that it was another example of the Adams family tradition of public service and private sacrifice. Both were right. "I was born for a controversial world," he had said in a flash of self-revelation, "and cannot escape my destiny."

THE AGE OF JACKSON, as it would come to be called, has meant many things to many historians. For some it signalled the transition from the "republicanism" of the eighteenth century to the "democracy" of the nineteenth—and further breakdown of the "deferential society." To others it meant the emergence of a free-wheeling "liberal capital-ism," replacing the more staid and restrictive economy of the earlier period. More recently it has come to represent a political counter-revolution against the forces of a "market economy" that threatened individual autonomy. But to Andrew Jackson and his followers at the time, it meant the opening of opportunity, especially political oppor-tunity, to groups and regions previously shut out.

Before 1828 no one had been elected President of the United States who was not a Virginian or an Adams. Small wonder, then, that for generations afterward, men talked of how the first "people's President" was sworn into office amidst a raucous throng of admir-ers who then descended upon the White House, tracked mud on the carpets, stood on the furniture, and trampled everything under foot in order to get a look at their hero. With the prospect of new appointments to many federal positions, the crowd that swirled around Jackson was full of high expectations. The new President did not disappoint them, promising that "reform" would be high on the agenda of the new administration. By this he meant an end to the "corruption" that had allegedly stigmatized the Adams administra-tion and its predecessors.

For John Quincy Adams, his first year out of office was anything but pleasant. Even before leaving the White House he managed to embroil himself in a journalistic brawl with the remnants of the old Federalist party in Massachusetts. During the election, the Jacksonians had charged that the late Thomas Jefferson had been a severe critic of the second Adams administration, implying that had he lived, he would have supported Jackson for president. In re-sponse, Adams outlined his support of Jefferson in 1803, and again

Thomas Sully's heroic portrait of Andrew Jackson shows the General with pen in hand, and a pensive expression on his face. *Courtesy of the Collection of The Corcoran Gallery of Art, Gift of William Wilson Corcoran.*

in 1807, in the face of Federalist disunionism. Surviving Federalists and their heirs indignantly demanded names and dates, and Adams spent much of the winter of 1828–29 composing a lengthy indictment of those who had toyed with secession during the presidencies of Jefferson and Madison. He decided not to publish it. In the end, Adams was persuaded that no good could come of a quarrel with some of the leading families in New England, most of whom had supported him in 1828. But it would be a long time before he would be welcome in the parlors of Boston's elite.

Then, in the spring, came news of the death of George Washington Adams. His eldest son was a troubled young man, as both parents knew, but they did not know how troubled. His law office, according to his disapproving brother Charles, had become a center of "loose-living and debauchery." George had involved himself with a female servant who had borne him a child. He had neglected the family finances and legal affairs entrusted to him. When his unknowing father summoned him to Washington to help with the move north, George knew that all would be revealed, and broke under the strain. While enroute to New York on the steamer *Benjamin Franklin* in late April, he either fell or jumped overboard. It was a month before his body was found.

George's death devastated both his parents. Consumed with guilt, Adams wandered about his rented home in a stupor for several days. Louisa now showed the greater strength, arranging for a brief funeral ceremony and refraining from the recriminations that must have surged within her. Her husband left Washington for Quincy, alone, as soon as he could.

The empty family mansion was in considerable disrepair, and it took most of the summer to make it habitable again. But it gave Adams something to do with his remaining two sons. He sent for the books and possessions that had been in storage since his return from England in 1817, and spent much of the summer happily unpacking and arranging them. "Of public affairs I take no thought," he reassured his wife soon after he settled in. "I wish to dismiss them forever."

At Charles's urging, he set about compiling his father's papers and correspondence in preparation for writing his biography, an exercise in the filial responsibility he had described to his late son George years before. He planned to spend three hours a day on the project and turn out a least one page of manuscript. When he wasn't writing, he called on old friends and neighbors in Quincy, revisiting the scenes of his youth and swimming in the ocean. He rarely went into Boston except to visit Charles, who in September married Abigail Brooks, daughter of Peter Chardon Brooks, one of the wealthiest men in New England. Adams remained in Quincy until December, when he rejoined his wife and the rest of the family in a new home on K Street, built for John Adams II and his family.

The Adams home drew a steady stream of visitors, most of them with a tale regarding the latest outrage in the Jackson administration. Adams at first counselled patience and forbearance. Andrew Jackson was an extraordinarily popular person, he reminded one correspondent, and "there is in his own character a fund of genuine public spirit" such that "we have every reason to hope that his Administration will be successful, not only to himself, but to the general welfare of the Union." But to his son Charles he predicted "there will be neither lofty meditations, nor comprehensive foresight, nor magnanimous purpose, nor the look for the horizons of future ages, presiding at the helm of State."

By the end of Jackson's first year, enough had taken place for Adams to drop any pretensions toward neutrality. In its pursuit of "reform", the administration had removed an unprecedented number of appointees of the former administrations. "To the victor belong the spoils," declared William L. Marcy, a Jacksonian Senator from New York, who was an ally of Martin Van Buren. To Adams it was a case of rewarding "sycophants and slanderers," unqualified and semiliterate "electioneering skunks," over dedicated nonpartisan public servants.

The new administration was also flexing its muscle in the new Congress, with the introduction of a comprehensive Indian Removal bill. Encouraged by Jackson's election, the white settlers of Georgia and Alabama hoped at last to sweep the Native Americans from the valuable lands of their states. Although the Cherokees successfully appealed to the Supreme Court for protection of their interests against the Georgia whites, they received no help from

President Jackson. Adams sensed it was a losing cause. The South-West alliance that had thrown him out of the presidency would also combine to throw the Indians out of their lands, he predicted. There was nothing to do, he told Alexander Hill Everett's younger brother Edward, now a Congressman, except record "the perfidy and tyranny of which the Indians are to be made the victims, and leave the punishment of it to Heaven."

At the same time, western leaders were arguing for a lowered price for frontier lands in order to speed up white settlement. They looked to Jackson, the first western president, for help. In South Carolina, Calhoun's friends were threatening to "nullify" the Tariff of 1828. They too expected Jackson, a native of South Carolina, to support them. At the end of the session Jackson vetoed a series of internal improvements bills, challenging their constitutionality. The reign of Andrew Jackson, Adams told his diary, "looks to decay, and not to improvement. Everything has an aspect of pulling down, and not of building up." Adams began re-reading the writings and speeches of Cicero, the Roman statesman whose attacks on despotism had inspired so many Americans during the Revolution. Now, for Adams at least, they began to take on a new meaning.

When his father returned to Quincy in June, 1830, Charles Francis Adams was disturbed. The former President seemed "full of care and depressed." He "thinks more of politics than I wish he did." That summer Adams was approached by Joseph Richardson, the retiring Congressman from his district, about the possibility of Adams replacing him. The ex-President did not reject the idea, indicating that his health and the nature of the opposition, if any, would have to be considered. He would not do anything that could be construed as soliciting votes or electioneering, and certainly would not be identified with any political party. The Congressman knew an Adams declaration of candidacy when he heard one. "Mr. Richardson said this was sufficient, and he would go to work."

Adams trounced the opposition, winning by better than a two-to-one margin over two opponents. And he had not lifted a finger on his own behalf. "My election as president of the United States was not half so gratifying to my inmost soul," he wrote when he heard the news. The same was not true of his family. Once again he had pulled the rug out from under his wife, just as she was looking forward to a sedate New England retirement. Charles was embarrassed too, both for himself and his father. "To neither of us can it prove beneficial to be always struggling before the public without rest or intermission."

The Congress to which Adams was elected in 1830 would not convene for over a year. Adams spent the winter in Washington amusing himself by writing poetry and watching the growing turmoil in Andrew Jackson's administration. He composed a curious "epic poem" entitled *Dermot MacMorrogh, or the Conquest of Ireland; an Historical Tale of the Twelfth Century*. It is unclear what or who inspired it, unless it was the fact that Dermot was a military hero who carried off another man's wife and then sold out his country. Some thought they saw Andrew Jackson in *Dermot*, but Adams never confirmed this. Although the poem went through three editions, few people read it. American literature, Adams decided, was like grape juice: it needed time to ferment into good wine. Unfortunately, it proved to be beyond his powers to provide the necessary sugar. He laid aside the biography of his father after having completed only two chapters. Charles completed the work in the 1850's.

That winter also saw the climax of the political struggle between Vice President Calhoun and Secretary of State Van Buren, each of whom hoped to succeed Andrew Jackson. Van Buren proved to be the winner, arranging for Jackson to discover what Adams had known for many years—that while Secretary of War in 1818, Calhoun had favored punishing Jackson following his invasion of Florida. Calhoun, who had kept his distance from Adams since 1825, now appealed to him via letter and intermediaries for evidence that would vindicate him. Adams refused to be drawn into the quarrel, exacerbated as it was by the continued defiance of Calhoun's own state over the tariff issue. In the spring, Jackson's entire Cabinet resigned. Adams was having a good time. His condition, he wrote, was "one of unparalleled comfort and enjoyment."

That year Adams delivered two formal orations, each of which attracted attention. The first was on the Fourth of July, at the request of the citizens of Quincy. The second was a eulogy of former President Monroe. Adams' target in the first was John C. Calhoun and the doctrine of Nullification; in the second it was Andrew Jackson and his obstruction of internal improvement.

The idea that a single state could "nullify," or opt out of enforcing a federal law thought to be unconstitutional, had its origin in the "compact" theory of the Constitution. Since the states had created the Constitution in 1787, said a long line of authorities from Jefferson through Calhoun, it followed that the states, not the federal government, should have the final say in constitutional matters. The idea had even blossomed for awhile among Federalists in New England during the Embargo and the War of 1812, when Timothy Pickering and others had called for the "interposition" of the commercial states of the North against the Jefferson and Madison administrations. Adams had challenged it when it came from his own region in 1808, and renewed the attack when it came from the South in 1831.

The Declaration of Independence, not the Constitution, created the Union, he told his fellow townspeople. The Declaration was "a social compact, by which the whole people covenanted with each citizen of the United Colonies . . . . To this compact, union was as vital as freedom or independence." The Constitution only strengthened and made "more perfect" a Union that already existed. Resistance to laws made under it was not an exercise of constitutional right, as the Nullifiers maintained, but simple rebellion, like that of Daniel Shays, inviting civil strife and bloodshed.

Like Jefferson and Adams, James Monroe also died on Independence Day, five years after his two predecessors. Adams owed much to him. By appointing him Secretary of State, the once-partisan Republican had set him on what turned out to be a somewhat convoluted road to the White House. In his eulogy Adams tried to redeem that debt by praising the Virginian for his non-partisan presidency, his expansionist vision, and his willingness, despite his states-rights background, to see federal money spent on internal improvements. How absurd, said Adams, without mentioning Jackson by name, to argue that a government could constitutionally annex the entire Louisiana Territory but "was incompetent to the construction of a post-road, the opening of a canal, or to the diffusion of the light of Heaven upon the mind of after-ages, by the institution of seminaries of learning." The eulogy was a virtual hymn to economic development and national "improvement."

Calhoun and Jackson were not his only targets in 1831. Five years earlier a fractious critic of the fraternal order of Masons by the name of William Morgan had been kidnapped in upstate New York and apparently murdered in retaliation for publishing some of the ritual oaths and secrets of the Order. No one was ever prosecuted for the crime. As a result, the Masons were accused of what a later generation of Americans might call a "cover-up." The Morgan episode persuaded thousands of citizens that the secret Masonic oaths and penalties led to Masonic juries that would not convict Masonic defendants, Masonic legislators who voted only for Masonic measures, and a Masonic network that would protect Masons everywhere. By 1831 the "anti-Masonic" movement had became a political party, spreading from western New York south to Pennsylvania, west to Ohio, and back east to New England. It was particularly strong in the Plymouth District of Massachusetts.

At first Adams had shown little interest in the anti-Masons, along with most Americans dismissing them as a passing phenomenon. But after his election he became more and more convinced of the justice of their cause. Men whom he respected, like his former Treasury Secretary Richard Rush, his former Attorney General William Wirt, and the Everett brothers endorsed the movement, as did younger Adams supporters like William H. Seward of New York and Thaddeus Stevens of Pennsylvania. In the spring of 1831, Adams attended an anti-Masonic convention in Boston, and from that point on he was identified with the movement.

Thus the Jackson administration, the Calhoun nullifiers, and the Masonic establishment all watched warily as the newest member of the Massachusetts delegation took his seat in Congress in late 1831. So too did his family, who for years would not reconcile themselves to what he had done. Adams resigned himself to his fate. "I go to Congress," he declared in the melodramatic fashion that often characterized his Congressional years, "with the opinions of those who are nearest and dearest to me in the world declared against the measure." But, he insisted, "my election to Congress was a *call*—unsolicited, unexpected, spontaneous, from a portion of my countrymen into the public service." No one with his background and family history could refuse a call.

ALTHOUGH IN LATER YEARS, new Congressmen (and Congresswomen) were expected to say little, defer to those with more seniority, and accept the most menial of committee assignments, in 1831 it was not expected that a former President would take a back seat. Adams hoped to be assigned to the Committee on Foreign Relations, but instead was appointed Chairman of the Committee on Manufactures, which would have the responsibility for devising a new tariff law in hopes of defusing the volatile situation in South Carolina. He begged unsuccessfully for another assignment, but the Jacksonians knew what they were doing. What better strategy than to pit the ultra-nationalist John Quincy Adams against the ultra-nullifier, John C. Calhoun?

Adams was nervous in his first few weeks. The former Senator and Professor of Rhetoric and Oratory remained unsure of himself when speaking without notes or preparation. He was as yet uncertain of the rules of the House. But he quickly gained respect, partly because of his background, but also because of his surprisingly conciliatory attitude in the tariff crisis. Although he had not the slightest doubt of the tariff's constitutionality (after all, he had signed it into law), Adams, like many of the Jacksonians, was looking for a way to accommodate at least some of the southern objections. He was not infatuated with the tariff, he told a South Carolina Congressman. Ever since his days in the Senate, as well as in his presidency, his main interest had been in internal improvements.

That winter, working closely with Jackson's Treasury Secretary Louis McLane, Adams and his committee slowly hammered out a modification of the existing tariff, with a provision for a reserve fund for internal improvements in the future. To Adams' surprise, the bill passed the House by a two-to-one margin, receiving more support in the South than in the North. Jackson immediately signed it into law.

The "Adams Tariff," was the ex-President's major achievement during his first term. "It was ridiculous," wrote Congressman Everett to his brother, "to hear men who but three years ago, were abusing Mr. Adams with all their might . . . now suddenly impressed with the belief, that he is the only man who can save the Union." Even the Richmond *Enquirer* found nice things to say about him.

Adams was also placed on a second key committee, this one selected to investigate the Bank of the United States. Nicholas Biddle, the president of the Bank, on the advice of Henry Clay, was seeking a renewal of the Bank's charter well in advance of its expiration in 1837. In spite of the fact that the Jacksonians were attacking the Bank as a corrupt monopoly and an unconstitutional menace, Clay was certain that Jackson would not veto its renewal in an election year. If he did, Clay was poised to campaign for the Bank and make it the issue in the election of 1832.

Adams had always been a firm friend of the Bank. He believed it to be a necessary control on the otherwise insatiable demand for easy credit with which to speculate in western lands. As expected, he found himself in a minority on the Jacksonian-appointed committee, but nonetheless worked harmoniously with it, accompanying the group on a junket to Philadelphia to interview Biddle and inspect the Bank first hand. Each side found what it was looking for, with the majority report calling for a denial of the Bank's application, and the minority, including Adams, supporting it. Neither report made much difference, since the Bank enjoyed a clear majority in Congress, who approved its re-charter. Nor did it matter to President Jackson, who stunned Clay and Biddle by vetoing the bill. The presidential election of 1832 would focus on the collision between Biddle's "Monster Bank" and "King Andrew the First."

The Jacksonians, now beginning to call themselves "Democratic" Republicans, or just "Democrats," had undergone some battering since 1828. They had lost the support of the Calhounites and extreme states-rights men in the South, and in the North, many who had supported Old Hickory in 1828 had been frightened by his attacks on the Bank and were looking elsewhere. The opposition, calling themselves "National" Republicans, chose Henry Clay as their presidential nominee. But they too had undergone some changes. Clay could not assume that everyone who voted for Adams in 1828 would automatically vote for him in 1832. He could not even count on Adams himself.

Adams had assumed that Clay would pick up the anti-Jackson standard, and wished him well. But the same "dogmatical and peremptory" manner Adams had noticed at Ghent in 1814 still characterized his behavior. Clay's strategy on the Bank had backfired, as Jackson's Veto Message became the rallying point for the Democrats against Biddle and his "Monster." Worst of all, Clay, a Mason himself, had refused to accommodate the anti-Masons. After giving some thought to nominating Adams himself for President, the Anti-Masonic party turned instead to William Wirt, his former Attorney General. Adams then enlisted in the cause by writing and publishing anti-Masonic letters that denounced the Masonic oaths and secrecy as inimical to a free society. While it is not clear how or even if he voted in 1832, Adams was far more sympathetic to the anti-Masons than to the National Republicans. "There is more pure principle in and sincere patriotism in the Antimasonic party than in all the rest put together," Adams told Charles. He believed that Clay might have won in 1832 if he had only come out against secret oaths and organizations in accordance with the anti-Masonic platform. Although Jackson was re-elected by a wider margin of electoral votes than in 1828, his percentage of the popular vote declined. Wirt and the Anti-Masons even carried the state of Vermont.

As CONGRESS RE-ASSEMBLED in December, confrontation loomed between Jackson and Calhoun, who had resigned as Vice President and returned as Senator from South Carolina. That state had declared the tariffs of 1828 and 1832 null and void within it borders, and called out its militia. Adams was certain that Jackson, notwithstanding his quarrel with Calhoun, would back down in order to placate the South, just as he had with Georgia against the Indians. When Adams read Jackson's Annual Message of 1832, he was sure of it. It was the ideological opposite of Adams' Message of 1825. Jackson called for a retreat from the role of the federal government in virtually everything. He called for an end to raising revenue through the sale of the public lands, suggesting instead that they be turned over to the settlers in the western states, whom he called "the best part of the population." He intimated that the public funds should be withdrawn from the expiring Bank of the United States, and once again challenged the constitutionality of federally-funded internal improvements. The federal government, said Jackson, should be reduced to the "simple machine" contemplated by the Founders. Finally, he advocated another reduction in the tariff. Calhoun may have lost the battle for the presidential succession, Adams told his friends, but he had won the far more important ideological war.

Then, a few days later, Jackson surprised everyone by issuing a proclamation denouncing nullification and threatening punishment for those who disobeyed federal law. In terms reminiscent of Adams' Quincy Address, the president gave a ringing endorsement to the nationalist interpretation of the Constitution, stating it was the product of the people, not the states, and that "before the declaration of independence, we were known in our aggregate character as the *United States of America.*"

Adams did not know what to make of it. The proclamation, he conceded, "contained much sound constitutional doctrine, more indeed than properly belonged to the source whence it originated." But since Jackson had already given in on the main question, by seeking a further reduction in the tariff, "between the Message and the Proclamation," Adams concluded, "Nullification is triumphant." To make matters worse, Henry Clay, who had been associated with protection of domestic industry for a generation, now reversed himself and joined hands with Calhoun to sponsor a "compromise" that steadily reduced tariffs over the next ten years.

As Chairman of the Committee on Manufactures, Adams attacked Jackson's Annual Message in a 12,000-word "minority report," later reprinted as a pamphlet. It was wrong, he said, to deny tariff protection to the manufacturers and workers, when importing merchants were "protected" by the navy against pirates and the planters and farmers of the frontier were "protected" against Indians. It was wrong to give away the public lands to the western states when the territory had been bought by Congress in the name of the whole people. And it was wrong to hobble the nation by denying Congress the power to build the canals, turnpikes, bridges, and harbors needed to advance civilization.

He zeroed in on Jackson's assertions that frontiersmen were "the best part of the population", and that government was a "simple machine." The first was a slight against the workers, craftsmen, merchants, and manufacturers of the nation, each of whom had equal rights with every other citizen. The second was a misreading of the purpose of the Constitution, whose preamble, among other things, pledged it to promote the general welfare and secure the blessings of liberty, not only to the present generation, but to its posterity. The authors of the Constitution did not believe this could be done by a mere simple machine. "Their purpose," Adams said, "in this great and solemn mutual covenant, was their own improvement —the improvement of the condition of the whole. The constitution itself is but one great organized engine of improvement—Physical, moral, political." That was the issue between Jackson and Adams. Was government a "simple machine" or an "engine of improvement?"

As the years went by, sitting at his desk in the House of Representatives, Adams reflected more and more on the significance of his doomed stand on internal improvements, expressed in his Annual Message of 1825. Its rejection, he concluded, was a turning-point, not only in the nation's constitutional history, but in its social and economic history as well. "The great effort of my administration," he told a friend in 1837, was "internal improvement, improvement which at this day would have afforded high wages and constant employment to hundreds of thousands of labourers. . . ," a nation "checkered over with rail Roads and canals." It might still happen, but it would take another fifty years, and with the "limping gait of State Legislation and private adventure. I would have had it done in the administration of the Affairs of the Nation."

Such still could have been the case, he continued, but

the Sable Genius of the South [slavery] saw the signs of his own inevitable downfall in the unparalleled progress of the general welfare of the North, and fell to cursing the tariff, and internal improvement, and raised the Standard of Free trade, Nullification, and State Rights. I fell, and with me fell . . . the system of internal improvement by National means and National energies—The great object of my life therefore as applied to the administration of the Government of the United States has *failed*. The American Union as a moral person in the family of Nations, is to live from hand to mouth, to cast away, instead of using for the improvement of its own condition, the bounties of Providence. . . .

To Adams, Andrew Jackson was becoming more than an ingrate whom he had more than once protected, more than a political opponent, and more than his own personal nemesis. Jackson increasingly represented the darker side of the American character. His legendary temper, his reputation for personal violence, his lack of education and dependence upon others to write his state papers for him, his alliance with southern slaveholders and western "adventurers" convinced Adams that the orderly republic envisioned by Washington, Jefferson, and his father was slipping away. There would be no making-up in their old age between John Quincy Adams and Andrew Jackson, as there had been with John Adams and Thomas Jefferson.

Not that some didn't try. Soon after his arrival in Congress, Adams was approached by Congressman Richard M. Johnson of Kentucky, a Jackson ally. The President, Johnson said, was anxious to restore relations with his former friend. He had been misled by Calhounites who told him Adams was responsible for the attacks on his beloved Rachel. Would he accept an invitation to dinner? asked Johnson. No, said Adams, there was nothing particularly conciliatory about that. Would he accept an invitation with a small group of friends? Again, the answer was no. What would he accept? That was up to the President to find out, said Adams. Martin Van Buren claimed in his Autobiography many years later that he had almost got the two together at the funeral of a mutual friend, but that Jackson reported back that as he went to shake hands with the "old gentleman," Adams assumed such a hostile look that the President feared he would be struck if he came nearer.

In 1833 the Harvard Board of Overseers voted to bestow an honorary degree upon Jackson on the occasion of his first (and only) foray into New England. Adams was visited at home by his cousin, the former Congressman Josiah Quincy, now president of Harvard. Would he, Harvard's most distinguished living alumnus, attend the ceremony? Certainly not, said Adams. "As an affectionate child of our Alma Mater, I would not be present to witness her disgrace in conferring her highest honors upon a barbarian who could not write a sentence of grammar and could hardly spell his own name." Quincy went home disappointed but not surprised. On the day of Jackson's arrival in Boston Adams heard the salute guns in the distance. He professed to relish "the solitary tranquillity of my own occupations."

That autumn, after several declinations, he consented to run for Governor of Massachusetts on the Anti-Masonic ticket. The Massachusetts constitution required a majority of the popular vote for election, otherwise the Legislature would choose from the highest candidates. The Anti-Masons hoped for a plurality over the Democrats and National Republicans and then subsequent election by the Legislature. But the results were disappointing, with Adams placing ahead of the Democrats but behind his fellow Congressman John Davis, the National Republican candidate. The situation was not unlike the presidential contest in 1824. This time, however, after receiving assurances that anti-Masonic concerns would be addressed, Adams withdrew in favor of Davis.

THE OPENING OF CONGRESS in December, 1833, saw yet another Jacksonian confrontation, this time between the President of the United States and the President of the Bank of the United States. Jackson had found the public funds to be unsafe in Nicholas Biddle's hands and thus proposed to remove them and place them in state banks. By the following spring, Jackson had produced a political crisis by removing two reluctant Treasury Secretaries before he removed the funds, and Biddle had provoked a financial crisis by calling in his Bank's loans.

Although Jackson had a majority in the House of Representatives, his enemies still controlled the Senate. There, led by Clay and

Daniel Webster and joined by Calhoun, the Senate denounced Jackson's "excesses" and formally censured him for his abuse of his office in removing the public funds from the Bank of the United States. His enemies compared him to the corrupt English monarchy of the seventeenth century, and forthwith began to call themselves "Whigs," after the English political party of that name who had fought for the rights of Parliament against the King. They hoped that all the enemies of "King" Andrew Jackson: National Republicans, anti-Masons, and Nullificationists, would join in the new party and prevent Jackson's heir, Vice President Van Buren, from succeeding him in 1836.

Adams at first was skeptical of the Whigs. The name itself was a mistake, he told Charles, because the old English Whigs had represented the aristocracy, not the people, and it made little political sense in an American context. It made even less sense for alleged nationalists like Clay and Webster to ally themselves with the nullifier Calhoun. The alliance lacked integrity, and the people would recognize it. Furthermore, Adams refused to support the Whig censure of Jackson, not because he respected the man, but because it smacked of the same contentious opposition and harassment he had experienced as President himself.

In spite of his rejections of Jackson's overtures, Adams refused to attack Old Hickory publicly during his presidency. It was Adams who advocated accommodation over the tariff in 1832. It was Adams who opposed the censure of Jackson. And in 1835, when a crisis brewed in foreign relations, Adams defended Jackson against his Whig critics. The result cost him a seat in the United States Senate.

Ever since Jefferson's presidency, the United States had insisted on French compensation to American citizens for losses inflicted during the Napoleonic Wars. With accrued interest, they amounted to several million dollars. For years the issue had lain dormant between the two nations, although Adams as President had made a futile attempt to obtain recognition of the claims in the 1820's. Jackson also had little success until 1830, when the reactionary Bourbon monarchy was overthrown in favor of a professedly more liberal branch of the family. A treaty recognizing the claims and making provision for payment was signed and ratified in 1831. But there matters stood for the next three years, until Jackson ran out of patience and in his Annual Message for 1834 urged retaliation against the French to force compliance with the treaty.

The Whigs thought Jackson had blundered. Daniel Webster, who had presidential ambitions of his own for 1836, was prepared to take a softer line against America's oldest ally. What would former Secretary of State and President John Quincy Adams do? His position was extremely delicate, not only because of his reputation as the most outstanding and the most informed American diplomat of the age, but because he had been selected to deliver a eulogy before Congress for the Marquis de La Fayette, who had died earlier that year. Jackson, as well as the entire diplomatic corps, was scheduled to attend the oration. What would Adams say?

As usual, he spent hours in research. He was conscious of his responsibility, not only because of the delicate state of Franco-American relations, but because he was the only American living who had actually known La Fayette since the days of the American Revolution. He confined himself to a three-hour, sweeping discourse covering Franco-American relations from the time of the American Revolution, with emphasis on La Fayette's role in it, coupled with a rousing attack on hereditary monarchies. When it was over, and Jackson and his cabinet filed out of the House chamber, Adams was pleased. "My voice held out far beyond my expectations," he reported to his diary. For the next few weeks he received many requests for copies, usually from Democrats. Whigs were disappointed.

They were even more disappointed a few weeks later when Adams backed Jackson's hard line. In the House he moved a call for the relevant papers dealing with the most recent diplomacy on the French claims. They were promptly provided. Nothing happened. Finally, the ex-Secretary of State reminded his colleagues of their responsibility. The Whig-controlled Senate might keep silent, but the House should not. Now that they had the required documents, they should "say to the nation and to the world, whether they will sustain the President" in his insistence on "maintaining the rights, interests, and honor of the country." Privately Adams thought that Jackson had handled the situation badly, but he was also convinced that both law and justice supported the United States. It was, he later noted, like 1807, when he reluctantly supported a President in whom he had little confidence.

The resemblance did not stop there. The Massachusetts Legislature was contemplating its choice for a new Senator, and Adams was more frequently mentioned than anyone else. Yet he continued to defend Jackson's stance against the French. It was a serious matter, he said, which "might possibly eventuate in war. . . ." He doubted it would happen, but it might. A garbled report of Adams' "war" speech was published in the Boston newspapers, and that was all Daniel Webster needed to persuade the Legislature to select someone else as his colleague. In 1807 Adams' support of Jefferson had cost him his Senate seat. Now, he noted ruefully, his support of Andrew Jackson had prevented his return. No matter. He persuaded himself that he was better off in the House. Near the end of the session that body unanimously passed a resolution, introduced by Adams and thereafter amended several times, supporting the President and enforcement of the treaty. Adams also urged passage of a Fortifications Bill to provide Jackson with a $3 million contingency fund in case of trouble while Congress was out of session. It was blocked by Webster and the Whigs in the Senate.

Adams did have his revenge the following year. Defending his opposition to the Fortifications Bill, Webster warned against placing too much power in executive hands. To this he added that even "if the proposition were now before us, and the guns of the enemy were battering against the walls of the Capitol, I would not agree to it." Adams went on the attack. If Webster was serious in his statement, "there was only one step more, and that a natural and easy one—*to join the enemy in battering down those walls.*" The stenographers recorded that a burst of applause broke out from all corners of the House, and it was from this point on that people started calling John Quincy Adams "Old Man Eloquent."

The new Whig party ran several candidates in different parts of the country that year, including Webster. They hoped to deny Vice President Van Buren a majority of the electoral votes, thus throwing the election into the House of Representatives, as in 1824. The strategy failed. Enough "plain republicans" in the North joined with enough planters of the South to elect Van Buren President in his own right. Webster barely carried his own state, with Charles Francis Adams and a number of his friends working for Van Buren. John Quincy, whom the Whigs declined to support, was re-elected to a fourth term on his own. He still resisted "the spirit of party."

DURING THESE YEARS, the Adamses had their share, perhaps more than their share, of personal tragedies, of which the death of their eldest son in 1829 was only a prelude. Thomas Boylston Adams died in 1832, leaving behind a widow and a large family. But Louisa and John Quincy were increasingly concerned with their second son, John Adams II. In the early 1820's Adams had purchased a flour mill on Rock Creek in Washington, but had never been able to make a go of it. He turned the operation over to his son John, with a similar result. Now the father of two daughters, John's health began to fail. Few of his letters survive; perhaps his brother Charles destroyed them in later years. By 1834 his parents were alarmed enough to plead with him to give up the mill and come north to live. But it was too late. In October, while the rest of the family was in Massachusetts, he collapsed. His father rushed to Washington only to find him in a coma. He died a few hours later, a victim, apparently, of overwork and possibly the alcoholism that had contributed to the deaths of both of his uncles and his older brother.

Adams now had outlived all of his siblings and all but one of his children. The obligations brought on by the purchase of the Quincy home and his responsibilities as executor of his father's estate required him to pay out quarterly dividends to the legatees, which now included all the children of his deceased brothers and sister. He sold some real estate in order to pay off debts, and the situation eased. In 1838 the family moved back to the home on F Street in Washington, where they had lived when Adams was Secretary of State, and the mill was turned over to Louisa's brother-in-law, who eventually made it a profitable business. Charles, who, unlike his father, had a head for figures and business, took over the management of the family's finances, collecting rents, finding tenants, and investing the proceeds in canal, bank, and insurance stock.

For Louisa Catherine Adams, her husband's continued presence in the limelight dashed any hopes she might have had for a tranquil old age. Although she never changed her mind about the folly of his return to public life, she accepted it, and for the rest of their life together, Louisa Adams loyally supported her husband, keeping abreast of political events, and regularly communicating the latest information, rumor, or gossip to her son in Boston. But privately she continued to mourn for her two oldest sons, never able to put out of her mind the feeling that she and her husband had erred by leaving them behind in 1809.

ALTHOUGH JOHN QUINCY ADAMS prided himself on his "independence" from partisanship, he in fact favored the National Republican and Whig positions on nearly every major issue, with the exception of his support of Jackson in the French crisis. He was pro-bank, pro-tariff, pro-internal improvement, and anti-Indian removal. He maintained his ties to the anti-Masons, but by 1836 they were in decline, drifting into and absorbed by the two major parties. By the late 1830's, other and more lasting issues were emerging.

The decade was marked by an increase in organizations devoted to the reform and "perfection" of American society. Spurred by the communication and transportation revolutions, organizations for the promotion of sobriety and temperance, for world peace, for a more strict observance of the Sabbath, for the closing of brothels, and for the advocacy of women's rights had sprung up in many parts of the North and to a lesser extent in the South. Most of these groups had religious origins, offshoots of the "Second Great Awakening" that was sweeping through the Protestant churches. The most spectacular, the most controversial, and from the standpoint of many, the most dangerous, was the movement to reform and perfect American society by ridding it of the curse of slavery.

One of the traditional means of expressing opinion and calling attention to any cause in the early nineteenth century was the petition to Congress. Indeed, John Quincy Adams' first act as Congressman was to present a petition from several Pennsylvanians in favor of abolishing slavery in the District of Columbia, being careful at the same time to note his own opposition to the measure. Over the next several years he and other northerners would introduce hundreds of antislavery petitions, which invariably were referred to committees and forgotten. But by the mid-1830's, a new militancy, combined with innovations in printing technology, changed the trickle of antislavery petitions into a flood, and the flood into a torrent. Southerners, alarmed for the state of their "peculiar institution," tried to choke off the petitions with a series of "gag rules" in Congress. This in turn brought more moderate Americans into the fray, who may have had reservations about the abolitionists, but who had none about civil liberties. John Quincy Adams was one of them.

At first, Adams had little time to commit to the slavery question, yet he privately complained of the "overseer ascendancy" of the Jackson Administration. Writing to a friend in the wake of the bloody Nat Turner insurrection in 1831, he declared that slavery lay at the bottom of all North-South divisions: the tariff, nullification, Indian removal, the public lands. It could well bring about a separation followed by emancipation, as he had contemplated privately in his diary as early as 1820. But it would not come with his help. "The preservation of the Union is to me what the destruction of Carthage was to Cato—the conclusion of every discourse."

In the course of the next year, Adams dined several times with the young Frenchman Alexis de Tocqueville, who was collecting material for his classic book, *Democracy in America*. Tocqueville was impressed by Adams' fluency in French and his willingness to talk about virtually anything, including slavery and the differences between North and South. In slavery, said the ex-President, were "almost all the embarrassments of the present and the fears of the future." To slavery he attributed the alleged laziness of white southerners, and their devotion to hunting, racing, and duelling. Was it possible for the South, asked Tocqueville, dependent as it was upon black labor in a torrid climate, to survive without slavery? Of course, said Adams. "The Europeans work in Greece and in Sicily, why should they not in Virginia and the Carolinas? It's no hotter there." He discoursed on a

number of other subjects: religion, political conventions, the settlement of the west. Then Tocqueville asked the crucial question. What
of the dangers posed by slavery to the future of the Union? "Mr.
Adams did not answer, but it was easy to see that on this point he had
no more confidence than I in the future."

Later, in the midst of the Nullification dispute, Adams pursued
the matter further. Anticipating Abraham Lincoln by a quarter of a
century, he told a New York Democrat that "the real question
convulsing the Union was, whether a population spread over an
immense territory, consisting of one great division all freemen, and
another of masters and slaves, could exist permanently together as
members of one community or not; that, to go a step further back,
the question at issue was slavery." Three months after that, Adams
went public. A Georgia Congressman, arguing against tariff protection, compared southern slaves to northern factories. "Our slaves
are our machinery," he said, "and we have as good a right to profit by
them as do the northern men to profit by the machinery they
employ." Taking him up on the unfortunate simile, Adams reminded
him how much his "machinery" was "protected" by federal power. It
was represented in Congress through the three-fifths clause in the
Constitution. It was bolstered by the North's obligation under the
Constitution to provide for the return of fugitive slaves. And, he
added, the United States Army was expected to help put down slave
rebellions. "That 'machinery,'" he said pointedly, "sometimes exerts a
self-moving power." Adams had "thrown a firebrand into the House"
cried a South Carolinian. He didn't care. His "machinery" speech
was published with approval in the northern newspapers, and Adams
was delighted.

Thus, while he continued as Chairman of the Committee on
Manufactures, defending the Bank, tariffs, and the public lands
against the Jacksonian onslaught, while he aligned himself with the
Jacksonians on the French question, and while he was denouncing
the Masonic order for its corrosive effect on free society, Adams was
also enlisting in the antislavery movement. After all, he told a
leading anti-Mason, there was "but one very imminent danger," and
it was not the Masonic Order. "The rottenness of the heart of our
Union is *Slavery*." As a nationalist, he accepted slavery as protected

by the compromises that had made possible the Constitution of 1787. It was perhaps a bad bargain, but one he was sworn to uphold. But that did not mean he was sworn to aid in its expansion, or in repression of its discussion. In late 1835, when the first attempts were made to stem the tide of antislavery petitions, his Congressional career moved into a new phase.

THE MOVE TO CUT OFF, or "gag," Congressional discussion of slavery was a political necessity for the Democratic Party. If Martin Van Buren's alliance of southern planters and northern plain republicans was to survive, it would not do for such a divisive issue to be constantly before Congress. Moreover, there were many in both sections who genuinely believed that "agitating" the slavery question jeopardized the Union by exacerbating the differences between north and south. Better to stifle discussion, even if it violated the Bill of Rights, than to threaten the Union. The increase in antislavery petitions in the mid-1830's made action necessary. Andrew Jackson himself led with a strong denunciation of abolitionism in his Annual Message of 1835, praising those who had mobbed abolitionists in the North, and calling for a national censorship law.

In December, after the routine tabling of a petition calling for the abolition of slavery in the District of Columbia, a South Carolinian moved to "peremptorily" reject in the future all such petitions, since Congress lacked the power to interfere with slavery anywhere. Most, including Adams, agreed that Congress lacked the power to abolish slavery in the states. But the District of Columbia was not a state; it was a political subdivision in which Congress itself was the governing power. In any event, the attempt to shut off petitions in the House was an attack on the rights of free expression, an issue entirely different from the antislavery crusade. The abolitionists played the issue for all it was worth. Their hero became John Quincy Adams, who was not an abolitionist in the sense that, like William Lloyd Garrison and other radicals, he demanded immediate emancipation of the slaves. But Adams was a radical in his determination to protect the right of petition.

At first he was reluctant, as he again put it, to "take the lead" in the matter. He was willing that petitions calling for abolition of slavery in the District be referred to a select committee with instructions to report that Congress ought not to act. But this was no longer good enough for the proslavery militants and their northern allies. In addition to a denial of Congressional power to interfere with slavery in the states or the District, they insisted on a third rule that "all petitions, memorials, resolutions, propositions, or papers, relating to in any way, or to any extent whatsoever, to the subject of slavery or the abolition of slavery, shall, without being printed or referred, be laid on the table, and that no further action whatever shall be had thereon."

The new Speaker was James K. Polk, a Tennessee slaveholder. He permitted several Congressmen to argue in favor of the rule, and then allowed the majority to shut off further discussion. Adams rose in his seat to protest, asking only a few minutes to explain his position. "Am I gagged or am I not?" he demanded. Overriding Adams' pleas, the House proceeded to adopt all three rules. His position now hardening, Adams voted against the first (that Congress had no power over slavery in the states), refused to vote on the second (that Congress ought not to interfere with it in the District), and when the third roll was called, shouted "I hold the resolution to be in direct violation of the Constitution of the United States, of the rules of this House, and of the rights of my constituents." But the resolution passed, 117–68.

For the next decade, Adams fought the "Gag Rule." Sometimes he fought alone, but more often he had the support of a growing number of "insurgent" northern Whigs who were elected from abolitionist-minded districts in New England and western New York. No longer uncomfortable with the rules and procedures of the House, he became adept at their use. Now, no one knew more than John Quincy Adams about motions to table, motions to reconsider, motions to recommit, and moving the previous question.

Of course the "Gag" backfired. Slavery's opponents could now claim that the tyrannical mentality of slavery was out to destroy the liberties of free white men and women as well as those of blacks. Using standardized printed forms, they descended upon northern cities and towns, invaded the churches, stalked the meeting halls, and went door to door, seeking new recruits. In the 1837–38 Congressional session, they dumped over 130,000 petitions calling for abolition in the District, following them up with 32,000 against the gag rule, 22,000 against the admission of new slave states, and 23,000 in favor of abolishing the domestic slave trade. Often they were piled high on Adams' desk in the House; in 1842 he had a single petition wrapped up in a wooden wheel, containing 51,863 signatures.

There were ways of getting around the rule. At the beginning of each session it had to be renewed, which meant that Adams and his friends could sneak through as many petitions as they could get away with until the House organized itself. And after it was re-enacted, there were still ways. Was a petition calling for the enforcement of the principles of the Declaration of Independence covered by the rule? What about one asking for the removal of the nation's capital to a free state? Or one calling for diplomatic recognition of the black republic of Haiti? Or a petition against the rule itself? There was of course no way of determining the object of a petition until its contents were described, and in spite of admonitions to be brief, Adams became an expert at cramming in as much of a petition's contents as he could before being declared out of order. Demands that Adams be disciplined led to more debate, in which slavery was bound to be mentioned.

One day in 1837 Adams goaded the slave interest into a series of self-defeating postures. First, he announced he had a petition that appeared to have been signed by nine women from Fredericksburg, Virginia, which he sent to the Speaker's desk for examination. Then he asked for a decision on a second petition "purporting to come from slaves." That did it. Speaker after speaker rose to denounce the "Massachusetts Madman" for insulting the House. The women from Fredericksburg, said a Virginia Congressman who claimed to know, were all free blacks or mulattoes, one of them "of infamous character." A South Carolina Whig suggested that Adams might be indictable by a grand jury for inciting slaves to rebellion. An Alabama Democrat demanded that his fellow southerners censure the ex-President. Others suggested that the petition be burnt. A series of resolutions followed, all with the same general purpose: censor

Adams for contempt of the House by attempting to submit a petition from slaves.

For awhile Adams let the debate run on. Then he let out his secret. The petition from the slaves *opposed* abolition as dangerous to the welfare of the signers and *favored* his own expulsion from the House if he persisted in submitting more petitions! That infuriated his opponents even more. They brought out new resolutions, including one that censured Adams for trifling with the House "by creating the impression" that the petition favored abolition. But this drew fire from Northern Democrats, who could not support the resolution, since Adams had said over and over that he himself did not favor immediate abolition. Then yet another resolution was submitted, censuring Adams for attempting to submit a petition from slaves. But that was not true, either, said Adams. He had not attempted to submit the petition, he had merely asked the Speaker for a ruling on it. Did Adams really think that slaves had the right of petition, asked a Marylander. Yes, he said, under certain circumstances. That brought forth more resolutions, censuring Adams for having *"given color to the idea"* that slaves have the right to petition. At last they had it right, said Adams, and he was ready to submit to their censure, provided of course, he was first given the right to defend himself.

The United States House of Representatives was on the verge of voting on a resolution censuring a member for the expression of an opinion. Even some southern Congressmen objected now. In retreat, the slaveholders offered three resolutions stating that 1) slaves did not have the right of petition, 2) anyone submitting petitions from slaves was to be considered, among other things, "as unfriendly to the Union," and 3) that since John Quincy Adams had disclaimed any disrespect for the House and promised not to present the petition if it was ruled out of order, the whole matter be dropped.

At last given the floor, Adams went on the offensive, invoking some of the most sacred principles of ordered liberty in defense of the right of petition, even for slaves. The right of petition is a human right, he said, "the right of petition is the right of prayer, not depending on the condition of the petitioner, . . . it is the cry of distress asking for relief. Did the gentleman from Virginia deny the right of petition to a woman in Fredericksburg simply because she was of infamous character, a prostitute perhaps? The Congressman hastily denied knowing any of the women. That was fortunate, said Adams, because he was about to ask who made these women infamous. "I have understood that there are those among the colored population of slaveholding states who bear the image of their masters." ("Great sensation" in the hall, reported the stenographer.) Did the gentleman from South Carolina really mean that a Representative could be hauled before a grand jury for something said in Congress? Not exactly, said the Congressman. But in South Carolina one could expect indictment. "God Almighty receive my thanks that I am not a citizen of South Carolina," replied Adams. ("Great sensation" again.)

Adams was having a field day. He closed by denying the implications of the third resolution and renounced any favors from the House. "I have retracted nothing: I have done my duty; and I should do it again, under the same circumstances, if it were to be done tomorrow!" He was unable to convince the House that slaves had the right of petition, but the other two resolutions went down to defeat by overwhelming margins. He was now attracting death threats from the South, promising to flog him, shoot him, hang him, or cut his "damned guts . . . out in the dark." Adams ignored them.

In 1838, Adams and the proslavery forces went at it again, this time over petitions from women in his own district. They did not call for abolition of slavery, but remonstrated instead against the annexation of Texas, now rapidly filling up with southerners and slaves. Petitions from women about anything usually inspired contempt among their opponents, and anti-Texas petitions were no exception. One Congressman had already suggested that husbands be provided for women presenting anti-slavery petitions to Congress. In the course of the debate over Texas, the Democratic Chairman of the Foreign Relations Committee criticized the women's petitions, regretting that they had abandoned "their duties to their fathers, their husbands, or their children," and had instead chosen to rush "into the fierce struggles of political life." He considered it "discreditable, not only to their own particular section of the country, but also to the national character . . . ."

Again, Adams struck back. Had the Congressman not read the Bible? Did he not know of Miriam, of Deborah, of Esther, whose petition to the King saved her country? Did he know his Greek and Roman history, of Aspasia, of Cornelia, of Portia, wife of Brutus and daughter of Cato? Knew he not Boadicea, who led the Anglo-Saxons against the Romans? Or of Queen Elizabeth I, or of Isabella of Castile who subsidized the voyages of Columbus? "Did she bring discredit on her sex by mingling in politics?" The son of Abigail Adams was just warming up. What of the heroic women of the American Revolution? What of the women of Philadelphia who helped clothe Washington's army? Or the women of South Carolina who in the darkest days of the war called themselves "rebel ladies" and risked their lives and health by caring for prisoners (among them Andrew Jackson's mother)? "Shall it be said here that such conduct was a national reproach, because it was the conduct of women, who left their 'domestic concerns,' and 'rushed into the vortex of politics?'" And lastly, what of the newly-crowned Queen Victoria, eighteen years old. Should she abdicate the throne of British Empire, since "affairs of state do not belong to women?" No one rose to defend the Chairman.

IN THE DEBATES OVER Texas annexation the issues of expansionism and the future of slavery would be intertwined, and no one better symbolized that entanglement than John Quincy Adams. As Secretary of State he had once claimed Texas for the United States. As President he had tried to buy it. And now as an antislavery Congressman, he became the leading opponent of its annexation.

Texans, said the annexationists, had strugged for their liberty against Mexico in 1836 just as the American colonists had against England in 1776. But "the fact is directly the reverse," said Adams. The Texas revolution had nothing to do with freedom, or liberty, or the ideals of 1776. "They are fighting for the establishment and perpetuation of slavery. . . ." The additional territory, said Adams and the anti-annexationists, was intended to offset the growth of the northern free states. The more Adams and the antislavery North thought about it, the more apparent it became to them that the Texas annexation movement was part of a larger movement, even a "conspiracy" to spread slavery throughout the remainder of North America. Though doubtful in actual fact, the belief in this "conspiracy" fueled much of the antislavery movement from the 1830's on.

Adams' apparent reversal on Texas made him a target for a double-barrelled attack by his proslavery critics and Democrats generally. First, they charged that Adams, while negotiating the Transcontinental Treaty in 1819, had needlessly settled for the Sabine River boundary, excluding Texas, when by a little hard bargaining he could have obtained the Rio Grande or some other line further south. Second, his new-found opposition to Texas annexation, said the Democrats, was only spitefulness, stemming from his desire for revenge against Andrew Jackson, the man who had humiliated him in 1828.

Of the two, the first charge was the easiest to refute. He was the last person in Monroe's cabinet to give up the idea of obtaining Texas, Adams said, and none other then Andrew Jackson himself had approved the Sabine boundary when consulted by Adams before the Treaty was concluded. Jackson, in his last year in office, professed to have no recollection of any such meeting. Adams cited his diary to prove it. As for the charge that his current opposition was based on nothing more than revenge, Adams reminded his critics that when he had tried to obtain Texas in the 1820's, there had been few slaves there. Since 1829, all Mexico, including Texas, was legally free territory. Now, to side with the slaveholding Texans against free Mexico was siding with oppression against liberty. If Texas were free, he implied, there would be no problem with its annexation.

On May 25, 1836, Adams attacked annexation in a speech that he later characterized as "one of the most hazardous that I ever made." It was one of his greatest, and probably stalled the annexation of Texas for several years. In one hour, and over the shouted protests of many of his colleagues, he tied together in one unpleasant package the gag rule, Texas, Indian removal, and slavery.

Having been denied the right to speak when the gag rule had been pushed through earlier, he now explained why he voted against the resolution that Congress had no power over slavery in the States.

There was one set of circumstances in which Congress would have power over slavery, he said, and that was in case of civil war. War was already raging among Indians and whites. The annexation of Texas might lead to war with Mexico. If it was a war for the re-imposition of slavery, it might involve Great Britain, now the leading abolitionist power in the western world. France, too, might join her. How ironic it would be if the United States of America, once thought to be the beacon of freedom to the world's oppressed peoples, would fight a war for slavery. He turned to Speaker Polk, a future president of the United States:

> Mr. Chairman, are you ready for all these wars? A Mexican War? A war with Great Britain, if not with France? A general Indian war? A servile war? And, as an inevitable consequence of them all, a civil war? . . . Do you imagine that your Congress will have no constitutional authority to interfere with the institution of slavery *in any way* in the States of this Confederacy? Sir, they must and will interfere with it.

From the minute that the southern states became the theater of war, declared Adams, "from that instant the war powers of Congress extend to the interference with the institution of slavery in every way by which it can be interfered with. . . ."

Emancipation through the war powers of Congress was a new concept in 1836, but Adams would refer to it again and again. If the South expected the North to sacrifice its young men in putting down a "servile rebellion," it should be prepared to accept the reality that slavery itself might expire in the resulting war. Although Abraham Lincoln's Emancipation Proclamation of 1863 invoked presidential and not congressional war powers, there were those who, a quarter of a century later, remembered what John Quincy Adams had said in 1836. He returned to the main point: "As to the annexation of Texas to your confederation, for what do you want it? Are you not large and unwieldy enough already? Do not two millions of square miles cover surface enough for the insatiate rapacity of your land-jobbers? . . . Have you not Indians enough to expel from the land of their fathers' sepulchres, and to exterminate?"

With that speech, Adams' expansionism, dating from the days of his Plymouth Oration and his support of Jefferson's Louisiana Purchase, gave way to his revulsion against slavery. He who had once lectured to his young friends that "Union" should be the watchword of their political career, now began to doubt the Union's future. He who had once aimed to be the "man of the whole nation" now believed that his mission was to "vindicate the New England character" against "the fraudulent pretenses of slave-holding democracy."

Not wishing to jeopardize the alliance between the planters and the "plain republicans" in an election year, the Jacksonians shelved the issue of Texas for the time being. But it remained in the background, waiting for a more favorable opportunity.

ALTHOUGH ADAMS CORRESPONDED with most of the leaders of the abolitionist movement, he kept his distance from them, refusing even to attend their conventions. Adams explained his position in a letter to an abolitionist, written in 1837. All organizations are concentrations of power, he said. "That power may be exercised for good or for evil, but political associations, for the purpose of promoting specific measures, or partial purposes, are subject to so many sinister influences, and in the exercise of their power are so apt to forget the rights of others" that he could never join any of them, even if he agreed with their purpose. He was uneasy about mass organizations. "It seems as if nothing could be done in this country but by association," he complained in 1839. For their part, many abolitionists remained ambivalent toward Adams. Prominent leaders like William Lloyd Garrison and James Gillespie Birney criticized him both publicly and privately. They could not understand how it was possible for him to denounce slavery in the manner that he did, and at the same time oppose what to them was the most modest of measures, its abolition in the District of Columbia.

In 1839 Adams clarified his positon in two long letters to the *National Intelligencer*. He examined the reasons for slavery's rise. It was the heritage of colonial America, he said, fixed later by the rise of the cotton culture and, ironically, by the end of the African slave trade, which drove up the price of domestic slaves. The South was now united in its defense. Slavery was protected by the Constitution that he literally was sworn to uphold. As for abolition in the District, Adams estimated that the whole South and at least half the North was opposed to it, to say nothing of the citizens of the District. While he had no doubt of Congress's constitutional authority, the project was "utterly impracticable." In reality, "the immediate abolition of slavery, therefore, in the District of Columbia, is no more in the power of any member of Congress to effect than the immediate abolition of polygamy at Constantinople, or the immediate abolition of widow burning in Hindostan. . . ." Should the measure even come close to a favorable vote in Congress, the owners of slaves in the District would move them to Virginia or Maryland. Without simultaneous abolition in those states, abolition in the District would be meaningless.

For Adams the struggle lay more in containment than in abolition. His opposition to the annexation of Texas was spurred by this. Likewise he resisted the extension of slavery's influence into the North through fugitive slave laws or the terrorizing of abolitionist meetings, or the suppression of antislavery literature in the mails. But "if the abolition of slavery is ever to be effected, in this country, it must be either by force, that is by a civil and servile war, or by the consent of the owners of the slaves." Most abolitionists disavowed the former; how much progress had they made with the latter? Since the slaveholders refused to be persuaded, and indeed abused and attacked their would-be persuaders, Adams was not optimistic. Slavery would end in the United States, he said, "because it has been explicitly promised in the holy Scriptures, and because the progress towards that improvement in the condition of man upon earth is clearly indicated by the whole tenor of human history." But it would not happen in his time, and would "be preceded by convulsions and revolutions in the moral, political, and physical world, from which I turn away my eyes to more cheering contemplations. . . ."

ON THE RELATED QUESTIONS of race and racial equality Adams was also a moderate. As President he had received free blacks socially with an ease that would not be seen again in the White House until

Lincoln's time. And yet, again like Lincoln, Adams fell short of racial equalitarianism. In his published conversation on Shakespeare with Fanny Kemble in 1836 he criticized *Othello* because he believed Desdemona's love for her African husband to be "contrary to the laws of nature." He was dubious about the capacity of blacks for self-government in republics like Haiti and Liberia. Yet he was curious about them as well. In 1837 he responded to a letter from Thomas Gaillard, the mulatto son of a man whose cousin had been a colleague of his in the Senate, sympathizing with Gaillard's argument for equal rights and seeking more information about his background, especially that of his slave mother. That same year he took an interest in the case of Dorcas Allen, a black woman who had killed her two children to prevent them from being sold into slavery and had tried to kill herself. Mrs. Allen had been free for many years, but owing to her lack of papers had been forced back into servitude. Because she was valuable "property," a jury had acquitted her of murder charges. The case attracted the attention not only of Adams, but of his cousin, Judge William Cranch, and Francis Scott Key. After visits from her husband, Adams donated $50 to a fund raised to buy Dorcas Allen's freedom.

His ambivalent relationship with the abolitionists was duplicated with other movements of the day. Following his defense of women's right to petition in 1838, many feminists may have thought in Adams they had a kindred spirit. Not so. In a letter to his cousin Anna Quincy Thaxter, he threw cold water on any idea that he thought women equal to men. It was true, he said, that his defense of women's right to petition Congress had something to do with the fact that in his youth he had grown up with some remarkable women, including of course his own mother. But, he continued, in the stilted language of the day, "my intercourse with the sex since that time has not left me ignorant of the imperfections in which they participate as a portion of the human race nor of the frailties incident to their physical and intellectual nature." In a brief address to a group of Quincy women who had gathered to honor him and his wife, Adams made clear that while he thought it appropriate for women to concern themselves with humanitarian matters like slavery, no one could expect them to have opinions on presumably more complex questions like banking, currency, or internal improvements. He remained opposed to women's suffrage.

The pattern repeated itself in other areas. He was sympathetic to the peace movements of the day, but was hardly a pacifist. He honored the sabbath and kept it holy by attending church, usually twice, but that did not prevent him from travelling or working when he found it necessary. He favored the temperance movement, as behooved one in whose family there lurked a tendency toward alcohol addiction, yet in an address to the Norfolk County Temperance Society, he reminded them that the Bible had not interdicted the consumption of wine, only its abuse. He once stunned his doctor when he told him that he took "one, sometimes two, and occasionally three glasses of Madeira wine after dinner." And after a meal at a friend's home in company with several others, he correctly identified eleven out of fourteen Madeiras as they came round the table. As his most famous biographer has remarked, "doubtless he could not have hung up such a score unless he kept in practice."

As a product of late eighteenth- and early nineteenth-century America, Adams did not escape the prejudices of the Anglo-Saxon Protestant "host culture." His diary is often marred by disparaging remarks about Jews and Catholics, especially since both groups seemed to have an affinity for the Democratic party. Yet when his coachman Jeremy Leary was fatally injured in a carriage accident he was deeply moved, and attended his Roman Catholic funeral. Over his long life he numbered many Catholics among his friends and once exasperated an evangelical Protestant minister by describing them as one of the most persecuted sects in America.

Men of his time therefore found John Quincy Adams difficult to classify: neither Whig nor Democrat, radical nor conservative, orthodox nor reformer. But he had not departed from the view stated during the Missouri debates that the color of a man's skin should not determine his rights. It was perhaps for this reason in 1840, that those who were seeking freedom for the captives arrested on the slave schooner *Amistad* turned to John Quincy Adams for help.

Chapter Eight

○

"A Stout Heart and a Clear Conscience, and Never Despair"

THE *AMISTAD* CASE was the major topic of conversation in antislavery circles from 1839 to 1841. Engaged in transporting Africans from one Cuban port to another, the captain and crew of the *Amistad* were attacked and killed by their "cargo" under the direction of Cinqué, who became the leader of the Africans, the two surviving whites forced to sail for Africa. Through a series of deceptions they in fact sailed up the American coast where they were captured near Long Island in August, 1839. Spanish authorities demanded that the vessel, Cinqué, and the Africans be turned over to them for return to Cuba and eventual punishment. Several treaties and precedents allegedly required the return of slave property in such cases. But abolitionists and their allies mobilized on behalf of Cinqué and the Africans of the *Amistad*, and for once public opinion in the North was on their side.

The issue was whether the captives were, in fact, slaves. The international slave trade had been outlawed by most nations, including Spain, for many years. Those caught and convicted of engaging in it were subject to the death penalty, and the victims were to be returned home. The inability of any of the *Amistad* captives to speak Spanish, plus their youth, clearly suggested that they had been abducted from Africa and therefore were not slaves. Yet the Spanish insisted that American courts had no business prying into the matter. In 1840 both the federal district and circuit courts decided in favor of the captives, but the Van Buren administration, always sensitive to the demands of the planters of the South in an election year, appealed the decision to the Supreme Court.

Adams had been following the *Amistad* affair since it first developed. He offered his legal services to Lewis Tappan, the wealthy New York abolitionist who was organizing support for the captives. When the case moved to the Supreme Court, Tappan accepted his offer, and asked him to appear along with Roger Baldwin, a well-known Connecticut attorney who had already shepherded the case through the lower courts. When he had made the offer of assistance, Adams had no idea of a personal court appearance. He had not argued before the Supreme Court since 1809, and had never had much confidence in himself as a lawyer. But Tappan persisted, and Adams finally agreed, hoping his age would not betray him. With the rest of the country absorbed in the presidential election of 1840, Adams and his son went over the merits of the *Amistad* case.

Distrusting the Democratic Van Buren administration, Adams had requested all the relevant papers in the *Amistad* affair from the State Department. The letters to the Spanish Minister from Secretary of State John Forsyth—a Georgia slaveholder—were clearly prejudiced against the captives. Moreover, anticipating a proslavery decision, Van Buren had ordered a naval vessel to be readied to transport the Africans back to Cuba, where they awaited trial for murder. The very fact that the administration was appealing the decision when it was not a party to the suit was proof enough for Adams of a proslavery bias. Nor did he have much confidence in the Supreme Court. All but two of its members were appointees of Jackson or Van Buren. Chief Justice Roger Taney sixteen years later would preside over the proslavery *Dred Scott* decision.

The hearing began in late February, 1841. The argument of the administration was simple enough. Treaties with Spain going back to 1795—and renewed by Secretary of State John Quincy Adams in

In this portrait of Cinqué, painted while he and his fellow Africans were awaiting trial in Connecticut, Nathaniel Jocelyn chose to portray his subject in a classical Roman Toga, rather than in the more colorful dress of the Mendi nation to which he belonged. *Courtesy of the New Haven Colony Historical Society, New Haven, Connecticut.*

1819—required respect for the property rights of the citizens of both nations. Slaves were property under both American and Spanish law. The Spanish Minister stipulated that the surviving whites legally owned the Africans, and international comity required that his word be final, lest in future cases a Spanish court decide not to take the word of an American Minister. The Court had no choice but to turn the captives over to the Spanish authorities for deportation.

Baldwin, in rebuttal, attacked the right of the federal government to participate in a case where it had no interest. Slaves and slavery were state matters, not national. The Africans of the *Amistad* were subject to the laws of the state of New York where they first were taken. None of the treaties cited applied to the *Amistad* since the Africans were not pirates, robbers, or assassins, nor was the vessel shipwrecked at the time of its capture. In spite of fraudulent attempts to classify them as slaves, Baldwin argued, the Africans were free men who had exercised their right of self-defense in capturing the vessel and forcing it back home.

Then came Adams, with a withering attack on the Van Buren Administration and the Spanish Minister's charge that the Africans were robbers and pirates. "Who were the merchandise and who were the robbers?" he asked. "According to the construction of the Spanish minister, the merchandise were the robbers and the robbers were the merchandise. The merchandise was rescued out of its own hands, and the robbers were rescued out of the hands of the robbers." At the end of the day, after four and a half hours, he was not finished.

That night one of the Justices died in his sleep, and the proceedings were postponed for a week. Adams then took up where he left off, hailing Cinqué and the Africans as liberators in the traditions of ancient Greece, and pointing dramatically at the Declaration of Independence, a copy of which hung on the wall of the courtroom. "The moment you come to the Declaration of Independence, that every man has a right to life and liberty, as an inalienable right, this case is decided," he said. "I ask nothing more on behalf of these unfortunate men, than this Declaration." Adams closed with an emotional account of his last appearance before the Court in 1809, in a case defending the rights of property. Now he was defending life and liberty. "Such has been the dictate of my destiny." He dramatically bade farewell to "this Honorable Court." Justice Joseph Story, one of the two non-Jacksonian appointees, wrote to his wife that the old man's argument was "extraordinary . . . for its power, for its bitter sarcasm, and its dealing with topics far beyond the record and points of discussion."

In the 1840's the Supreme Court moved faster than in later years, and within a week they were ready with their decision. Adams sat nervously in the courtroom, like a youthful attorney awaiting a decision in his first case. Justice Story rose to give the Court's opinion: a good sign. Ignoring for the most part Adams' contentions concerning executive bias, Story stayed close to the argument offered by Baldwin. The Africans had never been slaves, he said, therefore the treaties and precedents regarding the restoration of slave "property" did not apply. The essence of district and circuit court decisions was upheld, with the Court directing that Cinqué and his friends be released immediately. All but one of the justices concurred.

Adams and the abolitionists congratulated each other on the outcome, temporarily setting aside their differences over the abolition of slavery in the District. "Some of us may have at times done thee injustice. . . ," wrote the Quaker abolitionist poet John Greenleaf Whittier "but, I believe we now appreciate thy motives." Adams spent the next few weeks revising and expanding the text of his argument for publication. He franked and circulated hundreds of copies all over the United States, to members of Congress, to the American foreign service abroad, and to the foreign diplomatic corps at home.

He was now almost seventy-four. "With a shaking hand, a darkening eye, a drowsy brain, and with all my faculties dropping from me one by one, and the teeth . . . dropping from my head," he felt perhaps it was time to quit. The census of 1840 had resulted in a loss of two seats for Massachusetts, and his district had been redrawn so that it contained mostly new constituents. He could make a graceful exit, coming after such an important victory. But, as he told a correspondent earlier, he had spent nearly his entire life in public service; he was no longer fit for anything else. "More than sixty years of incessant active intercourse with the world has made political movement to me as much a necessity of life as atmospheric air. This is the weakness of my nature, which I have intellect enough to perceive, but not energy to control." From Massachusetts an admiring Ralph Waldo Emerson wrote in his diary that Adams seemed to gain strength from controversy. "He is like one of those old cardinals, who, as quick as he is chosen Pope, throws away his crutches and his crookedness, and is as straight as a boy. He is an old roué, who cannot live on slops, but must have sulphuric acid in his tea."

By now nearly everything he said or did in public was noted and reported. He received so many invitations to speak that he had to put a notice in the papers that he could not even respond to the invitations, let alone accept them. Time and again he would be called from his seat in the House by a colleague who had a constituent insisting on shaking hands with John Quincy Adams. Young ladies, in the fashion of the day, would present him their autograph albums, often asking in addition to his signature a few lines of poetry, for which he was also building a reputation. His lengthy poem, *The Wants of Man* appeared in several newspapers in 1841. Even his youthful verses about "A Vision", written about the long-dead Mary Frazier and other Newburyport girls in the 1780's now surfaced in the press. Adams did not know what to make of it. "I am so tickled with professions of veneration that I believe them all sincere," he confessed to his diary in 1841. But were they? "It might be wiser to treat them all with contempt; but it would not be so good-natured."

He set a model of commitment to his job in an era of congressional absenteeism. Usually he was the first to take his seat in the House each day, and among the last to leave. As Edward Everett later remarked, he would hardly have been more surprised to see one of the columns of the House chamber missing from its pedestal than John Quincy Adams missing from his seat. His status did not mean he was universally beloved, but even southern Congressmen recognized his standing. For them, to go home and report that they had tangled with John Quincy Adams was a badge of courage, if not of good judgment.

Ever since New Year's Day, 1831, when they were surprised by some three hundred visitors who stopped by to pay their respects, the Adamses celebrated the new year by holding an open house. Adams kept a close watch on attendance. In 1832 there were "foreign legations, members of Congress, citizens, Shawanese Indians, and Quakers, officers of the army and navy, and some strangers." The numbers increased with the passage of time. True, most well-wishers had just come from shaking hands with Andrew Jackson or Martin Van Buren a few blocks away, but it was a source of satisfaction nonetheless.

On matters not having to do with slavery or Texas, Adams' impartiality was trusted by nearly everyone. If there was a disputed election, or a contested boundary line between two new states, Adams would be asked to help settle the matter. When the House of Representatives was unable to select a Speaker in 1839, owing to a close division between Whigs and Democrats, Adams was drafted to preside while the matter was settled. Escorted to the Speaker's chair by two southerners, Adams presided over the House for the next several days, sipping coffee and munching toast until the work was done.

Two of Charles Francis Adams' children left pen portraits of their grandfather. Charles Francis Adams, Jr., born in 1835, remembered him as "a very old-looking gentleman, with a bald head and a white fringe of hair—writing, writing—with a perpetual inkstain on the fore-finger and thumb of the right hand." His most vivid memories were of Adams standing or sitting on the front porch of his son's home "watch in hand, noting the earliest and last rays of the summer day." Henry Adams, in his famous *Education of Henry Adams*, recounted his forays into his grandfather's study and dressing-closet "where a row of tumblers, inverted on the shelf, covered caterpillars which were supposed to become moths or butterflies, but never did." He told how as a youngster he had almost succeeded in a rebellion against going to school, when the door to Adams' library opened, his grandfather slowly descended, took his hand without a word, and escorted him down the road until the young Henry "found himself seated inside the school, and obviously the centre of curious if not malevolent criticism."

In spite of the publicity generated by his antislavery stance and his attacks on the Gag Rule, at no time was Adams a one-issue Congressman. The record shows that he participated fully in nearly every matter brought before the House. He joined in the attacks upon the Van Buren administration's banking policies, repeatedly (and futilely) exposed the fraud and cruelty of Van Buren's Indian policies, sponsored a bill for the more efficient collection of the revenue. He took a particular interest in the disposition of the unusual bequest to Congress by the Englishman James Smithson, to be used for "the increase and diffusion of knowledge among men." It took ten years for the funds to be properly put to use, but the creation of the Smithsonian Institution in 1846 owes as much to John Quincy Adams as to anyone else in public life.

No nineteenth-century President, not even Thomas Jefferson, was more familiar with the progress and possibilities of science than John Quincy Adams. Although as President he failed to persuade Congress that the federal government should play a greater role in supporting research, he never abandoned the idea. When he learned of the Smithson bequest in 1836, he saw an opportunity. He moved a resolution to dispatch an agent to London to collect the funds— over half a million dollars in gold. "The earth was given to man for cultivation, to the improvement of his own condition," he argued. "Whoever increases his knowledge, multiplies the uses to which he is enabled to turn the gift of his Creator to his own benefit." The resolution passed without opposition. He made the matter a pet project, so much so that he was appointed Chairman of a special Smithsonian Committee in the House. He met with President Van Buren and members of his cabinet, urging them to implement the bequest. But as Adams had reason to know, the Jacksonians, with their view of government as a "simple machine," were not favorable to the use of federal power for "improvement." Some Democrats even favored returning the money, lest government be expanded into illegitimate areas. Often the Smithsonian Committee's meetings had to be adjourned owing to the lack of a quorum. Pending their disposition, Van Buren's administration invested the Smithson funds in state bonds, which promptly declined in value.

There was disagreement, too, as to the precise use of the funds. Adams was determined that only the income from the bequest should be spent, not the capital. He also opposed the creation of a school or university with the money. America already had schools and universities, he said. Smithson's will demanded an institution that would serve needs of the public, not the elite; Adams wanted "no monkish stalls for lazy idlers." Finally, he was determined that the money be used, at least in part, to create a national astronomical observatory, along the lines of that at Greenwich, in England. The mockery of his "lighthouses of the skies" in 1825 still rankled him. Adams kept up the pressure, writing countless letters and composing two lectures on the bequest. They could not let James Smithson down, he told his audiences. The following year his bill for the creation of the Institution failed, owing largely to the disagreements over the observatory, and the national university. Dismayed, Adams did not give up.

PASSING OVER KNOWN QUANTITIES like Henry Clay and Daniel Webster, the Whig party in 1840 nominated a war hero, William Henry Harrison, and swept to victory over Van Buren and the Democrats. They adopted the techniques first used by the Jacksonians: mass meetings, parades, bonfires, and hoopla. The age of "mass politics" had arrived, as tens of thousands marched for Van Buren or "Tippecanoe and Tyler too."

While many applauded the new trend in politics, as demonstrated by record-high turnouts in most states, Adams did not. He saw instead a greater potential for violence, as when a Whig parade marshal was killed in Baltimore following a Democratic attempt to break up the procession. Most might approve of the conventions that had replaced the old party caucuses; Adams denounced them as frauds: "an immense unwieldy mass of political machinery to accomplish nothing." Many might be excited at the prospect of bringing political campaigning down to the grass roots; Adams was shocked instead by national political leaders like Clay, Webster, Calhoun, and others "travelling about the country like Methodist preachers. . . ." How could serious matters be discussed in such an atmosphere? Where would it end? "Immense assemblages of people are held—of twenty, thirty, fifty thousand souls—where the first orators of the nation address the multitude, not one in ten of whom can hear them. . . ." At times he was sure he was witnessing "a revolution in the habits and manners of the people" that would end in civil war. There was, he feared, a degeneration in American political institutions and a "change in the manners of the people."

Indeed, political life and American society in general had taken on a more violent tone since he first appeared in Congress. Assaults, fistfights, and duels among Congressmen had accompanied the rise of sectional and partisan rivalries. Fistfights were harmless, but duels were another matter. Most of them involved southerners, influenced by the "code of honor" still enjoying popularity in their section. Adams linked the practice to the South and its "peculiar institution." It was an "appendage of slavery" used to threaten and bully those who voiced their disagreement with southern ways. Northerners usually turned down challenges, which left them open to the charge of cowardice. Adams was tired of it. He sponsored anti-duelling legislation following a particularly senseless affair in 1838, in which the Kentucky Whig William Graves killed the Maine Democrat Jonathan Cilley. He wanted duelling made punishable by death, but his bill was watered down before it became law.

Duelling was only the most obvious of the several trends Adams thought were disrupting the legislative and executive process. Andrew Jackson himself had been physically assaulted once and later was the object of an unsuccessful assassination attempt. The violence in Washington reflected, Adams believed, the society as a whole, for which Jackson himself, the duellist and frontier brawler, was partly to blame. In 1834 a mob in Boston sacked and burned a Catholic convent, provoked by hysterical attacks on the Catholic religion and wild tales of deviant behavior taking place behind convent walls. There were riots in Baltimore in 1835, and in 1838 a Philadelphia mob burned down an abolitionist meeting house that had just opened a few days earlier in the name of free speech. Out in Illinois, another mob attacked the printing house of the abolitionist Elijah Lovejoy, killed him, and threw his press into the Mississippi. Adams wrote the Introduction for the *Memoir* published in Lovejoy's honor. Yet when a protest meeting was called in Boston over the

Lovejoy affair, the Attorney General for Massachusetts defended the mob.

Yet, in spite of his reservations, Adams could hardly disapprove of the result of the election of 1840: a humiliating defeat for Martin Van Buren, the architect of his own downfall in 1828. And by then Adams had to admit that of the two parties, the Whigs were the less objectionable to him. Many friends and allies were elected or re-elected that year, including several antislavery Congressmen. As he watched from the sidelines, his criticisms of the raucous nature of mass politics were tempered by the result. Perhaps, he mused, after twelve years of retreat, his principles of economic nationalism and the use of government as an "engine of improvement" would be revived. Perhaps, after twelve years of clouds, the sun was breaking through. "Is the time arriving for me to speak?" he asked his diary— as if he had been silent all those years.

Adams did not have a high opinion of the new President. He had reluctantly appointed Harrison Minister to Colombia when he himself was President, but described the General as a "shallow mind, a political adventurer, not without talents, but self-sufficient, vain, and indiscreet." Since then the Whigs had converted him into a hero, like Andrew Jackson, who had left his humble surroundings to serve his nation. In vain did Democrats point out that, as a member of an old Virginia family and the son of a signer of the Declaration of Independence, Harrison's origins were far from humble. Now that "Old Tippecanoe" was elected, Adams was willing to give him another chance. "If he is not found time-serving, demagogical, unsteady, and Western-sectional," he wrote, "he will more than satisfy my present expectations."

Declining an invitation to attend Harrison's inaugural, he watched the parade as it went past his house. There was "not the slightest symptom of conflicting passion" he conceded, and everything was conducted "in perfect order." Two weeks later he reported gleefully that the spoils system was being turned against the Democrats, that "the removals from office have commenced and they are going along swimmingly." With the *Amistad* victory under his belt, and a Whig-controlled Congress about to meet in special session at Harrison's request, surely this was no time to quit. Now the

Smithsonian bequest could be realized, the giveaway of the public lands could be halted, and internal improvements restored.

After barely a month in office, the sixty-eight-year-old Harrison died. Fate's pendulum had swung again, carrying a cruel lesson for John Quincy Adams and all who had hoped for a repeal of the Jackson era. If he thought little of Harrison, Adams thought far less of his successor John Tyler, a states-rights man who was put on the ticket to placate the South: "a political sectarian, of the slave-driving, Virginian, Jeffersonian school, principled against all improvement." Harrison's death, said Adams, "brings to a test that provision of the Constitution which places in the Executive Chair a man never thought of it by anybody." He even thought Tyler should call himself "Acting President," but few agreed.

Within a year, the Whig victory, the Whig hopes, and very nearly the Whig party itself lay in ruins. True to his states' rights views, which were closer to those of Jackson and Van Buren than to most Whigs, Tyler vetoed two bank bills and a tariff bill passed by the special session in the summer of 1841. His entire cabinet resigned in protest, save Secretary of State Daniel Webster. The Whigs then split, most of them rallying around Henry Clay and his economic nationalism, a minority sticking with Tyler, who eventually was read out of the party. His actions, wrote Adams bitterly, returned the country once again to "the political swindlers so recently driven from power."

Adams, too, suffered as a result of the Tyler succession. He had hoped to be named Chairman of the Foreign Relations Committee, a position which had eluded him under the Jacksonians. Instead, he was named Chairman of the Indian Affairs Committee, apparently in recognition of his past attacks on Jacksonian Indian policy. After thinking it over, he asked to be relieved of the assignment. If there was any area he wished to avoid, it was the "sickening mass of putrefaction" that constituted Indian affairs. By 1841 nearly all of the Indians east of the Mississippi had been either exterminated or driven west. To serve on this committee now "would keep a perpetual harrow upon my feelings, with a total impotence to render any useful service."

Only in the fight against the Gag Rule were there signs of

progress. In the special session Adams once again served notice that he would move to rescind the Rule, and proceeded to do so, following up with a three-hour speech that went over the entire ground of the Rule's violation of the Bill of Rights, the shame that it brought to the House, and the linkage between the slaveholding mentality and the denial of civil liberties to American citizens. To his surprise and delight, his motion was adopted by a vote of 112–104. Three days later a motion by a northern Democrat to reconsider the matter failed, 116–110. Then the slaveholders brought in their heavy artillery and launched an attack on Adams that lasted two days. They changed enough votes to force a reconsideration, after which his motion was defeated, 107–104. But it was close, closer than it had ever been. Northern Democrats who in the past had stood with their southern allies were beginning to defect in the face of pressure from their constituents. Adams tried again in the regular session the following December, but this time his opponents were ready for him and he was beaten immediately. He did not care personally about these defeats. "It is the disgrace and degradation of my country. This is the iron that enters into my soul."

Although defeated on the Gag Rule, Adams finally became Chairman of the House Foreign Relations committee after Henry Clay's friends summarily removed the incumbent Tylerite Chairman. At last Adams held the position in Congress that he thought he deserved.

IN LATE 1841 THE MOST pressing foreign policy issues again involved Great Britain. There was continued disagreement over the northeastern boundary of the United States with Canada, a potentially explosive issue in Maine and northern New England. There was the right of "visitation," claimed by the British, of ships attempting to evade the ban on the international slave trade by illegally flying the American flag. This aggravated southerners. There was the matter of Alexander McLeod, a British citizen currently on trial for murder in New York state for actions that occurred while he was an agent of Her Majesty's Government. Britain warned that if McLeod was executed, there would be war. And there was the British opposition to Texas annexation, which irritated annexationists everywhere. Except for the Maine boundary question, Adams, who had built his earlier diplomatic career as an Anglophobe, who had once said the right of search on the high seas was worse than slavery, sympathized with the British position. And now he was Chairman of the Foreign Relations Committee. Thus southerners, annexationists, and Democrats viewed his ascendancy with hostility and looked for ways to topple him.

Adams provided them with an opportunity in January, 1842, when he introduced a petition from Haverhill, Massachusetts, calling for a peaceable dissolution of the Union. The petitioners were abolitionists who believed that the benefits from a union with slaveholders were not worth the moral and economic cost. As with the petitions on slavery in the District of Columbia, Adams was careful to disassociate himself from the content of the petition, urging that it be given to a special committee with instructions to report against it. It was "not yet time" he said, ambiguously, for such drastic action. Thomas W. Gilmer, a Tylerite Whig from Virginia, promptly moved a resolution stating that Adams had "justly incurred the censure of this House."

It was 1837 all over again. Word spread quickly that John Quincy Adams was single-handedly taking on the House of Representatives. The galleries filled. Stenographers reported they missed a good portion of the debate because of the disorder in the hall. Feelings and emotions ran high, and it was resolved to adjourn the House before nightfall lest, in the words of one correspondent "a candle-light sitting would bring in riot, fighting, the use of knives and pistols, and murder. . . ." Henry Clay left his seat in the Senate to watch the ex-President. "The papers will inform you of the afflicting scenes passing in the House of Representatives," he wrote to a friend. "They will fill every patriot bosom with distress."

Democrats and Tylerites met and resolved to both censure Adams and remove him from the Foreign Relations Committee. The next day Congressman Thomas Marshall, nephew of the late Chief Justice, introduced a resolution accusing Adams of encouraging high treason. "Again my dear Charles we are plunged in hot water by

the old question of the right of Petition perhaps too warmly maintained by your Father," wrote Louisa Adams wearily.

In his defense, Adams once more fell back upon the Declaration
of Independence, which he had the Clerk of the House read aloud.
That document, written by a slaveholding Virginian, upheld the
right of any people to "peacefully dissolve the bands that had
connected them with another." As for Marshall's resolution, he
claimed the right of defense under the Sixth Amendment. After all,
high treason was a serious crime. He made it clear that if they
insisted on going through with the censure proceedings, his "defense" might take weeks.

After two weeks of wrangling, with time out to deal with essential business, the House realized it was in a hopeless muddle.
Tylerite Whigs and Democrats were willing to stretch out the
proceedings to embarrass and paralyze the national Whigs. Finally
enough southern Whigs agreed to call it a day, and voted with their
northern colleagues to table the censure motions. Unabashed, Adams
then proceeded to present nearly two hundred more petitions, most
of which were rejected under the Gag Rule.

In reporting the censure "trial" of John Quincy Adams, most
Whig newspapers were sympathetic; Democratic journals were not.
The Democratic papers usually omitted any mention of his opposition to the Haverhill petition. To them it made no difference. They
believed Adams was less interested in the right of petition than he
was in stirring up trouble. Adams, they claimed, who had once stood
for the Union over everything, who had said in 1831 that Calhoun's
ideas of nullification were treasonous, had now become a disunionist, pure and simple. As the Democratic Washington *Globe* put it,
"He hastens others on, but is in no haste himself. He does not take
positions himself until he has made them by others, and then points
to them as things that *will* be. Surely and diligently he digs at the
foundations of the Union, and prepares the dark mine for its
overthrow."

Had they been able to read his diary, of course, they would have
learned that as early as 1820 he believed that if the Union were to
dissolve, slavery would be the solvent. For nearly a generation it had
been southerners and defenders of slavery who had threatened, as

they put it, to "calculate the value of the Union." The Haverhill petition was a hint that disunionist sentiment over slavery was not a southern monopoly. "When a Union fails of the ends for which it was formed, why should not freemen be allowed to 'right the wrong'" asked a correspondent from abolitionist-minded Rochester, New York. "Mr. Adams' movement has caused much excitement," reported the ever-watchful John C. Calhoun. "It is the first open development of abolition towards disunion."

The aftermath saw five southern Congressmen resign from the Foreign Relations Committee, professing to be unable to work with Adams. Five new members were named, three of whom also asked to be excused. Three more were added, who agreed to serve for the rest of the Congress. No more attempts were made to sabotage Adams' position as Chairman. It was clear that he was the target of the Texas annexationists, and that if the Democrats regained control in the next congressional election, he would be removed.

By the summer of 1842 all semblance of leadership among the Whigs in Congress had disappeared. They had failed to enact any part of their nationalist program, thanks to Tyler's use of the veto. Henry Clay had resigned from the Senate and gone home in disgust—and to prepare for the election of 1844. From the comfort of his farm in Kentucky, Clay wrote to Adams, urging him to assert leadership over the Whigs, and confront Tyler's abuse of the office he held only by accident. In every past national crisis, he told his former chief, there had always been someone step forward "who was adequate to the service of conducting us in safety through the impending danger. Upon the present occasion that noble office is yours."

Adams did what he could, although he was again reluctant to "take the lead" at this stage of his life. But after Tyler twice vetoed a tariff bill because it provided for sharing the proceeds of the sale of public lands to the states, thus spreading the wealth throughout the whole Union, Adams led the furious Whig reply. Appointed Chairman of a select committee to consider Tyler's veto message, he reported out a constitutional amendment that would make a major-

ity of each house of Congress, not two-thirds, sufficient to override
a presidential veto.

This was another change of heart for Adams. For most of his life,
from the days of the "Publicola" letters in 1791, to his opposition to
the Jackson censure in 1834, he had thought the tendency of
American politics was to weaken executive power. But not in the
summer of 1842. It was not only the matter of his vetoes, but Tyler's
insistence that in the absence of any tariff law—the old one having
expired—he could still collect duties, that caused the Whigs to view
him as a tyrant worse than Jackson himself. Adams' report, signed by
a majority of the select committee, hinted at an impeachment of
Tyler, but recognized that the votes were not there, no more than
they were for a constitutional amendment. A third tariff bill, minus
the provision for sharing land revenues, was finally passed. "The
long agony was over," Adams wrote, "and the lands are lost forever."

That autumn Adams went home to uncertain prospects for
re-election in his new district, which contained more Democratic
voters than his old one. A series of maladies and discomforts that
summer he interpreted to be warnings of "a sudden termination to
my life." By all odds he should be planning for retirement or worse,
he again told himself. "I see my duty, but I procrastinate." He
prepared what he called a "take-leave" address to the constituents of
his old district. Should he be defeated by his new electors, it would
serve as a Farewell Address.

On September 17, Adams was escorted to the Congregational
church in Braintree, where his parents lay entombed. The building
was, according to his account, "crowded in all its parts almost to
suffocation." In the custom of the day, men were seated on the first
floor, the women and children in the galleries. Banners hung on the
right and left which read "Welcome defender of the right of petition," and "Shame on the nation that fosters and sustains an institution, which dares assail and would destroy the sacred right of
petition." There he delivered a three-hour speech, "without inter-
ruption, and without a moment's flagging of attention."

He concentrated his fire upon John Tyler, the accidental President, and Andrew Jackson, his old nemesis. First, there was Texas.
Once, as Secretary of State, he had insisted that some day the North

American continent and the United States would be the same; now he was fully convinced of the plot to spread slavery throughout the remaining territories. Texas annexation was but the first step. The "dismemberment" of Mexico, he warned, and the acquisition of her territory from the Rio Grande north to San Francisco, had long been the "gigantic and darling project of Andrew Jackson." And for what purpose? To "restore" slavery to Texas and to surround the North "with a girdle of slave states." American expansion to the southwest no longer meant expanding the empire of freedom, but rather extending the chains of slavery.

Slavery was not just a menace in distant territories, he continued. It was threatening to strangle freedom in the North was well. The minority slaveholding interest was unified when it came to protecting itself; the majority free states were not. Slave property was represented in Congress and the Electoral College under the "three-fifths" clause; northern property was not. The result was all too apparent. The President of the United States was a slaveholder. So was the President of the Senate, the Speaker of the House, the Chief Justice of the United States, a majority of the Supreme Court, and half the President's cabinet. It had always been this way, almost since the founding of the Republic. "With such consequences staring us in the face, what are we to think when we are told that the Government of the United States is a democracy of numbers; a Government of the majority of the People?" Yet those who called themselves "Democrats" were remarkable for their appeal to the poor against the rich, "provided their skins are white." Democracy? "Why upon what foundation can Democracy find a foothold to stand, but upon the rights of man; upon the self-evident truths of the Declaration of Independence? Democracy and Slavery! . . . Are not fraud and hypocrisy the religion of the man who calls himself a democrat and holds his fellow-man in bondage?"

Finally he turned to the Tyler administration: the president's use of the veto to frustrate the will of the majority, his warmongering against Mexico and Britain, his allies' attempts to censure and remove Adams from the Foreign Relations Committee, his illegal collection of the tariff, but above all his veto of the distribution of land sales revenue to all the states. Adams looked out at his audience and began his lament for the lost public lands and the chance for their improvement. "I had long entertained and cherished the hope," he declared

> that these public lands were among the chosen instruments of Almighty power, not only of promoting the virtue, welfare, and happiness of millions upon millions of individuals and families of the human race, but of improving the condition of man, by establishing the practical, self-evident truth of the natural equality of all mankind, as the foundation of human government, and by banishing Slavery and War from the earth. . . . Was all this an Utopian daydream? Is the one talent, entrusted by the Lord of the harvest, for the improvement of the condition of man, to be extinguished by the blasting breath of Slavery?

He had been accused, said Adams, of using "violent and passionate language" on the floor of the House. Possibly it was true, for which he apologized. But they should remember the circumstances, remember that twice in five years there had been a plan to censure and even expel him from Congress. No one else had attracted such attention. He concluded by reading from a toast given in South Carolina on the last Fourth of July: "May we never want a Democrat to trip up the heels of a Federalist, or a hangman to prepare a halter for John Quincy Adams."

No toasts were offered that day in the church, but resolutions of thanks were adopted, and the crowd concluded by singing a special "Ode" to J. Q. Adams, written to the tune of "America":

> But time shall touch the page
> That tells how Quincy's sage
> Has dared to live. . . .

Adams was narrowly re-elected that year, but the Whigs were soundly defeated, losing control of Congress. A month later he was back in Washington, ready to move again against the Gag Rule. But his opponents were ready too, and they tabled his motion, 106–102.

President Tyler now stepped up the pressure for Texas annexation. Resolutions favoring it were sent to Congress from the legislatures of Mississippi and Alabama, countered by resolutions of opposition from Massachusetts, Vermont, Connecticut, and Ohio. As the outgoing chairman of a committee of an expiring Congress, Adams was in a weakened position to resist. Out of desperation he offered resolutions that denied the power of Congress or any other branch of government to annex a foreign country and implied that resistance by the free states to annexation would be proper and constitutional. After these failed, he signed a protest issued by twelve other antislavery Congressmen declaring annexation "identical with dissolution" of the Union. As he had with the Haverhill petition the year before, Adams was now flirting with the "nullification" and disunionist ideas he had denounced earlier in his life.

That summer he turned down an invitation to appear with President Tyler at the dedication of the Bunker Hill Monument in Massachusetts. He regretted, too, that he could not go to Bangor, Maine, to observe the tenth anniversary of the abolition of slavery in the British Empire, but sent them a rousing antislavery letter nonetheless. He did relent in the case of the Massachusetts Historical Society, who had asked for a lecture on an appropriate topic dealing with New England history. He seized the occasion to praise New Englanders for having laid the foundations of human freedom, justice, and democracy in America. No longer was the nation threatened by outside powers, as she had been in the years following the Revolution. Now, he said, the threat came from within itself, from the nation's very success and "temptation to aggrandizement." There were those who might look forward to conquering all of Mexico in a war over Texas, but Adams warned against assimilating "men of other races, the children of other blood, bred to other opinions, accustomed to other institutions, trained to other prejudices, and disciplined to other principles."

When the day of Tyler's arrival in Boston came, as with Jackson ten years earlier, John Quincy Adams stayed at home. The new Bunker Hill Monument was carved out of Quincy granite, and he would have liked to have attended, but the presence of the slaveholding Tyler was too much. From the porch of Charles' house he could see the monument and hear the cannon. Memories of 1775 stirred within him.

Other memories were soon to come. Charles had been selected to give the annual Fourth of July oration in Boston at Faneuil Hall, just fifty years to the day when Adams himself had delivered it in 1793. Already being compared to his father, the thirty-six-year-old younger Adams was beginning to lose his hair and resemble him physically as well. John Quincy Adams rode into Boston to hear his son, and then back to Quincy. "I went up the hill at sunset, witnessed the fireworks on the common of Boston. No language can express the agitation of my feelings and the remembrances of this day."

TWO DAYS LATER HE LEFT for an extended trip by stagecoach, boat, and railroad that turned into one of the most remarkable journeys of his life. Originally planned as an excursion to benefit the health of his daughter-in-law Abigail, it turned into a triumphant procession for "Old Man Eloquent." The Adams party travelled westward to New York state, where they turned north and travelled down the Canadian side of Lake Ontario, crossing back to New York at Niagara Falls. After viewing the Falls, they moved up the river to Buffalo, where they were met at the dock "by shouting multitudes," the puzzled ex-President wrote in his diary. At Buffalo he was invited to speak at Rochester, but not before he stopped at Batavia on the way. At Rochester he was met by the thunder of cannon and the ringing of bells, and toured the city much in the manner of visiting royalty.

This was John Quincy Adams country. Yankees had first settled there in the 1790's, and they were followed by others who had taken advantage of the Erie Canal. They had voted heavily for him in 1828 and needed no lectures on the virtues of "internal improvement." This was also the "burnt-over district," where anti-Masonry had ignited, and where abolitionism and other reform movements were still strong. At Auburn he was met by former Governor Seward, at Utica he was met by a torchlight procession. The next day he visited the Utica Female Seminary, where he dissolved into tears as one of the speakers read from the recently-published collection of letters from Abigail Adams to her son, edited by her grandson, Charles Francis Adams.

That was not the end of it. While at Niagara Falls he received an invitation to come to Cincinnati, Ohio, to dedicate the new astronomical observatory there. After thinking it over for a day, Adams accepted, promising to come sometime in November, before the opening of the new Congress. He had a reason for accepting this invitation above all others. For more than forty years, from the days when he dabbled in scientific experiments with his friends in Boston, to when he had watched the sun set and rise from his bedroom in St. Petersburg, to when he had gathered his children about him in England to watch the heavens through a telescope, to his authorship of the *Report on Weights and Measures*, John Quincy Adams had maintained his interest in astronomy. The Cincinnati invitation gave him a new opportunity to travel to the west and make a statement on behalf of science and scientific discovery, that would stand as a testament to his faith in "improvement" of the American mind and spirit, and encourage others to stand with him.

As he sped across New York by train in prematurely cold October weather, there were no crowds at first. At Buffalo he climbed aboard a steamer that was to take him to Cleveland, where he would travel by stage and canal boat south to Cincinnati. But the boat stopped at Erie, Pennsylvania, where word had leaked out of his arrival, and a reception was hastily organized. At Cleveland he was recognized in a barber shop, whereupon a crowd soon descended upon his hotel, resulting in another reception and speech. In Akron, he was greeted at the Town Hall by a large throng and kissed by "a very pretty" young woman. Thinking it perhaps an Ohio custom, the septuagenarian proceeded to kiss every woman that followed, "at which some made faces, but none refused." At each of the towns on his route there was the same ritual—a crowd, a reception, and a short speech. The strangeness of the proceedings, he told his diary, "increases like a ball of snow." Now, near the end of his life, he was beginning to appreciate the warmth and exhilaration that could be generated by the friendly crowds that had so often disturbed him in the past.

When he arrived in Cincinnati, he was thoroughly exhausted, and suffering from what he called "tussis senilis"—an old man's cough. This did not bode well. Nor did it the next day when the rains came and turned the site of the new observatory into a sea of mud. Adams gave a short speech to a mass of umbrellas, and it was decided to postpone the main address until the following day. Once again his speech proved to be too long, and he delivered about half of his written remarks in a two-hour address at a crowded Methodist church.

He treated his listeners and readers to a learned historical discourse on astronomy that went from Pythagoras to Newton, combined with a lecture on the failure of most Americans to appreciate the importance of science and scientific discovery. In 1825, when he had compared America unfavorably to Europe in this regard, he had paid heavily for it. But he had not changed his mind. Even the Russians, he said, afflicted as they were by the despotism of the tsars, had recently constructed an observatory, to say nothing of the French, the Italians, and the English. "But what, in the meantime, have *we* been doing?" Adams asked his audience. The political independence proclaimed in 1776 carried with it a responsibility for intellectual independence as well. Yet Americans remained inattentive and indifferent. As for observatories: "Look around you, fellow-citizens—look from the St. John to the Sabine— look from the Neversink to the Columbia, and you will find, not one! not one!" Even if the Smithsonian funds were used to build one, it would be British, not American funding. So John Quincy Adams had come to Cincinnati to congratulate its citizens for taking the initiative themselves, to "wipe that reproach on us away."

After concluding, Adams was followed by another crowd to his hotel, where he had dinner, accepted several invitations to cross the river into Kentucky, and attended a play. The next day he met with a delegation of black citizens of the city, and attended a meeting of the local bar association. When he crossed the river, he was greeted by another "very pretty woman" who gave him "the first kiss in Kentucky." He proceeded up the Ohio to Maysville where he delivered a heartfelt tribute to his colleague, rival, friend, and former Secretary of State, Henry Clay, denying once and for all the charges of corrupt bargains between the two. From there it was on to Pittsburgh and another tumultuous reception, and then to Washington via Harper's Ferry and Baltimore. "I have performed my task, I have executed my undertaking, and am returned safe to my family and my home" he wrote upon his return.

Adams paid a price for his travels. "My strength is prostrated beyond anything that I ever experienced before, even to total impotence," he told his diary. "I have little life left in me. . . . Although it took longer than usual for him to recover, he still had strength to confront the new Democratic Congress on the issue of the Gag Rule. Since the Democrats had a nearly two-thirds majority in the House, he expected to lose by a big margin, but the vote was close again, 94 to 91. Adams studied the tally sheet carefully. Over half of the northern Democrats were now opposing the Gag. Three months later Adams was presented with a silver-tipped ivory cane, with the motto "Right of Petition Triumphant." Below it was a blank space, designed so that Adams could record the date of the Gag Rule's abolition. But would he live long enough to see it? As expected, the Democrats not only dropped him from the Chairmanship of the Foreign Relations Committee, they dropped him from the Committee altogether. They were willing to re-appoint him Chairman of the Manufactures Committee, but Adams declined, pleading his poor health and "other reasons, with which it was not necessary for me to trouble the House."

ANOTHER PRESIDENTIAL ELECTION loomed ahead, which Texas annexation threatened to dominate. President Tyler instructed his new Secretary of State, Abel P. Upshur, to negotiate a treaty of annexation with the Texas Republic. At the same time he demanded additional expenditures for the army and navy, in preparation for war with Mexico, or with Great Britain, or both, should those nations seek to prevent annexation.

As part of their preparedness campaign, the administration brought the warship *Princeton* to Washington, along with its new super-guns, the "Peacemaker" and the "Orator." Key members of Congress, including Adams, were invited to see the guns fired. In Adams' view it was only a device to "fire their souls with patriotic ardor for a naval war." Nonetheless he went to see the guns in mid-February. A week

One of only two or three daguerreotypes known to have been taken of John Quincy Adams, this one was probably made in 1843 at his home in Quincy by Philip Haas. Adams would have been seventy-six years old. *Courtesy of the The Metropolitan Museum of Art, Gift of I. N. Phelps Stokes, Edward S. Hawes, Alice Mary Hawes, Marion Hawes, 1937.*

later he turned down a second invitation, which probably saved his life, for this time the "Peacemaker" exploded, killing Secretary Upshur and several others. For his new Secretary of State, President Tyler then turned to none other than John C. Calhoun.

If anyone needed proof of the "conspiracy" to expand slavery in the United States by annexing Texas, the appointment of slavery's most powerful defender in Congress seemed to provide it. Adams was not one of those requiring proof. When Calhoun sent the Texas annexation treaty to the Senate, he fully expected it to be approved, even after the Secretary unwisely defended it as necessary to preserve slavery in America. "The impulse of national aggrandizement," Adams wrote in April, "spurred by private avarice and corruption, cannot be resisted." For Adams, the fight against annexing additional slave territory now took on monumental proportions. Forgetting or ignoring his own role in annexing slaveholding Florida in 1819, he convinced himself that "the freedom of the human race" now hung in the balance. He was delighted when Calhoun's bungling and the near unanimity of the Whigs in the Senate torpedoed the treaty. Then the two expected presidential nominees, Henry Clay and Martin Van Buren, published simultaneous letters opposing Texas annexation. For the time being, the anti-annexationists had won, but would they be able to hold on?

They would not. Van Buren's rejection of Texas cost him the Democratic nomination. Instead, the Democrats nominated Adams' old adversary, former Speaker James K. Polk. Polk was a protege of Andrew Jackson, committed to expansion and "Manifest Destiny," which for him included not only the annexation of Texas, but California and Oregon as well. Adams and others followed the Democratic convention in Baltimore by means of the new "electro-magnetic telegraph of Professor Morse," in the east end of the Capitol. When the machine tapped out the news of Polk's victory, he was despondent. The nomination was another example of "the degeneracy of my country from the principles which gave her existence, and the ruin irreparable of them all, under the transcendent power of slavery and the slave representation." The annexation of Texas, he later predicted, would transform the United States "into a conquering and warlike nation. Aggrandizement will be its passion and its policy. A military government, a large army, a costly navy, distant colonies, and associate islands in every sea, will follow of course in rapid succession."

Although he always maintained that ex-Presidents should stay out of presidential elections, Adams came closer in 1844 than he ever had before to an outright endorsement of the Whigs and Henry Clay. He warned a group of abolitionists who were advancing the cause of the new Liberty Party that there was a "great difference" between the Whigs and the Democrats, "and that placing them on the same level of exclusion was to secure the triumph of the worst party." His feelings were exacerbated by Democratic attacks on him during the campaign. Once again they charged that he deliberately gave away Texas when he negotiated the Transcontinental Treaty with Spain. But this time the accusations came from none other than Andrew Jackson himself.

If Adams was convinced that Old Hickory instigated the plot to snatch Texas from Mexico, Jackson was persuaded that Old Man Eloquent had been, and always was, the key obstacle to its acquisition. After Jackson left office in 1837, Adams became less restrained in his public treatment of him. For his part, Jackson warned annexationists that they needed to move quickly lest that "scamp", that "wretched old man", circulate his petitions and memorials against it once again. "Mr. Adams' object," the General told a friend, "was to keep down the growing ascendancy of the South and West." Jackson, prompted by some letters from George W. Erving, the American Minister to Spain in 1818, now joined those who said that Texas was rightfully United States territory, and would be then were it not for the bungling and biases of John Quincy Adams. For good measure, Democrats also attacked the Anglo-American Convention of 1818, in which the United States and Britain agreed to a joint occupation of Oregon. The Democratic campaign that rallied in 1844 under the twin demands for the "re-annexation of Texas and the re-occupation of Oregon" was an attack on the diplomacy of John Quincy Adams.

If there was one part of his life about which Adams was sensitive enough to challenge anyone to a duel, it was his career as a diplomat in the service of the United States. But he was not a duellist, and now he was seventy-seven years old. So he did the next best thing: he went after Jackson in public speeches. He spent weeks toward the end of the election preparing an address to the Boston Young Men's Whig Club, an address that was designed to vindicate himself, skewer Jackson once and for all, and advance the cause of Clay and the Whigs.

After practicing his speech in front of his son, who warned him that his language might be too violent, Adams went off to Boston where he spoke for over two hours, "much to the amusement of the auditory." He had a young man read from his diary the account of his meetings with Jackson in 1819. He denounced and ridiculed former Minister Erving. He went over the charges of the proslavery "plot," and closed with what he called an "apostrophe to the young men of Boston," warning them that their trial was approaching, as the forces of slavery and those of freedom prepared for battle. "Young men of Boston: burnish your armor, prepare for the conflict, and I say to you . . . think of your forefathers! Think of your posterity!" The speech created a sensation in Boston, and in Tennessee. "Who but a traitor to his country," said Jackson, "can appeal as Mr. Adams does to the youth of Boston?" And any claim by Adams that he had approved the Transcontinental Treaty was absolutely "*False, False, False* his diary to the contrary notwithstanding."

Adams may have had the better of their last argument, but Jackson's party won the election of 1844, albeit by the narrowest of margins. The Democrats' combination of Texas with a pledge to "re-occupy" Oregon blunted the argument that expansion was a southern proslavery plot. Indeed, Polk failed to carry many southern states, including his own state of Tennessee, while he carried many free states, including New York. It was a bitter disappointment, Adams told Henry Clay, for he "had hoped under your guidance the country would have recovered from the downward tendency into which it had been sinking." Adams himself did quite well, handily defeating both the Democrats and the Liberty party candidate, for whom his antislavery stance was not militant enough.

Paradoxically, the Democratic victory opened the door to rescinding the Gag Rule. The year before, many northern Democrats had been pressured in the name of party unity to support their southern colleagues one more time lest the party appear to be divided in the forthcoming election. Since then, the southerner Polk had snatched the presidential nomination from the northerner Van Buren and had gone on to victory. With nothing to hold them in check, more northern Democrats were at last ready to vote against the Gag Rule. Adams' motion to rescind passed easily, 108 to 80. "Blessed, ever blessed be the name of God," he wrote in his diary. The ivory cane given to him earlier in the year could now receive its date: December 3, 1844.

Then the pendulum swung again. Reading Polk's razor-thin victory as a favorable vote on Texas annexation, the outgoing Tyler proceeded to push it through, not by treaty, but by a joint resolution of both houses of Congress. Adams and the Whigs were outraged, but there was nothing they could do. The resolution passed easily in the House, very narrowly in the Senate. "I regard it as the apoplexy of the Constitution," Adams wrote. "Our Country, if we have a country, is no longer the same." Conquest, not justice, now governed America's foreign policy.

Even so, to the confusion of both friends and enemies, Adams threw his support to the Polk administration's determination to abrogate the joint occupation agreement with Britain and claim all of Oregon up to the fifty-fourth parallel, even if it meant war. Here, he explained, somewhat disingenuously, there was no "conquest" involved. Oregon was not slave territory, and the Americans had a better claim to it than the British, an Old World power. Polk's invocation of the "Monroe Doctrine" against European influence in the New World had Adams' hearty approval, since he had inspired much of it himself. Now he was criticized as a warmonger by Quakers and pacifists, even by some southern Democrats who were having second thoughts about expanding free territory. There was no need to worry, said Adams. He was convinced that the Polk administration would not fight for all of Oregon, but would compromise, as it eventually did.

The real danger of war, as he had said so often before, was with Mexico. The Mexicans may have had a better claim to Texas than the British had to Oregon, but Mexico had an unstable government incapable of defending its claim. Adams' fears were realized in 1846, when Polk used a border skirmish in which American troops were attacked on disputed soil as the pretext for a war which eventually would result in the loss of over a third of Mexico's lands to the United States. Adams was one of only fourteen Congressmen, nearly all from New England or of Yankee background, to vote against funding what he called a "most unrighteous war."

His opposition to the Mexican war, from literally its start to its finish, was the last significant public role. His attendance in the House remained regular, but he left the denunciations of Polk's war to others. He had even been replaced as Chairman of the Smithsonian Committee by Robert Dale Owen, son of the great Scottish reformer. Owen saw no need for an observatory, but he did agree to throw in a reference to astronomy in his Report to the House, to humor "the old man," as he told a colleague. Nevertheless, Adams reluctantly voted for the Smithsonian in 1846. Only the income from the fund was to be spent, as he had wished. As for the "lighthouses of the skies," Adams had to content himself the 42-inch telescope that belonged to the Navy in Washington, and with watching the sun rise and set from his son's house on the hill in Quincy. It was for him a religious as well as a scientific experience. "The pleasure that I take in witnessing these magnificent phenomena of nature never tires," he told himself in the summer of 1845. "It is a part of my own nature, unintelligible to others, and, I suppose, a singularity which I should suppress or renounce."

Now he often found himself reminiscing about days long since past, of long-dead friends and enemies, triumphs and failures. In that same summer, a simple picnic in Quincy triggered a succession of childhood and youthful memories, as did the occasion of his forty-eighth wedding anniversary a month later. "A small remnant only can be before us," he wrote of himself and Louisa in July, 1845. "We have enjoyed much. We have suffered not a little." He set aside much of the gloom that he felt over national affairs. "With regard to what is called the wheel of Fortune, my career in life has been, with severe vicissitudes, on the whole highly auspicious." Given the advantages he had in education and family background, he perhaps was more successful than he deserved. He listed his friends and enemies—some of them—of whom Andrew Jackson led the latter list. The General had died the previous month, followed by a nation-wide mourning unmatched since Washington's death. But Adams had not been fooled. The Tennessean remained "a hero" but also "a murderer, and adulterer, and a profoundly pious presbyterian, who, in the last days of his life belied and slandered me before the world."

One day in the summer of 1846, with the nation at war and Congress still in session, Adams found himself "drawn by an irresistible impulse" to swim in the Potomac once again, something he had not done for a long time. He was now in his eightieth year. As he slipped into the water, he heard one of three youths nearby say, no [...] with some wonder, "There is John Quincy Adams." They had [...] ir clothes "at one of my old standard rocks" but he found [...] Two days later he was back at five in the morning, with no [...] im his rock. After a brief dip, he walked home warming [...] the rising sun. It was to be one of his last swims. "The [...] f my life is a long disease. . ." he wrote toward the end of [...] th. "I no sooner seem to recover from one, than I am stricken down by another."

He returned to Quincy later that summer. Upon the invitation of two young abolitionists, Charles Sumner and Samuel Gridley Howe, he presided at a meeting at Faneuil Hall called to express outrage over the kidnapping of an alleged runaway slave, who had been hustled off to New Orleans with no semblance of due process. He doubted if his health would allow it, and in any event his voice was almost gone. His son, now a leader of the Massachusetts "conscience" (as opposed to the "cotton") Whigs, was to be one of the speakers. Five thousand people had crammed themselves into the old building, and they cheered as he slowly walked to the rostrum. Nearly forty years before, he reminded them in what was virtually a whisper, he had also presided at a protest meeting in that very Hall. That was when the British had attacked the *Chesapeake*, when many had been willing to overlook the violation of American rights. Now it was a question whether the laws of Massachusetts applied to those who lived there, whether "my native Commonwealth is to maintain its independence or not."

His native Commonwealth had no hesitation in returning him to his seat in Congress in the elections of that year, and by a

1600-vote majority, one of his largest. Nationally, the Whigs were victorious in a backlash against the Mexican War. Adams planned to spend a few weeks in his son's Boston home before heading south. But on November 20, 1846, as he set out with friends to tour the new Harvard Medical School, he felt his knees collapse and was unable to go any further. He was put to bed and spent several days in a semi-conscious state, probably the result of a mild stroke. He recovered soon enough, but in a "posthumous memoir" written the following March, he claimed that from the date of his stroke "I date my decease, and consider myself, for every useful purpose to myself or my fellow-creatures, dead."

Not quite dead. When he returned to Washington in February, 1847, and walked into the House chamber, the proceedings stopped until he was seated. From then on, though his attendance was almost as regular as it had ever been, the frail man said little. Only one subject stirred him to anything like his old-time passion, and that was when someone attempted to slip through an appropriation to compensate the owners of the *Amistad*. For those whose memories were short, Adams recounted the whole affair, and the appropriation was defeated, 28–94.

He remained a staunch opponent of the war with Mexico. He voted for the Pennsylvania Democrat David Wilmot's "proviso" excluding slavery from any territory conquered from Mexico. When in December the Whigs elected as Speaker of the House Robert Winthrop, a man with a name that went back in Massachusetts history even before his own, John Quincy Adams administered the oath of office.

"A stout heart and a clear conscience, and never despair." So wrote Adams to his son on January 1, 1848. By now his diary had dwindled to little more than brief notes and scraps of poetry. He confided to a friend that he did not expect to see the end of the present session of Congress, and reminded Louisa more than once of where his will might be found when she needed it. At last death found him at his desk in the House, but, as Senator Benton said, "where else could it have found him, at any stage of his career, for the fifty years of his illustrious public life?"

THE MODERN VISITOR TO THE Capitol building in Washington may stop at Statuary Hall, once the room in which John Quincy Adams' House of Representatives met and debated. Here there are busts of varying quality depicting important men and women from each of the fifty states. Adams is not among them. But if the visitor will look carefully, there lies imbedded on the floor of the Hall a small bronze disk, marking the spot where John Quincy Adams last sat. No other memorial may be found in Washington.

Inscribed on the wall of the church in Quincy where Adams was interred, his son chose the following words:

Near this place
Reposes all that could die of
JOHN QUINCY ADAMS,
Son of John and Abigail (Smith) Adams,
Sixth President of the United States.
Born 11 July 1767,
Amidst the storms of Civil Commotion,
He nursed the vigor
Which nerves a Statesman and a Patriot,
And the Faith
Which inspires a Christian.
For more than half a century,
Whenever his Country called for his Labors,
He never spared them in her Cause.
On the Twenty-fourth of December, 1814,
He signed the second Treaty with Great Britain,
Which restored peace within her borders;
On the Twenty-third of February, 1848,
He closed sixteen years of eloquent Defence
Of the lessons of his Youth,
By dying at his Post,
In her Great National Council.

A son, worthy of his Father,
A Citizen, shedding glory on his Country,
A Scholar, ambitious to advance mankind,
This Christian sought to walk humbly
In the sight of his God.

Epilogue

The first and greatest qualification of a statesman in my estimation is the mastery of the whole theory of morals which makes the foundation of human society. The great and everlasting question of the right and wrong of every act, whether of individual men or of collective bodies. The next is the application of the knowledge thus gained to the events of his time in a continuous and systematic way. . . . In my opinion no man who has lived in America had so thoroughly constructed a foundation for his life as your grandfather.

So wrote Charles Francis Adams late in life to one of his own sons. Indeed, it was the assuredness with which the Adamses in general always knew the "right and wrong of every act," that tended to set them apart from their contemporaries. It earned them the respect and admiration of many, and the disdain and contempt of others.

In his diplomatic career, John Quincy Adams' penchant for wrapping himself in morality, while defending positions that were clearly determined by his country's self-interest, often infuriated his counterparts. Paradoxically, his second career as President of the United States was undercut by his refusal to use the weapons at his command to shore up support for an admittedly visionary program. Perhaps too, his reluctance sprang from the lingering doubt that his office had been won in a way consistent with his own rigorous standards for the "calling" to public service.

His third career, in Congress, saw a return to the previous pattern.

Unencumbered by partisan constraints, he was free to enter into controversy with all the righteousness of which he was capable. Yet his third career was often touched by despair, both personal and political. The ideal of an American republic, an orderly, stable community, united around common political, moral, and religious convictions, a shining example set apart from the corrupt Old World, retreated steadily before the raucous democracy of the nineteenth century.

AFTER HER HUSBAND'S DEATH, Louisa Catherine Adams lived on in the house on F street for four more years. Each New Year's Day, she was visited by Presidents, Generals, Senators, and Congressmen: a surviving relic of an age that most of them knew only through books and reminiscences. She died on May 15, 1852. Her son took her remains back to Quincy, where they were laid beside those of her husband, father-in-law, and mother-in-law.

Many expected Charles Francis Adams, who came to resemble his father physically if not temperamentally, to take up his cause. Indeed, the summer following John Quincy's death, he ran for Vice President of the United States on the "Free Soil" ticket, headed by none other than Martin Van Buren. His father would have swallowed hard at the alliance, but would have had no reservations about its purpose: the containment and curtailment of slavery's growth in North America.

After editing ten volumes of his grandfather John Adams' letters and papers in the early 1850's, Charles Francis Adams joined the new antislavery Republican party, and was elected Congressman from Massachusetts in 1858 and 1860. Then, at the behest of his father's long-time admirer Secretary of State William H. Seward, President Abraham Lincoln appointed him Minister to Great Britain. He was the third Adams to go to London at a difficult juncture in American history. After serving as Minister during the Civil War, Adams represented the United States in the international tribunal that settled the *Alabama* claims. He then returned to Quincy and devoted most of the rest of his life to editing his father's diary, portions of which were published in twelve volumes as the *Memoirs of John Quincy Adams*.

While John and John Quincy Adams may have had their problems with the American electorate, their descendants did their best to square accounts in later years. Three grandsons of John Quincy Adams—Charles Francis Adams, Jr., Henry Adams, and Brooks Adams—made their contributions to the story of the Adams family in the form of memoirs, essays, biography, and history, most notably Henry's famous *Education of Henry Adams*, and his multi-volume *History of the Administrations of Thomas Jefferson and James Madison*.

For all the Adamses, the underlying theme of their public lives was unrequited love—a love of country that was never fully returned. Brooks Adams, the most eccentric of all of John Quincy's descendants, was persuaded that his grandfather forsook his earlier religious faith and died an agnostic, convinced that no God who had permitted Andrew Jackson to triumph, the public lands to be plundered, slavery to expand, and half of Mexico to be conquered by the United States, could be counted upon to exist. But there is no evidence that John Quincy Adams lost his faith in God—if anything, it seems to have increased in his last years. It was his faith in the Union that faltered. It remained for the next generation to preserve and solidify the Union, confronting the forces against which John Quincy Adams had battled during most of his lifetime.

Suggested Reading

OVER A GENERATION AGO, Samuel Flagg Bemis won the Pulitzer Prize for his *John Quincy Adams and the Foundations of American Foreign Policy* (New York, 1949), which was followed by his *John Quincy Adams and the Union* (New York, 1956). The two volumes together comprise the most complete account of Adams' life. Although Bemis wrote from a rousing, nationalist viewpoint no longer in vogue, his volumes still set the pace for any Adams biographer. Marie Hecht, in her *John Quincy Adams: a Personal History of an Independent Man* (New York, 1972), added personal details left out by Bemis, as did Paul Nagel in his *Descent from Glory: Four Generations of the John Adams Family* (New York, 1983). Most recently, Nagel has added a full-length study: *John Quincy Adams: A Public Life, a Private Life* (New York, 1997).

Adams' early years are dealt with in Robert East's overly saccharine *John Quincy Adams: The Critical Years* (New York, 1962) and in David Musto's article "The Youth of John Quincy Adams" in the American Philosophical Society *Proceedings* 113, 269–82 (August 15, 1969). Although there is little on Adams' diplomatic career in the Netherlands and Prussia that cannot be found in Bemis, see Bradford Perkins's *The First Rapprochement: England and the United States, 1795–1805* (Berkeley, 1955), *Prologue to War, 1805–1812* (Berkeley, 1961), and *Castlereagh and Adams* (Berkeley, 1964), for Adams' increasing role in Anglo-American affairs. Adams in Russia is dealt with in Nikolai N. Bolkhovitinov, *The Beginnings of Russian-American*

Relations, 1775–1815 (Cambridge, MA, 1975) and in Norman Saul, *Distant Friends: the United States and Russia, 1763–1867* (Lawrence, KS, 1991). For the story of the negotiating of the Treaty of Ghent, nothing beats George Dangerfield's account in *The Era of Good Feelings* (New York, 1952).

For a revisionist account of Adams as Secretary of State, see William Weeks, *John Quincy Adams and American Global Empire* (Lexington, KY, 1992). A somewhat different analysis, written by a political scientist, is Greg Russell's *John Quincy Adams and the Public Virtues of Diplomacy* (Columbia, MO, 1995). Ernest May's *The Making of the Monroe Doctrine* (Cambridge, MA, 1975) offers a brilliant analysis of Adams' motivations in influencing Monroe's foreign policy, just a year before the presidential election of 1824. The election itself is discussed in James Hopkins' essay in Arthur Schlesinger, Jr., ed., *History of American Presidential Elections* (New York, 1971), 1, 349–409.

The most thorough account of Adams' ill-fated presidency is Mary Hargreaves, *The Presidency of John Quincy Adams* (Lawrence, KS, 1985), supplemented by Dangerfield's *Era of Good Feelings*. The blunders of the election of 1828 are best described in Robert Remini's *The Election of Andrew Jackson* (Philadelphia, 1963, and Westport, CT, 1980), and in his highly partisan *Andrew Jackson and the Course of American Freedom* (New York, 1981). Sidelights on the Adams presidency may be found in Edwin Miles' "President Adams' Billiard Table" in the *New England Quarterly,* 45 (March 1972), 31–43, and Lynn Hudson Parsons, "'A Perpetual Harrow on My Feelings': John Quincy Adams and the American Indian," also in the *New England Quarterly,* 46 (September 1973), 339–79. The latter documents Adams' slow change of heart regarding the Native American.

Adams' Congressional career is best described in Leonard Richards' *The Life and Times of Congressman John Quincy Adams* (New York, 1986), a trenchant and concise analysis that seeks to offset some of the mythology about Adams handed down by his descendants. See also William Lee Miller's able if somewhat eccentric *Arguing About Slavery: The Great Battle in the United States Congress* (New York, 1996), in which Adams plays the lead role. Daniel Walker Howe fits Adams into the broader pattern of Whig thought in his *Political Culture of the American Whigs* (Chicago, 1979), especially Chapter Three. Other, more specialized studies include Wendell Glick, "The Best Possible World of John Quincy Adams," *New England Quarterly,* 37 (March 1974), 3–17, and William Jerry Maclean, "Othello Scorned: The Racial Thought of John Quincy Adams," *Journal of the Early American Republic,* 4 (Summer 1994), 143–60. The solemnities following Adams' death in 1848 are described in Parsons, "The 'Splendid Pageant': Observations on the Death of John Quincy Adams," *The New England Quarterly,* 53 (December 1980), 464–82.

There is no published full-length biography of Louisa Catherine Adams. Jack Shephard's *Cannibals of the Heart: A Personal Biography of Louisa Catherine and John Quincy Adams* (New York, 1980) comes the closest. See also Lyman Butterfield's essay on Louisa in *Notable American Women 1607–1950: A Biographical Dictionary* (Cambridge, 1971), and L. H. Parsons on the same subject in *American First Ladies* (New York, 1996).

One cannot fully fathom any of the Adamses unless one reads their diaries. Charles Francis Adams published most of the public side of his father's diary in twelve volumes in the 1870's as *Memoirs of John Quincy Adams* (Philadelphia, 1874–77), and in the 1920's Allan Nevins condensed these into one volume as *The Diary of John Quincy Adams* (New York, 1928). The Massachusetts Historical Society intends to publish the complete diary, but only the first two volumes have appeared as *The Diary of John Quincy Adams 1779– 1788* (Cambridge, 1981). *The Writings of John Quincy Adams,* 7 vols. (New York, 1913–17), the only collection of his letters available, regrettably ends at 1823. However, the 608 microfilm reels of the Adams Manuscript Trust, including the entire J. Q. Adams diary, his papers and correspondence—both incoming and outgoing—are available in most major research libraries throughout the United States.

Index